Why Are We Attracted to Sad Music?

Sandra Garrido

Why Are We Attracted to Sad Music?

palgrave
macmillan

Sandra Garrido
MARCS Institute for Brain Behaviour and Development
Western Sydney University
Milperra, NSW, Australia

ISBN 978-3-319-39665-1 ISBN 978-3-319-39666-8 (eBook)
DOI 10.1007/978-3-319-39666-8

Library of Congress Control Number: 2016957737

Printed on acid-free paper

This Palgrave Macmillan imprint is published by Springer Nature
This Palgrave Macmillan imprint is Springer International Publishing AG
The registered company address is: Gewerbestrasse 11, 6330 Cham, Switzerland

Contents

About the Author

Sandra Garrido is a researcher in music psychology, a pianist and violinist and the mother of two small boys. After completing her PhD, she spent several years in research at the Melbourne Conservatorium of Music and the Australian Research Council's Centre of Excellence for the History of Emotions. She is currently a Dementia Research Fellow at the MARCS Institute for Brain, Behaviour and Development at Western Sydney University. She has authored over 30 academic publications and co-authored a book entitled *My Life As A Playlist* (2014).

List of Figures

1

Introduction

Many of us who love music generally have no difficulty believing in its power to stir the heart and change our mood. However, popular beliefs in the mind-altering power of music tend to fall into two divergent camps: a passionate optimism about the universally beneficial effects of music on the listener, or an equally fervent belief that music—particularly unfamiliar music—is a tool of evil by which the young and impressionable can be induced to aggression, violence and self-harm.

Key minds throughout the centuries, however, have argued for a more balanced viewpoint with regard to music's effect on the listener. Aristotle (384–322 BC), for example, argued that for some people music can "excite the soul to a mystic frenzy", while others would "find their souls lightened and delighted" or would enjoy "an innocent pleasure" in the music (*Politics*, Book VIII, Section VII). Aristotle argued, therefore, that music of all rhythmic and tonal modes should be employed, "but not all of them in the same manner". In other words, Aristotle acknowledged that different musical features had different effects on the mood, and that these effects would vary from individual to individual. Similarly, Dr Robert Burton, a seventeenth-century medical practitioner, wrote in his book *Anatomy of Melancholy* that some music can "make melancholy

S. Garrido, *Why Are We Attracted to Sad Music?*,
DOI 10.1007/978-3-319-39666-8_1

persons mad", while others may experience a "pleasing melancholy" when listening to music which "expels care, alters their grieved mind and easeth in an instant" (Memb VI, Subs III). Apparently based on his own experiences, Burton here recognizes the fact that experiences of melancholy in music can be pleasant at times, but can have an unpleasant effect at other times or in other individuals.

Tragedy was a popular art form in ancient Greece during the time of Aristotle. Tens of thousands of people in ancient Greece would pack the arenas of large cities to witness popular tragedies Similarly, the seventeenth century, in which Robert Burton lived, witnessed a period known as 'Elizabethan melancholy', in which melancholic afflictions seemed to be widespread and a general preoccupation with melancholic topics could be observed in the arts. While music itself, as well as our ways of interacting with it, have changed a great deal since the time of Aristotle, or indeed, of Robert Burton, their words cited above suggest a response to music that that has considerable similarities with what we experience today. While we might not think of it as a "mystic frenzy", some modern music genres, such as electronic trance, are specifically designed to induce dissociative, trance-like states in the listener or in dancers (Becker-Blease, 2004). The phenomenon of feeling pleasant emotions when listening to sad music is also acknowledged by many music listeners in the twenty-first century (Kawakami, Furukawa, Katahira, & Okanoya, 2013).

In fact, it is the attraction to "melancholy" music, in particular, that is the focus of this volume. The mystery of why we are attracted to sad music is a particularly fascinating paradox that has puzzled philosophers for centuries, with very little empirical research on the subject until the last decade. 'Negative' emotions such as sadness are generally held to involve avoidance behaviours according to most models of emotion, impelling us to escape from situations or people that make us feel sad, thus protecting us from potential danger. We could expect, therefore, that people would usually display a preference for listening to happy music. Research supports this idea, with findings that people do mostly prefer to listen to uptempo music in major keys, music which is usually perceived as happy (Husain, Thompson, & Schellenberg, 2002; Thompson, Schellenberg, & Husain, 2001). Counterintuitively, however, in the case of music or other aesthetic experiences, the evidence suggests that we also willingly seek out experiences of sadness, even seeming to enjoy them (Schubert, 1996). As David Hume says "[t]hey are pleased as they are afflicted, and never so happy as when they employ tears, sobs and cries to give bent to their sorrow" (Essay XXII, 1742–1754).

Just as it was in ancient Greece and seventeenth-century England, sad music remains popular in the twenty-first century. A study by Glenn Schellenberg and Christian von Scheve (2012) demonstrated that in the 45 years from 1965 to 2009, popular songs from the US Top 40 charts became increasingly slower and made more frequent use of minor modes, confirming that sad-sounding music was becoming increasingly popular as the decades passed. The fact that sad music and music about heartbreak and unrequited love is increasingly popular seems all the more paradoxical when we consider the preoccupation that Western societies have with the pursuit of happiness. The multitude of popular books available on how to find happiness and the prevalence of websites devoted to the same topic attest to this fascination.

Sad music is not only found in Western cultures, of course. Sad songs are also an important part of the musical culture in many parts of the world. Many Chinese and Korean pop songs focus on the sadness of separation and long-distance love. The tango, which originated in Argentina, is not just the sensual dance that many non-Spanish speakers presume it to be. The lyrics are often, in fact, all about unrequited love and tragedy of the highest proportions. In some cultures particular musical genres have sprung up around themes of longing and loss, including the *fado* from Portugal, the *morna* from Cape Verde and the Blues amongst African-Americans. Thus, sad music forms a key part of musical cultures all around the world, despite the fact that pursuit of happiness and *avoidance* of sadness is such a pervasive interest, particularly in Western cultures.

The seemingly unassailable nature of this contradictory behaviour, described as "the paradox of tragedy" by Aristotle, has led to centuries of lengthy debate by philosophers about the very nature of emotion and what is experienced in response to music. In the modern day, the debate often becomes quite heated, particularly when the lives of young people become involved, as appears to be the case in situations where music is implicated in the suicide of members of musical subcultures such as the 'emo' subculture.

Yet, despite centuries of discussion, philosophers have reached little consensus on the issue, as I shall demonstrate in subsequent chapters. Their lack of agreement suggests that there is perhaps no single definitive answer to this question. Rather, as I shall argue in this volume, our attraction to sad music and the impact that it has on our mood and mental health are influenced by a complex interaction of musical, personal and situational variables.

More than eight years ago, when I first began to read the literature on the subject of why we listen to sad music, I was struck by the fact that the majority of writings on the subject were to be found in the philosophical literature. None of these writers appeared to me to consider the fact that people responded to music differently, nor did they appear to consider the fact that music could sometimes have a negative effect on people's moods. When I stumbled across the words of Aristotle and Robert Burton cited above that allude to the personalized nature of emotional response to music, they immediately "struck a chord" with me based on my own observations of how people respond to music. Thus, the importance of individual differences and the possibility of negative effects from music listening form the premises on which the research presented in this volume is built. In this text, an attempt is made to shift the debate from the purely philosophical to the empirical, taking individual differences in psychology as a theoretical framework for the investigation. In contrast to the two divergent viewpoints about the power of music presented at the outset of this chapter, it will be argued in the subsequent chapters that music is neither universally beneficial, nor can certain musical genres be vilified as universally dangerous to emotional health and wellbeing. Rather, the music, the individual and the context in which the music is heard all come together to create distinctly different affective experiences. As well as surveying the empirical evidence emerging from various parts of the world in relation to the 'paradox of tragedy', this volume will present original research that further explores the potential of sad music to provide important psychological benefits to the listener, and outlines the cases in which its impact may be less beneficial.

The discussion begins in Chapter 2 with an overview of some of the theoretical difficulties inherent in a discussion of 'sad music'. Can something intangible like music, which is not a psychological agent, be said to express emotion? Is what we feel in response to music 'real' emotion? Can current emotion models encompass the complexity of sadness as experienced in aesthetic contexts? The chapter will then examine what it is about music that makes it seem sad or that evokes sadness in the listener. Chapter 3 will follow on from this with a discussion of the various philosophical explanations that have been proposed over the centuries for why we are attracted to sad music.

Chapter 4 will cover the topic of the biological and chemical processes occurring in the brain and the body when we experience sadness in response to music and will examine how this compares to experiences of sadness in everyday life. It is argued that this evidence tends to put an end to much of the philosophical debate over whether the emotions experienced in response to music are real or not. One of the primary reasons reported by listeners for choosing to listen to sad music is to improve their mood. Chapter 5 will thus discuss the historical use of sad music as a tool for mood regulation, while Chapter 6 will examine more recent empirical evidence, examining these in the light of modern-day theories of mood management.

Building further on the theme of individual differences, Chapter 7 will discuss findings in recent research about the relationship between personality and the attraction to sad music. Two case studies presented in Chapter 8 will demonstrate the contrast between the different ways people use sad music for mood regulation purposes, and will illuminate the fact that mood regulation disorders such as depression can influence the way people both use and respond to sad music. Having established that music can be used so as to both improve and worsen mood, in Chapter 9. I will consider the question of whether it is possible to 'prescribe' music for mood improvement purposes in much the same way as Aristotle described, using particular musical modes to produce various affective outcomes. The use of music in health contexts and original research by the author in relation to its use with young adults will be discussed. Chapter 10 will consider the impact of contextual variables such as group music listening or involvement in musical subcultures.

The next three chapters will then explore in more detail three distinct experiences of sadness in which music is often employed: nostalgia, heartbreak and grief. Chapter 11 will investigate the experience of mixed emotions such as nostalgia in response to music, while Chapter 12 will discuss the case of love songs and our attraction to them in times of heartbreak. Chapter 13 will then explore the use of music both historically and cross-culturally in coping with grief.

Chapter 14 will summarize the arguments made throughout the volume, proposing a model for conceptualizing the complex interplay of variables that influence our attraction to sad music and the impact it has on our mood and mental health.

Not only is the answer to the question of why people are attracted to sad music philosophically interesting, but it also has important implications for understanding human emotion, the function of music in society and the role of music in controlling moods and emotions. It is hoped that this volume will demonstrate the exquisite variability in the human experience of sadness in music, providing information of practical use to health practitioners, educators and music lovers alike about the value of music to enhance our emotional lives.

References

Becker-Blease, K. A. (2004). Dissociative states through New Age and electronic trance music. *Journal of Trauma & Dissociation, 5*(2), 89–100.

Hume, D. (1742–1754). *Essays moral, political and literary.*

Husain, G., Thompson, W. F., & Schellenberg, E. G. (2002). Effects of musical tempo and mode on arousal, mood, and spatial abilities. *Music Perception, 20*(2), 151–171.

Kawakami, A., Furukawa, K., Katahira, K., & Okanoya, K. (2013). Sad music induces pleasant emotion. *Frontiers in Psychology.* doi:10.3389/fpsyg.2013.00311.

Schellenberg, E. G., & von Scheve, C. (2012). Emotional cues in American popular music: Five decades of the top 40. *Psychology of Aesthetic, Creativity and the Arts, 6*(3), 196–203.

Schubert, E. (1996). Enjoyment of negative emotions in music: An associative network explanation. *Psychology of Music, 24*, 18–28.

Thompson, W. F., Schellenberg, E. G., & Husain, G. (2001). Arousal, mood and the Mozart effect. *Psychological Science, 12*, 248–251.

2

What Is Sad Music?

Theoretical Issues

While the reader may well be able to imagine that the *answer* to the question of 'why we are attracted to sad music' is a complex one, what is perhaps not at first apparent, is that the *question* itself is inherently problematic from a theoretical perspective. Even if we choose to sidestep the debate about how to define music, we must still confront the difficulty of defining 'sad' music. This is challenging on several levels.

Firstly, given that music is not a psychological agent that is capable of feeling or expressing emotions in the same way as a human, some philosophers have argued that music by its very nature is not able to 'express' anything at all. They therefore object to the use of emotion words in relation to music altogether, arguing that pure or absolute music contains no meaning external to its own formal features. Proponents of this viewpoint, known as formalism, include the nineteenth-century music critic Eduard Hanslick and the composer Igor Stravinsky. Stravinsky said: "For I consider that music is, by its very nature, essentially powerless to express anything at all, whether a feeling, an attitude of mind, a psychological mood, a phenomenon of nature, etc. Expression has never been

S. Garrido, *Why Are We Attracted to Sad Music?*,
DOI 10.1007/978-3-319-39666-8_2

an inherent property of music. That is by no means the purpose of its existence. If, as is nearly always the case, music appears to express something, this is only an illusion and not a reality" (Stravinsky, 1936, p. 53).

There is logic in the argument that music is incapable of having or expressing emotions in the same way a person would. However, most listeners would probably argue that they both perceive and experience emotion in connection with music. If the expression of emotion in music is "an illusion", as Stravinsky claims, the illusion is so pervasive amongst music listeners that it has, to all intents and purposes, become the accepted reality. Other theorists thus suggest that music is expressive in that it arouses corresponding emotions in the listener (arousal theory), embodies an agent or musical persona that expresses emotion (persona theory), or that it represents or symbolizes certain emotional states (Packalen, 2008; Seitz, 2005). Therefore, despite the logic in the argument that music is not of itself "sad", the term "sad music" will be used throughout this volume for simplicity's sake, in reference to music that the listener perceives or experiences as sad.

However, the conceptual conundrums do not end there. Even if it is agreed that the reality of human response to music provides sufficient grounds for using emotion words in connection with music, we now face a second problem in defining the concept of sad music. This is the question of whether or not what we experience in response to music are real emotions.

Emotion theorists generally argue that certain components must be present in order for the experience to be categorized as an emotion. For example, one psychology text defines emotions as: "feelings states with physiological, cognitive, and behavioral components" (Rathus, 2002, p. 304). Similarly, Georges Rey (1980) states that emotions consist of seven components: cognitive, qualitative, behavioural, physiological, contextual, etiological and relational.

In other words, it is generally understood that emotions are typically directed towards an object and influenced by our beliefs about that object. The emotions then motivate us to take certain actions in response to the object, i.e. to protect ourselves, to escape a threat etc., behaviours that enhance our biological chances of survival and reproductive success. For example, the emotion of sadness may be directed toward a particular person in response to behaviour or an event that we perceive and believe to have caused us loss or disappointment. It is our appraisal of the behaviour or event that leads to the emotional response of sadness, which in turn motivates us to take action to either escape the situation or the person who has caused it, or to otherwise change the situation.

When we consider the example of music, however, this understanding of emotion as being comprised of certain components becomes problematic. Who or what exactly is the object of our emotional response? There is no human involved who has behaved in such a way as to evoke an emotion in the listener. We could argue that the object of the emotion is the music itself. If that is the case, emotion theorists might respond, of what is the cognitive component comprised? In our example above, it was the appraisal of the behaviour of the object as causing loss or disappointment that gave rise to the emotional response. In the case of sad music, however, no actual loss or disappointment has occurred. Furthermore, as is apparent from our discussion in Chap. 1 about the popularity of sad music and films, there is often no motivation to escape from the object (the music or film) that is causing the sad response.

Thus, some theorists conclude that we do not experience real emotions in response to music. Since it seems implausible that listeners could actually be enjoying the experience of sadness in music, many philosophers argue that we are not—that in fact, something else is happening. As Stephen Davies (1997) writes: "If we enjoy the sadness that we claim to feel, then it is not plainly sadness" (p. 242). Nick Zangwill (2007), for example, claims that theories that promote the arousal of emotions as a main function of music have little plausibility because "the essential features of emotion preclude such essential relations between music and emotion" (p. 391). Elsewhere he states that "music, in itself, has nothing to do with emotion" (Zangwill, 2004, p. 29). The philosophical arguments that attempt to explain how we seem to be experiencing sadness in the context of music can be broadly divided into two camps: the cognitivists and emotivists.[1]

[1] While this dichotomy tends to oversimplify the multiple theories in existence, it provides a useful way of understanding the differences between them, and thus will be retained here.

Broadly speaking, cognitivists tend to argue that we do not experience sadness at all in relation to sad music. Peter Kivy (2002), for example, calls himself an "enhanced formalist" (p. 109). In contrast to the extreme views of formalists such as Stravinsky, Kivy does believe that music can be expressive of definite emotions. However, he argues that although we can recognize emotions in music, we never actually feel the corresponding emotions ourselves. Rather, he argues, that listeners are emotionally aroused or excited by the beauty, magnificence or aesthetic desirability of the music, but mistake their emotional excitement for the emotions they perceive as being expressed in the music. In Kivy's view, the only emotions experienced in relation to music are "'excitement' or 'exhilaration' or 'awe'" (p. 13). For example, if the music is representational of sadness, listeners may perceive the sadness in the music but will not experience sadness themselves. Rather, they experience pleasure from an appreciation of the aesthetic features of the music but mistakenly believe their emotional experience to be one of sadness since that is what they perceive the music to be expressing. According to Kivy, sadness can never be elicited in us unless it is the features of the music itself, such as a fault or some kind of aesthetically unpleasant feature that arouses such an emotion.

This is similar to other arguments by aestheticians such as Andy Hamilton (2007) and Rose Subotnik (1991) who argue that listeners engage with the 'acousmatic' or 'structural' features of the music rather than the emotions perceived. Similarly, scholars such as Klaus Scherer (2004), for example, distinguish between 'utilitarian' and 'aesthetic' emotions, arguing that while the former are adaptive reactions to one's environment, the latter are prompted only by appreciation of the aesthetic qualities of the music and are thus unrelated to any immediate real-life concerns, typically invoking pleasant-unpleasant type reactions.

In contrast to cognitivists such as Kivy, on the other hand, emotivists argue that we do experience sadness in response to sad music. However, they too agree that what we experience are not real emotions. While differing according to the detail of their theories, emotivists argue that what we experience are a special set of 'aesthetic emotions' (see for example Bell, 1913; Gurney, 1880). Prominent aesthetic philosopher Jerrold Levinson (1990a), for example, states that he finds it hard to accept Kivy's idea that the only emotion experienced in relation to music is 'aesthetic awe'. He is unwilling to admit that 'being moved' is all we ever experience in relation to music (Levinson, 1996a). Rather, he argues that what we experience are emotions that are not "full-fledged" (p. 308).

Levinson (1990a) draws his conclusions that the emotions we experience in response to music are not real emotions on the basis that such emotions are objectless. He argues that they share some aspects of ordinary emotions, such as their characteristic affective states, but lack others, such as a specific intentional object. He states that the cognitive element of emotions—that is, a belief directed towards a particular object—is absent in the case of music since there is no object towards which it can be directed. It is thus by the physiological and affective elements of an emotion that the particular emotion is recognized in the music. His conclusion is thus that, lacking the cognitive element, what listeners experience are not "garden-variety" emotions (Levinson, 2006, p. 54).

Other emotivists argue along similar lines. Jenefer Robinson (1994) for example, agrees that Kivy is wrong in thinking that his analysis of the one emotion—'being moved'—demonstrates that no other connection exists between emotions and music. She argues that there may be other "more primitive emotions aroused by music, perhaps requiring less developed cognitive mediation" (p. 18). Similar arguments are that what we experience are weaker versions of ordinary emotions (Davies, 1997), or 'quasi-emotions', that is, affective components of fully-fledged emotions that we *imagine* to be genuine.

Both the cognitivist and emotivist perspectives approach the paradox in question by attempting to show how the phenomenon of listening to music differs from the experience of emotions in real life. Precluded from their arguments from the outset is the possibility that there may be an explanation that allows for the existence of real emotions as a response to music. Some of these arguments will be covered in more detail in Chap. 3. However, the contention that what we experience in response to music is not real emotion again denies the reality of the human experience. To many of us, what we experience when listening to music feels just as real as anything experienced in response to real life events. As Patricia Greenspan (1988) says, these attempts to force our experiences to fit certain definitions such as by insisting that emotions must have a clearly defined object, seems to result in the exclusion of states that we commonly "recognize as emotions" (p. 44).

Revisionist explanations, therefore, argue for an understanding of emotion broad enough to encompass what is experienced when listening to music. For example, Peter Mew's (1985) view is that music can arouse emotion without the mediation of emotional objects. He believes that this makes music a "fascinating counter example to the widely held philosophical view that the core emotions cited always take objects" (p. 34). Donald Callen (1982), too, remains unconvinced that all emotions must have objects. Callen uses empathetic identification and imagination to support his argument, pointing out that we can be grieved at the sadness of others without knowing the object of their sadness. In fact, we generally believe it is "morally right or praiseworthy to be grieved in the presence of sadness" (p. 383). Similarly, Georges Rey (1980) states that one may have beliefs and preferences without emotions and vice versa. Robert Roberts (1988) agrees that typically emotions involve beliefs, but that this need not always be the case: "Sometimes we experience an emotion despite not believing its propositional content" (p. 183).

If, as Greenspan suggests, narrower definitions of emotion tend to exclude experiences that are commonly experienced as real emotions, perhaps the difficulty lies with the definitions themselves. Broader definitions of emotion, such as that proposed by Paul and Anne Kleinginna (1981), may be more helpful. They describe emotions as "a complex set of interactions among subjective and objective factors" which may or may not include affective experiences, cognitive processes, physiological responses, and lead to goal-directed behaviour (p. 355). Such a broad understanding of emotion allows us to avoid the philosophical contortions needed to make human response to aesthetic experiences 'fit', allowing us to focus on the phenomenon itself.

In any case, whether or not our response to music is without either object or behavioural response is not something that is completely agreed upon by philosophers. As Kendall Walton argues (1997), it could be said that there are behavioural responses involved, since listeners may typically tap their feet, sway with the music, or display facial expressions of agitation or anguish. He compares this to the filmgoer who involuntarily flinches, despite knowing that the events on-screen pose no actual threat.

Walton's conclusion is that the listener's imagination elicits the behavioural response, which, in turn, causes them to imagine that they are actually feeling the emotion. He argues that since the situation is not real, the emotion must be only imagined. However, it does not seem clear how Walton's imagined emotions differ from real emotions, given that that there is an object, and there are affective and behavioural responses. It seems entirely possible as Greenspan (1988) argues that these are real emotions although induced by an imagined situation (p. 42). Perhaps, as Greenspan suggests, continuing the example of someone viewing a film, we see the film from the perspective of a character in a film, or some invented character who is also viewing the events in the film and feel real emotions in empathy with this imaginary character.

Explanations such as Greenspan's are persuasive. It is by no means certain, as many philosophers assert, that what are experienced in relation to music are not true emotions. According to some, real emotions may be present even in the absence of an object and a set of beliefs directed toward that object. Furthermore, it does not seem too far-fetched to claim that real emotions can be experienced in relation to an imaginary object. It is arguable that even in the case of 'pure music', or music with no programmatic content, there may in fact be an object, although an imaginary one for at least some listeners. Thus, for the purposes of this volume, it will be assumed that, subjectively at least, real emotions are experienced in response to music.

Defining 'Sadness' in the Context of Music

The third conceptual difficulty is in defining 'sadness' itself in relation to music. Emotion theorists often categorize emotions on two dimensions: arousal (from low to high) and valence (from negative to positive). According to these approaches, the valence dimension of an emotion indicates its relative pleasantness or unpleasantness (Colombetti, 2005), while the arousal dimension indicates the level of activation or alertness that the emotion involves. Bipolar models of emotion, such as Russell's (1979) circumplex model, therefore place sadness within the lower left quadrant, defining it as an emotion of negative valence and low arousal, or an unpleasant emotion involving relatively low activation or alertness. However, categorizing sadness in terms of such models is problematic across the emotion literature and particularly when we consider aesthetic situations such as listening to music.

The term 'arousal' itself is notoriously difficult to define and is not always consistently used within the literature. It can refer to physiological arousal or activation of the autonomic nervous system (Glass & Holyoak, 1986; Juslin & Västfjäll, 2008), or to "a continuum of sensitivity to environmental stimuli," ranging from sleeping to various states of waking alertness (Berridge, 2008, p. 1). Arousal can also relate to the intensity with which an emotion is experienced rather than its quality. For example, one can be more or less happy, more or less angry, or more or less disgusted (Benjafield, 1997; Duffy, 1962).

According to this latter understanding, a single emotion could be experienced at either high or low levels of arousal. As sadness increased in intensity it would also increase in arousal, with intense forms of sadness involving correspondingly higher levels of physiological activation. That the intensity of an emotion is related to the level of arousal finds empirical support from various studies. A consistent theme across general theories of emotion is that intense emotions are indeed accompanied by increased levels of physiological arousal (see, e.g., Rickard, 2004). Such increased arousal is reported by study participants when listening to 'sad' music (Garrido & Schubert, 2011a). That a single emotion can differ in intensity and experienced arousal also tends to be confirmed by a recent study in which it was reported that older adults rate experiences of happiness as lower in arousal than do younger participants (Bjalkebring, Västfjäll, & Johansson, 2015). Thus, it seems possible that, in contrast to the usual understanding of sadness as involving low levels of arousal, very intense sadness could be accompanied by high levels of arousal.

Similar complications exist with the valence dimension in bipolar models of emotion. As discussed above, so-called 'negative emotions', such as sadness, are generally believed to stimulate avoidance behaviours. Izard (1991) and Lazarus (1991), for example, define positive and negative emotions according to whether their consequences are desirable or undesirable, beneficial or harmful. However, as Colombetti (2005) points out, just because an emotion feels good it does not follow that it is positive or beneficial, involves approach behaviours or even that it is positively evaluated. She cites anger as an example, which is typically understood to involve unpleasantness but approach behavior.

As discussed above, the same paradox exists with sad music in that rather than being perceived as unpleasant and motivating avoidance behaviours, people actually seem to enjoy it and to be strongly attracted to it, a phenomenon that will be further demonstrated by much of the empirical evidence presented in this volume. Thus, Greenspan (1988) argues that emotions defy easy categorization into positive and negative because they can at times be mixed and layered, featuring both "comfort" and "discomfort" (p. 31), and therefore involve both positive and negative evaluations.

That this 'mixing and layering' does occur in response to music is borne out by a study that I conducted in collaboration with colleagues Tuomas Eerola, Jane Davidson and Waldo Garrido.[2] The study involved a survey of audience members who attended a live choral performance in Saint Cuthbert's Chapel at Ushaw College, in Durham, UK in 2014. Held to commemorate the centenary of the First World War, the heart of the performance was William Byrd's *Mass for Five Voices*. The programme also included two sarabandes from the solo cello suites of J.S. Bach, a short choral work by Francis Pott: *A Lament*, and the Lamento from Benjamin Britten's Opus 72 cello suite.

All of these were works designed to highlight themes of grief and conflict. Byrd has himself been called the "Master of Grief" (Lam, 1973), since so many of his works are set to sombre Latin texts and were written as expressions of grief and protest at the persecution of Catholics in England towards the end of the reign of Queen Elizabeth I (Harley, 1997; Kerman, 1981). The two Bach sarabandes (from suites No. 2 and No. 5) are also among the most mournful of Bach's works, and the Britten cello work—played *piangendo* (weeping plaintively)—is reminiscent of the Bach. Pott's *A Lament* was also inspired by death and grief, Pott having been moved to compose it by the death of a soldier in the war in Afghanistan in 2009. These prevailing themes of grief and loss provided a useful opportunity to explore the audience's response to sadness in music.

---

[2] Unpublished.

We asked members of the audience to complete a survey during the intermission in which they answered questions about their response to the first half of the programme. The survey asked participants to answer questions about the part of the programme that had represented the most emotional point of the performance so far for them. As well as freely describing why they thought that section had produced the greatest emotional response, participants also indicated the emotions they had experienced at that point using the Geneva Emotional Music Scale (GEMS; Zentner, Grandjean, & Scherer, 2008), a scale that contains nine emotions believed to be commonly experienced in the context of music listening, including sadness.

If participants indicated that they had experienced sadness we then asked them to further specify what the experience of sadness had been like for them by rating a list of eight sadness-related adjectives or compound adjectives. The terms selected were drawn from a study by Warriner and colleagues (2013) who created valence and arousal scores for thousands of words from the English lexicon. We deliberately selected sadness-related terms that could represent the four quadrants of a bipolar affective space (Fig. 2.1), and thus both pleasant and unpleasant, and high and low arousal experiences of sadness. For example, the terms 'depressed' and 'downhearted' were used to represent sadness that fell into the lower left quadrant of the model—the traditional placement of sadness—while

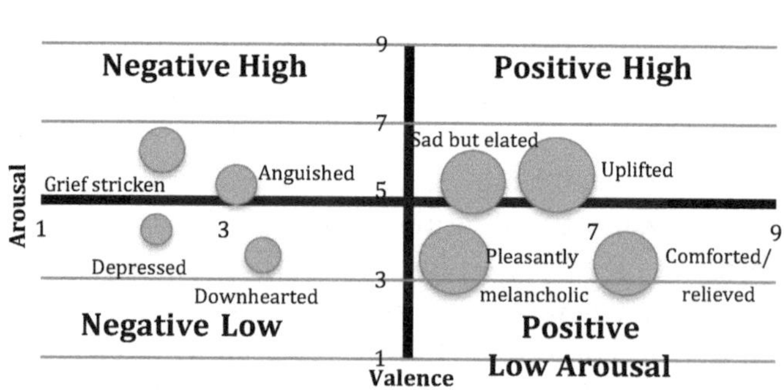

Fig. 2.1 Sadness adjectives in a 2-dimensional model showing the median term values. (Circle size indicates the relative proportion of participants who selected the term)

'grief-stricken' and 'anguished' were used to represent unpleasant but high arousal experiences of sadness. We used terms to represent more pleasant experiences of sadness as well, such as 'pleasantly melancholic' for the pleasant/low arousal quadrant, and 'sad but elated' for the pleasant/high arousal quadrant.

Of the 63 participants, 32 answered these questions about their experience of sadness in relation to the music. As can be seen in Fig. 2.1, most participants reported pleasant or positive experiences of sadness, of both high and low arousal, with 'uplifted' being the most highly rated term. In fact, negative valence and low arousal sadness items that fall within the lower left quadrant, where most emotion theorists would put sadness, received the lowest rating of all. Factor analyses revealed that while unpleasant forms of sadness could probably be measured using a combination of items on the GEMS such as 'Sadness' and 'Tension', the more pleasant experiences of sadness were not accounted for by the GEMS at all, suggesting that such measures are insufficiently complex to pick up the varied ways in which sadness is experienced in the context of listening to music.

We cannot be certain from these results whether what participants experienced were distinct forms of sadness or whether they involved the simultaneous experience of various emotions, i.e. mixed emotions. However, what it does suggest is that current emotion models are inadequate for explaining or measuring the complex variations of sadness that can be experienced when listening to music. Thus, the term 'sad music' in this volume is used to refer to music that is perceived by the listener as sad or that induces sadness in the listener in all its variants, whether or not such sadness fits traditional understandings of sadness as a negative, low arousal emotion.

What Makes Music Sad to the Listener?

This brings us to a final question: what kind of music is perceived or experienced as sad by listeners? The answer is again a complex one, since there are many ways in which music can evoke emotions in the listener. Patrik Juslin and colleagues (Juslin, Harmat, & Eerola, 2013; Juslin,

Liljestrom, Vastfjall, & Lundqvist, 2010; Juslin & Västfjäll, 2008) have proposed that there are eight mechanisms by which music can induce an emotional response in the listener:

i. *Brain stem reflexes*—an unconscious and automatic activation of physiological systems in response to signals of danger from the acoustic environment.
ii. *Rhythmic entrainment*—the unconscious compulsion to adjust bodily rhythms to externally heard rhythms.
iii. *Emotional contagion*—the activation of mirror neurons that cause an automatic empathic response to emotions expressed by others.
iv. *Evaluative conditioning*—the automatic emotional responses elicited by the repeated pairing of a musical stimulus with something else leading to a response by association.
v. *Episodic memory*—the triggering of specific memories that themselves evoke emotions.
vi. *Visual imagery*—the conjuring up of visual images that produce an emotional response.
vii. *Musical expectancy*—the violation of culturally acquired knowledge of musical conventions and syntax.
viii. *Aesthetic judgement*—a subjective evaluation of the aesthetic beauty of the music.

As can be seen from this list, emotions can be induced in the listener through both biological processes that are likely related to the evolutionary functions of music in the development of human society (Huron, 2001) and also cognitive responses that are mediated by individual experiences and context-specific knowledge. That biological mechanisms may be involved is also suggested by the fact that people from most cultures tend to recognize sadness in music via the same cues. For example, Laura-Lee Balkwill and William Forde Thompson (1999) asked thirty participants of Western origin who were unfamiliar with Hindustani ragas to listen to raga excerpts. Despite their lack of familiarity with the tonal system of ragas, the participants were able to accurately identify the excerpts intended to express sadness, joy and anger. They appeared to do so by their assessment of certain psychophysical cues in the music. In particular, sadness was associated with a slower tempo and higher levels of musical complexity, i.e. music with complex harmonies, and a high degree of melodic variation throughout. Thus, the authors concluded that certain primary emotions, such as sadness, can be conveyed both by means of psychophysical cues that are cross-culturally understood, and by means of culturally specific conventions of expression.

While we cannot necessarily assume that something that is universally perceived indicates the operation of biological mechanisms—in this case, arguments about the evolutionary origins of music lend plausibility to the case for a certain degree of innate response to music. One of the strongest arguments about the evolutionary origins of music relates to its relationship to other forms of communication such as speech (Patel, 2008). For example, music processing has been found to involve parts of the brain specifically used to process and produce speech, such as Broca's and Wernicke's areas (Maess, Koelsch, Gunter, & Friederici, 2001; Nan, Knosche, & Zysset, 2008).

In fact, many of the cues that have been found to convey sadness in music are related to the prosodic qualities of sad speech. Some of the features common to both sad speech and music include: a low overall pitch and relatively small pitch range (Fairbanks & Provonost, 1939; Huron, 2008a); weak articulation (Dalla Bella, Peretz, Rousseau, & Gosselin, 2001); softness or low levels of intensity (Juslin & Laukka, 2003; Siegman & Boyle, 1993), and darker timbres (Schutz, Huron, Keeton, & Loewer, 2008). Slower tempos are also associated with sadness and depression in both speech and music (Breitenstien, van Lancker, & Daum, 2001). David Huron argues that what these acoustic features have in common is that they suggest low physiological arousal (Huron, 2011). For example, the reduced muscle tone in the mouth and throat that accompany low levels of arousal results in lower voice pitch. Similarly, sluggish muscle activity in the same areas also result in less variation in vocal pitch, or a monotone, as well as slurred articulation.

Where expressions of sadness are more intense or higher in arousal, the prosodic features of vocal expressions may differ—as in the higher pitched expressions and alternations between modal and falsetto voices produced by a constricted pharynx (Huron, 2015a). Known as a 'breaking' or 'cracking' voice, this is a feature often utilized by singers to create particularly emotive expressions of grief and sadness. Brandon Paul and David Huron (2010) found, for example, significant correlations between the use of a cracking voice and grief-related lyrics in country music. Thus, it may be that much of what we perceive as sad in music stems from the biological effects that sadness has on the human voice, a fact that many would argue suggests an evolutionary connection between vocal communication of emotion and music.

A small proportion of music listeners have particularly intense reactions to music, called "chills" or "frissons". These can include tears, chills down the spine, and piloerection or goosebumps, as well as heightened states of consciousness and trance-like experiences (Gabrielsson, 2011). Sad music is twice as likely to produce these chills as happy music, and it may be brought on by particular features of the music such as sudden changes in harmony or other unexpected variations. It is also associated with the sudden entry of a solo soprano voice or instrument emerging from a relatively richer musical background. Researchers have found that the chills tend to peak at intense and dramatic crescendos (Gabrielsson, 2001). Songs that have been reported as inducing this effect in listeners include Pink Floyd's 'The Final Cut', Schoenberg's *Verklärte Nacht* and Whitney Houston's 'I Will Always Love You'.

One of the most intriguing explanations for these chill effects has been offered by neuroscientist Jaak Panksepp (1995). He argues that chills may emerge from deeply ingrained and automatic responses to calls signaling distress or sadness, such as separation calls. More recent experimental work on piloerection and the chill phenomenon by Mathias Benedek and Christian Kaernbach (2011) offers some support for Panksepp's hypothesis. Subjects in their study listened to four short musical selections and four short audio excerpts from film soundtracks, while physiological measures were being recorded. They found that heart rate and respiration measures were consistent with the presence of non-crying sadness. However, Benedek and Kaernbach argued that "sadness" is probably a term that only inadequately describes the specific emotional state associated with piloerection, since it can be associated with thrilling as well as frightening events. In animals, piloerection is often triggered in situations of threat, and thus, the authors argue, thrills and chills responses in humans may be an evolutionary relic of the threatening aspect of being "moved" or "touched". It seems, therefore, that many of our emotional responses to music as well as our perception of music as sad is related to some degree to our biological programming to respond to acoustic cues that signal needed information about our environment or that represent emotional communications by those around us.

However, a single musical cue such as tempo does not in itself appear to convey sadness to the listener. After all, music that is considered peaceful or relaxing can also be slow in tempo. Stephanie Khalfa and colleagues (2008a, 2008b) thus found that while physiological responses of participants differed for 'sad' and 'happy' music that contained a number of musical cues, when pitch, mode and rhythmic variations were removed, leaving tempo as the only cue, the difference in response was lost. Thus, it appears that although biological responses such as entrainment form part of our emotional response to music, listeners rely on a combination of cues to make an assessment of emotional intent, and that these can include context-specific knowledge of the musical conventions applicable as well (Balkwill, Thompson, & Matsunaga, 2004).

Even those musical cues based on speech patterns may differ from culture to culture, since prosodic expressions of emotion in speech also differ across cultures (Burkhardt et al., 2006). Ani Patel and Joseph Daniele (2003), for example, found that the rhythmic differences between English and French speech were mirrored by musical themes originating in the same cultures. Thus, while the mechanisms for responding to these cues may be biological, the specific features of the cues themselves may vary at least slightly from culture to culture, knowledge of which is acquired over time with continued exposure to the conventions of emotional expression in one's cultural context.

In addition to those linked to expression of emotion in human speech a number of other conventions of musical expression have come to signify sadness and may act as acoustic cues to the listener in different cultural contexts. For example, minor keys are generally perceived as expressing sadness in Western music. Obviously, the use of minor keys to signify sadness is not a universal element of music since other cultures do not use the same major/minor tonal systems as Western classical music. Sadness is in fact communicated in laments, elegies, dirges and other song forms throughout the world in music not based on diatonic harmonies (see, e.g., Feld, 1990; Wilce, 2009). That this understanding of minor modes is culturally acquired was further demonstrated by Simone Dalla Bella and colleagues (2001) who showed that, while adults and children around 6–8 years old are able to distinguish happy and sad music on the basis of both tempo and mode, children of the age of 5 tend to only be influenced by tempo. Thus, it is evident that an understanding of mode is something that is acquired gradually through acquaintance with the music of a given culture.

Even within a specific cultural context one person may perceive certain songs to be sad where another would see them differently. In addition to biological mechanisms and culturally acquired knowledge, personal factors—including both disposition and life experiences—play a role in the type of music that we will see or experience as 'sad'. For example, in a survey of British funeral music conducted by Cooperative Funeralcare (2013) it was revealed that among the top ten most popular songs for use in funerals in 2012 was Frank Sinatra's "My Way". For most people this song probably represents a stirring anthem of personal strength and individualism. However, for a person who has continually heard the song at funerals, the song could easily come to be associated with grief and mourning. Thus, in much the same way as Pavlov's dogs eventually began to salivate at the mere sound of a bell, such a listener may automatically feel sadness as soon as they hear the song even before consciously registering any of the musical features of the song. Conversely, if a group of friends were to sit around a campfire humorously parodying the expressions of grief and heartbreak by a country singer, for example, it is likely that when the friends hear the song on future occasions they would be reminded of an evening of fun and camaraderie and would experience positive emotions in response to what would otherwise be considered a sad song. Thus, personal experiences shape emotional responses to music through both conditioning and by evoking particular memories.

One's disposition or state of mind can also influence how a listener perceives music. For example, one person might hear a piece of music such as the "Méditation" from the opera *Thäis* by Jules Massenet and view it as an expression of tenderness and quiet joy, while another would see it as a heart-wrenching expression of sadness. Such differences in perspective between people are found in a variety of contexts, depending on the individuals' current state of mind or overall disposition. This was made evident to me one day when I enthusiastically asked a friend to listen to a recording of a violin performance by Joshua Bell that I had personally found inspiring and joyful. After about half a minute, she asked me to turn it off, saying that she felt too depressed to listen to something that was so disheartening. I can still remember my surprise that our own individual moods at the time had such a strong impact not only on our emotional response to the music, but also even on our perception of the emotion being expressed in the music.

The tendency to view things in a negative light when we are ourselves in a negative mood is borne out by numerous studies. Richard Wenzlaff and Danielle Bates (1998), for example, found that people with a dysphoric disposition tended to form more negative sentences from scrambled words than happier people, suggesting an attentional bias towards negative thoughts. People with tendencies to depression are also more likely to interpret facial expressions as conveying negative emotions (Raes, Hermans, & Williams, 2006), to perceive interpersonal feedback as having been more negative (Gotlib, Krasnoperova, Neubauer Yue, & Joormann, 2004), and to recall negatively biased memories (Lyubomirsky, Caldwell, & Nolen-Hoeksema, 1998), than is the case for happier participants. Thus, Huron (2011) argues that in addition to the biological mechanisms and the culturally acquired knowledge, a cognitive element relating to the thoughts and memories that are triggered also influence what music an individual will perceive as sad or will experience sadness in response to.

This was also suggested by the results of the study described in the above subheading that I conducted in Durham along with my colleagues. In that study we also found that the nature of the sadness experienced by members of the audience depended, to a large extent, on the mechanisms that appeared to have been involved in their emotional response. Participants were more likely to rate their experience of sadness as having been of the negative, low- arousal type (see Fig. 2.1), such as depression or feeling downhearted, when the music triggered personal memories or thoughts, or where the individual was already in a low mood prior to the concert. High-arousal negative emotions such as grief and anguish were related to the triggering of visual images by the music, whereas positive high-arousal experiences of sadness that included elation and being uplifted were related to an appreciation of the musical features themselves. These results tend to indicate that it is more than the music itself that influences one's emotional response to the music.

I further explored the question of what makes a 'sad song' in a study in which I asked over 500 participants to name a song that made them feel sad. Participants included undergraduate students and a non-student group, and ranged in age from 15 to 88 years (with a mean age of 28). The music they nominated was from a variety of genres, including rock, classical, folk, electronic, jazz, and pop. Samuel Barber's "Adagio for Strings" was among the most frequently nominated songs, along with "Danny Boy", Jeff Buckley's version of "Hallelujah", and Eric Clapton's "Tears in Heaven".

I also asked the participants to nominate a song that made them happy in order to see whether there were any significant differences between the 'happy' and 'sad' songs. Surprisingly, an analysis of the songs revealed no significant differences in tempo (beats per minute) between the two groups. Both the sad and happy song nominations contained roughly equal numbers of slow and fast music. Even more surprising was the finding that both the 'happy' and 'sad' song nominations were predominantly in major keys, and that the 'happy' song category contained just as many songs in a minor key as the 'sad song' nominations. Some songs, such as Eva Cassidy's version of 'Somewhere Over the Rainbow', even appeared several times in both categories. So it appears that the musical cues of tempo and mode were not the most important detail in determining what affective impact the music would have on participants.

As it turned out, more important than tempo or modality was the lyrical content. I used Linguistic Inquiry and Word Count software (LIWC; Pennebaker, 1993) to explore the lyrics of the songs nominated by participants in both the 'sad' and 'happy' categories. This software is useful for investigating patterns of word use, providing word counts for several word categories used in the text, including words that express positive or negative affective content, or words relating to specific topics such as money or death, for example. What this analysis showed is that the happy song category contained significantly more words in the present tense than the sad song group, suggesting that these songs tended to focus on the here and now rather than on the past or the worries about the future.[3] It also contained more words expressing positive emotions than the sad song category and more words expressing assent (i.e., words such as "OK", "yes" or "agree"), while the sad songs contained significantly more words expressing negative emotions, particularly anger and sadness.

These results suggest that, in the case of non-instrumental music at least, the lyrical content plays an important role in determining whether a participant will experience sadness in response to it. These results thus confirm the findings of studies such as that by Elvira Brattico and colleagues (2011) in which it was found that although some differences in musical cues were found between happy and sad music (either with or without lyrics), in general, the message conveyed by the lyrics was of more importance than the acoustic cues in the music itself.

These results also tend to point once again to the cognitive element, implying that thoughts that may be triggered by the music, i.e. either positive or negative, present- or past-focused, also play a role in the emotions that will be evoked by the music. Thus, while musical cues such as minor keys and slow tempos may be conventionally considered to be sad, it is evident that a wide variety of music can induce sadness in the listener. In this analysis I did not look at the pitch of the music or the vocal qualities or techniques of the singers. It may be that other acoustic cues such as instrumental timbre or pitch range may provide stronger cues than culture-specific ones such as mode, given their relationship to prosodic emotion indicators in speech.

In any case, it is evident from the empirical research by many academics outlined above that a complex interplay of biological, cultural, environmental and personal variables is at work in determining whether a person will both perceive a piece of music as sad and experience sadness in response to it. These multiple influences including personality and the social circumstances of music listening will be discussed in more details in subsequent chapters. However, the hierarchy of cues or mechanisms, i.e. the relative importance and strength of various cues and mechanisms, is something that has not been completely established. It

[3] All findings were significant at $p < .01$.

may be that while biological mechanisms such as the startle response or the chill response are activated automatically and powerfully within milliseconds of hearing a piece of music, these are soon overridden by our own temperament and our current mood, which in turn interact with the lyrical content and our personal associations with the music. Musical cues that signal emotion via similar acoustic qualities as speech in our culture are also significant in our perception and response to emotion in music, but are perhaps secondary to our own mood and memories of a song. It may be that culturally acquired knowledge, such as the idea that minor keys represent sadness in Western cultures, will turn out to have the least significant impact on how we perceive and respond to music.

References

Balkwill, L.-L., & Thompson, W. F. (1999). A cross-cultural investigaton of the perception of emotion in music: Psychophysical and cultural cues. *Music Perception, 17*(1), 43–64.

Balkwill, L.-L., Thompson, W. F., & Matsunaga, R. (2004). Recognition of emotion in Japanese, Western and Hindustani music by Japanese listeners. *Japanese Psychological Research, 46*(4), 337–349.

Bell, C. (1913). Art. Retrieved from http://www.gutenberg.net/dirs/1/6/9/1/16917/16917-h/16917-h.htm

Benedek, M., & Kaernbach, C. (2011). Physiological correlates and emotional specificity of human piloerection. *Biological Psychology, 86*, 320–329.

Benjafield, J. G. (1997). *Cognition* (2nd ed.). Upper Saddle River, NJ: Prentice Hall.

Berridge, C. W. (2008). Noradrenergic modulation of arousal. *Brain Research Reviews, 58*(1), 1–17.

Bjalkebring, P., Västfjäll, D., & Johansson, B. E. A. (2015). Happiness and arousal: Framing happiness as arousing results in lower happiness ratings for older adults. *Frontiers in Psychology, 6*(706). doi:10.3389/fpsyg.2015.00706.

Brattico, E., Alluri, V., Bogert, B., Jacobsen, T., Nartiainen, N., Nieminen, S., & Tervaniemi, M. (2011). A functional MRI study of happy and sad emotions in music with and without lyrics. *Frontiers in Psychology, 2*, 308.

Breitenstien, C., van Lancker, D., & Daum, I. (2001). The contribution of speech rate and pitch variation to the perception of vocal emotions in a German and an American sample. *Cognition & Emotion, 15*, 57–79.

Burkhardt, F., Audibert, N., Malatesta, L., Turk, O., Arslan, L., & Auberge, V. (2006). *Emotional prosody—Does culture make a difference?* Paper presented at *Speech Prosody*, Dresden, Germany.

Callen, D. (1982). The sentiment in musical sensibility. *Journal of Aesthetics and Art Criticism, 40*, 381–393.

Colombetti, G. (2005). Appraising valence. *Journal of Consciousness Studies, 12*(8), 103–126.

Dalla Bella, S., Peretz, I., Rousseau, L., & Gosselin, N. (2001). A developmental study of the affective value of tempo and mode in music. *Cognition, 80*, B1–B10.

Davies, S. (1997). Why listen to sad music if it makes one feel sad? In J. Robinson (Ed.), *Music and meaning*. New York: Cornell University Press.

Duffy, E. (1962). *Activation and behavior*. Oxford, England: Wiley.

Fairbanks, G., & Provonost, W. (1939). An experimental study of the pitch characteristics of the voice during the expression of emotion. *Speech Monographs, 6*, 87–104.

Feld, S. (1990). *Sound and sentiment: Birds, weeping, poetics and song in Kaluli expression*. Philadelphia, PA: University of Pennsylvania Press.

Funeralcare, C.-o. (2013). *Funeral Music*. Retrieved from http://www.co-operative.coop/funeralcare/arranging-a-funeral/your-guide-to-arranging-a-funeral/Funeral-Music/

Gabrielsson, A. (2001). Emotions in strong experiences with music. In P. N. Juslin & J. A. Sloboda (Eds.), *Music and emotion: Theory and research* (pp. 431–449). Oxford: Oxford University Press.

Gabrielsson, A. (2011). Strong experiences with music. In P. N. Juslin & J. Sloboda (Eds.), *Handbook of music and emotion: Theory, research, applications* (pp. 547–574). New York: Oxford University Press.

Garrido, S., & Schubert, E. (2011a). Individual differences in the enjoyment of negative emotion in music: A literature review and experiment. *Music Perception, 28*(3), 279–295.

Glass, A. L., & Holyoak, K. J. (1986). *Cognition* (2nd ed.). New York: Random House.

Gotlib, I. H., Krasnoperova, E., Neubauer Yue, D., & Joormann, J. (2004). Attentional biases for negative interpersonal stimuli in clinical depression. *Journal of Abnormal Psychology, 113*(1), 127–135.

Greenspan, P. (1988). *Emotions and reasons.* New York: Routledge.
Gurney, E. (1880). *The power of sound.* London: Smith, Elder.
Hamilton, A. (2007). *Aesthetics and music.* London and New York: Continuum International Publishing.
Harley, J. (1997). *William Byrd: Gentleman of the Chapel Royal.* Hants, UK: Scolar Press.
Huron, D. (2001). Is music an evolutionary adaptation? *Annals of the New York Academy of Sciences, 930*, 43–61.
Huron, D. (2008a). A comparison of average pitch height and interval size in major and minor key themes: Evidence consistent with affect-related pitch prosody. *Empirical Musicology Review, 3*(2), 59–63.
Huron, D. (2011). Why is sad music pleasurable? A possible role for prolactin. *Musicae Scientiae, 15*(2), 146–158.
Huron, D. (2015a). Musical semiotics and analogical reference. In C. Maeder & M. Reybrouck (Eds.), *Music, analysis, experience: New perspectives in musical semiotics.* Leuven: Leuven University Press.
Izard, C. E. (1991). *The psychology of emotions.* New York: Plenum.
Juslin, P. N., Harmat, L., & Eerola, T. (2013). What makes music emotionally significant? Exploring the underlying mechanisms. *Psychology of Music.* doi:10.1177/0305735613484548.
Juslin, P. N., & Laukka, P. (2003). Emotional expression in speech and music: Evidence of cross-modal similarities. *Annals of the New York Academy of Science, 1000*, 279–282.
Juslin, P. N., Liljestrom, S., Vastfjall, D., & Lundqvist, L.-O. (2010). How does music evoke emotions? Exploring the underlying mechanisms. In P. N. Juslin & J. A. Sloboda (Eds.), *Handbook of music and emotion: Theory, research, applications.* Oxford: Oxford University Press.
Juslin, P. N., & Vastfjall, D. (2008). Emotional response to music: The need to consider underlying mechanisms. *Behavioral and Brain Sciences, 31*, 559–621.
Kerman, J. (1981). *The Masses and Motets of William Byrd.* Berkeley: University of California Press.
Khalfa, S., Guye, M., Peretz, I., Chapon, F., Girard, N., Chauvel, P., & Liegeois-Chauvel, C. (2008a). Evidence of lateralized anteromedial temporal structures involvement in musical emotion processing. *Neuropsychologia, 46*, 2485–2493.
Khalfa, S., Roy, M., Rainville, P., Dalla Bella, S., & Peretz, I. (2008b). Role of tempo entrainment in psychophysiological differentiation of happy and sad music? *International Journal of Psychophysiology, 68*, 17–26.

Kivy, P. (2002). *Introduction to a philosophy of music*. Oxford: Clarendon Press.

Kleinginna, P. R. J., & Kleinginna, A. M. (1981). A categorized list of emotion definitions, with suggestions for a consensual definition. *Motivation and Emotion, 5*(4), 345–379.

Lam, B. (1973). Master of grief. *Listener, 89*, 874.

Lazarus, R. S. (1991). *Emotion and adaptation*. New York: Oxford University Press.

Levinson, J. (1990b). Music and negative emotions. In J. Levinson (Ed.), *Music, art and metaphysics: Essays in emotional aesthetics* (pp. 306–335). Ithaca: Cornell University Press.

Levinson, J. (1996a). Music and negative emotions. In J. Robinson (Ed.), *Music and meaning*. New York: Cornell University Press.

Levinson, J. (2006). *Contemplating art: Essays in aesthetics*. Oxford: Oxford University Press.

Lyubomirsky, S., Caldwell, N. D., & Nolen-Hoeksema, S. (1998). Effects of ruminative and distractive responses to depressed mood on retrieval of autobiographical memories. *Journal of Personality and Social Psychology, 75*(1), 166–177.

Maess, B., Koelsch, S., Gunter, T. C., & Friederici, A. D. (2001). Musical syntax is processed in Broca's area: An MEG study. *Nature Neuroscience, 4*(5), 540–545.

Mew, P. (1985). The expression of emotion in music. *British Journal of Aesthetics, 25*, 357–361.

Nan, Y., Knosche, T. R., & Zysset, S. (2008). Cross-cultural music phrase processing: An fMRI study. *Human Brain Mapping, 29*, 312–328.

Packalen, E. (2008). Music, emotions and truth. *Philosophy of Music Education Review, 16*(1), 41–59.

Panksepp, J. (1995). The emotional sources of "chills" induced by music. *Music Perception, 13*(2), 171–201.

Patel, A. D. (2008). Music as a transformative technology of the mind. Paper presented at the *Music: Its Evolution, Cognitive Basis, and Spiritual Dimensions symposium*, Wolfson College, Cambridge University.

Patel, A. D., & Daniele, J. R. (2003). An empirical comparison of rhythm in language and music. *Cognition, 87*, B35–B45.

Paul, B., & Huron, D. (2010). An association between breaking voice and grief-related lyrics in country music. *Empirical Musicology Review, 5*(2), 27–35.

Pennebaker, J. W. (1993). Putting stress into words: Health, linguistic, and therapeutic implications. *Behaviour Research and Therapy, 31*(6), 539–548.

Raes, F., Hermans, D., & Williams, J. M. G. (2006). Negative bias in the perception of others' facial emotional expressions in major depression: The role of depressive rumination. *Journal of Nervous and Mental Disease, 194*(10), 796–799.

Rathus, S. A. (2002). *Psychology in the New Millenium* (8th ed.). Orlando: Harcourt College Publishers.

Rey, G. (1980). Functionalism and the emotions. In A. O. Rorty (Ed.), *Explaining emotions*. Berkeley: University of California Press.

Rickard, N. S. (2004). Intense emotional responses to music: A test of the physiological arousal hypothesis. *Psychology of Music, 32*(4), 371–388.

Roberts, R. (1988). What an emotion is: A sketch. *Philosophical Review, 97*, 183–209.

Robinson, J. (1994). The expression and arousal of emotion in music. *Journal of Aesthetics and Art Criticism, 52*(1), 13–22.

Russell, J. A. (1979). Affective space is bipolar. *Journal of Personality and Social Psychology, 37*, 345–356.

Scherer, K. R. (2004). Which emotions can be induced by music? What are the underlying mechanisms? And how can we measure them? *Journal of New Music Research, 33*, 239–251.

Schutz, M., Huron, D., Keeton, K., & Loewer, G. (2008). The happy xylophone: Acoustic affordances restrict an emotional palate. *Empirical Musicology Review, 3*, 126–135.

Seitz, J. A. (2005). Dalcroze, the body, movement and musicality. *Psychology of Music, 33*, 419–435.

Siegman, A., & Boyle, S. (1993). Voices of fear and anxiety and sadness and depression: The effects of speech rate and loudness on fear and anxiety and sadness and depression. *Journal of Abnormal Psychology, 102*, 430–437.

Stravinsky, I. (1936). *An Autobiography*. Retrieved from https://archive.org/details/igorstravinskyan011583mbp

Subotnik, R. R. (1991). *Developing variations: Style and ideology in Western music*. Minneapolis: University of Minnesota Press.

Walton, K. (1997). Listening with imagination: Is music representational? In J. Robinson (Ed.), *Music and meaning*. New York: Cornell University Press.

Warriner, A. B., Kuperman, V., & Brysbaert, M. (2013). Norms of valence, arousal and dominance for 13,915 English lemmas. *Behavior Research Methods, 45*, 1191–1207.

Wenzlaff, R. M., & Bates, D. E. (1998). Unmasking a cognitive vulnerability to depression: How lapses in mental control reveal depressive thinking. *Journal of Personality and Social Psychology, 75*(6), 1559–1571.
Wilce, J. M. (2009). *Crying shame: Metaculture, modernity, and the exaggerated death of lament.* Chichester: Wiley-Blackwell.
Zangwill, N. (2004). Against emotion: Hanslick was right about music. *British Journal of Aesthetics, 44*(1), 29–43.
Zangwill, N. (2007). Music, metaphor and emotion. *Journal of Aesthetics and Art Criticism, 65*(4), 391–400.
Zentner, M., Grandjean, D., & Scherer, K., R. (2008). Emotions evoked by the sound of music: Characterization, classification and measurement. *Emotion,* 8, 494–521.

3

The Philosophical Debate

Why We Like Music

A logical starting point for our consideration of why we are attracted to sad music is to consider why we like music at all. Why is music cultivated in human society? Steven Pinker (1997) has notoriously referred to music as "auditory cheesecake", claiming that music is nothing but a pleasant artifact of the processes of evolutionary selection, rather than something that is necessary for our survival. However, most activities that are important for survival of the species, such as eating and reproduction, are also pleasurable, since the brain is geared up to reward adaptive behaviour. A number of reasons for the widespread interest in music in human cultures have thus been based on ideas arising from evolutionary theory.

Theories about the evolutionary functions of music date right back to Charles Darwin. Darwin proposed, in his book *Descent of Man*, that music was important in processes of sexual selection, arguing that musical ability was, in essence, the human equivalent of the peacock's tail. Since this idea will be discussed at length in Chap. 12, when we consider the topic of music and love, we will not consider it further here.

S. Garrido, *Why Are We Attracted to Sad Music?*,
DOI 10.1007/978-3-319-39666-8_3

However, other theorists have proposed convincing explanations for the role of music in promoting human survival.

Many of these theories argue that music conferred some kind of social benefit on our ancestors, which promoted survival by assisting individuals to form alliances in group settings. For example, one theory suggests that music developed as a kind of pre-verbal communication between parents and children and a way of checking the wellbeing of offspring when caregivers had to move away from a child in order to gather food, for example (Dissanayake, 2000). The fact that singing is still important in parent–child bonding today and that children are born with some innate abilities to decode and remember music tends to support this argument (Hallam, 2010; Trehub, 2003).

Other theories focus on how music, particularly its rhythmic aspect, can help to train the co-ordination of movement in group activities that may have been important for hunting and gathering. Entrainment—the capacity to synchronize to an external rhythm—is present in very few animal species. Even primates show little ability to move their fingers in time to an external beat (Zarco, Merchant, Prado, & Mendez, 2009). However, humans are able to entrain to beats of varying tempi and often do so quite unconsciously—a capacity that would have made it easier for members of groups to work together to achieve common goals. Other social benefits that music is argued to have conferred on our ancestors are the enhancement of cognitive and social skills (Cross, 2001), the ability to tune in to the emotions that other people are expressing (Livingstone & Thompson, 2009), and the power to confer a sense of importance within rituals as well as to enhance learning (Patel, 2008).

Thus, there are many reasons that can be proposed to explain why we find music so pleasurable and enjoyable. However, this still leaves us with the intriguing question of why we should be attracted to sad music. If negative emotions are biologically designed to motivate us to escape from uncomfortable or threatening situations, why then should we be so willing to listen to music that makes us cry? Some of the reasons proposed by philosophers throughout the centuries will be discussed in the next section of this chapter.

The Paradox of Our Attraction to Sad Music

As we have seen in the previous chapters, the experience of listening to sad music seems to defy conventional understandings of sadness as a 'negative' emotion, with sad music and films being among the most popular with both their creators and audiences. This has evidently been the case since at least the time of Aristotle, since he himself commented on the paradox both in relation to the tragic theatre of his day and to music.

In Aristotle's time plays such as Sophocles' *Oedipus the King*, first performed around 429 BC, would have been played in large outdoor theatres such as the Theatre of Dionysus in Athens, which probably held around 12,000–17,000 people. The story of Oedipus is a famous one: an oracle predicted that Oedipus would kill his father and marry his mother and Oedipus subsequently spends much of his life wrestling with fate in an attempt to avoid the destiny predicted for him. Oedipus eventually learns the terrible truth that he has indeed killed his own father and married his mother. He then pokes out his own eyes and his wife (and mother) commits suicide. The play ends with an empty stage and the repetition by the chorus of a rather depressing Greek maxim, that 'no man should be considered fortunate until he is dead'.

At its original performance Sophocles' play won second prize in the city Dionysia. Aristotle, in his *Poetics*, lauded it as the best example of drama in existence. It has remained popular ever since, with the play having been performed and filmed countless times as well as being adapted to modern political stories. All of which begs the question: Why has such a dark tale retained its popularity?

This question has been the subject of much discussion. Aristotle concluded that tragedies held their appeal in that they gave the viewer an opportunity to experience catharsis, or to release their own negative emotions. Freud also considered the popularity of this play, arguing that the tale illustrated the supposedly universal desire of a son to possess his mother and to eliminate his father. Nevertheless, Oedipus is not the only tragic story to achieve such a level of popularity. Friedrich Nietzsche was thus more interested in the phenomenon of Greek tragedy in general and why the ancient Greeks would create such an art form. His conclusions were that true art must reflect life and must thus be amoral because life in its very core is not moral. The attraction of the ancient Greek tragedy, according to Nietzsche, lay in the way it celebrated life unconditionally and captured its essence without flinching.

The ancient Greeks were, of course, not the only civilization to value tragedy and expressions of sadness in the arts. The all-time highest-grossing film on record (when box office figures are adjusted for inflation) is the 1939 film *Gone With the Wind*. In real figures, the second highest-grossing film of all time is the 1997 film *Titanic*, which grossed over $2 billion internationally at the box office. Both of these films could be described as "tear-jerkers", being highly likely to draw tears in the viewer. Sad music seems to be equally popular. The *Guinness Book of Records* of 2009 states that Elton John's "Candle in the Wind"—a song famously associated with the tragic death of Diana, Princess of Wales in 1997—is the world's biggest-selling single of all time, having sold over 33 million copies. A quick perusal of the most popular songs in Australia in the year 2015 confirms a similar phenomenon: number 3 on the list is a song by Wiz Khalifa called "See You Again" and number 5 is a track by Adele called "Hello", both of which consider themes of loss, separation and broken relationships.

In fact, the aesthetic enjoyment of sadness in music seems to be something experienced by all kinds of people, no matter what genre of music they prefer. Levinson (1996b) comments that art which expresses negative emotions is often held to be the most rewarding art of all. This is borne out in empirical research as well. Emery Schubert (2007) reports that most subjects in his study experienced reactions of greater emotional strength when listening to pieces expressing negative emotions than to other types of music, and that the strength of the emotion elicited was a key factor in participants' liking for a piece of music.

Thus, it is apparent that the human love of tragedy is almost equal to our preoccupation with happiness, and that this has been the case throughout much of history, from the time of the ancient Greeks until today. Since Aristotle first proposed his 'catharsis' theory, countless numbers of philosophers have written on the subject of why we listen to sad music. As discussed in Chap. 2, cognitive theorists argue that we do not actually experience 'garden-variety' emotions as expressed in the music, but rather experience 'aesthetic awe' which is then mistaken for the sadness perceived in the music (Kivy, 2002). Emotivists, on the other hand, although their arguments may differing in detail, tend to agree that there is some connection between the emotions expressed in the music and those experienced by the listener.

However, on the point of whether the emotions experienced are the same as real-life emotions and what our motivations may be for seeking out negative emotions in music, emotivist theories disagree. In an article on the subject of emotional response to art in general, Levinson (1996a) categorizes the various explanations for our attraction to negative emotions in aesthetic contexts into five groups: deflationary and revisionist explanations, compensatory (also known as functional), organicist, and conversionary explanations.

We have already encountered 'deflationary' and 'revisionist' explanations in Chap. 2. The former include arguments by Kivy and other cognitivists, who deny that the emotions evoked in the listener are anything like real-life emotions, while the latter include those who, like Patricia Greenspan, argue for a broader understanding of emotion that can encompass what is experienced in response to music. We will now consider the other categories mentioned by Levinson a little more closely.

Compensatory or Functional Explanations

Compensatory or functional explanations present the idea that there are benefits obtained when listening to sad music that somehow compensate for the negative emotions experienced. Aristotle's argument about catharsis—that aesthetic engagement with tragedy allows people to vent their own feelings of sadness—is one of the oldest of these types of explanations. It is generally believed that the venting of strong emotions results in a beneficial lessening of tension (Rathus, 2002, p. 303). Crying also may result in the production of prolactin, a hormone that can induce a feeling of calmness and comfort (Huron, 2011). Thus, listening to sad music when one is feeling sad could provide an important psychological release of tension and correspondingly increased sensations of calm and wellbeing. Aristotle's explanation was thus perceptive although written more than 2000 years ago.

However, despite the strength of this argument, it does not offer an entire solution to the paradox. Catharsis is a process mostly useful to people who are experiencing strong negative emotions at the time of listening to the music. It still leaves us without an adequate explanation for its strong attraction for people who are not dealing with sadness or grief. It also implies that the greatest value or pleasure to be found in listening to sad music is in the relief that we feel when the music (and our emotional experience) comes to an end. This does not account for the fact that people often enjoy the experience of the sadness itself during the listening, nor does it account for the fact that even people who are not currently feeling sad may enjoy listening to sad music.

Levinson proposes several other rewards that may accrue from listening to sad music that offer some kind of 'compensation' for the experience of a negative emotion. One other benefit that may be enjoyed is the reward of 'emotional resolution', or the feeling that comes from a happy ending. A happy ending or a happy resolution to a piece of music may be all the more pleasurable if it occurs at the end of a sad song, movie or story. The triumph of good over evil is a popular theme in narratives of all kind, including musical ones. However, once again, this explanation, although plausible, leaves more questions unanswered than are answered. If this is the answer, why, then, do we also enjoy music that does not resolve happily? Why, also, do we enjoy the sad part of the music before it has resolved? As Kivy (1989) argues, we do not experience our satisfaction only when the work concludes, but rather enjoy the music all the way through, suggesting that there is more to the picture.

A further functional explanation described by Levinson is the reward to be enjoyed from 'expressive potency', or, in other words, the reassurance received of our own power to feel and express deep emotion. As some theorists have expressed it, music and other art forms give us an arena for 'practicing' emotions that are commonly experienced in human life. The implication of Levinson's argument is that listening to sad music somehow helps listeners to become more emotionally adjusted. Both Davies (1997) and Kivy (1989) object to this argument, countering that there is little evidence that people who listen to such music end up with a greater understanding of emotion than others or that they are better able to cope with tragic situations in life. However, some support for the idea of expressive potency is suggested by evolutionary arguments about the value of music in allowing us to engage with other people emotionally and to understand emotions when expressed by others (Livingstone & Thompson, 2009).

In fact, there is some evidence that the ability to recognize the emotions being expressed in music is related to emotional intelligence (Reniscow, Salovey, & Repp, 2004). Emotional intelligence is a multidimensional group of abilities that includes the ability to recognize and monitor expressions of emotion in oneself and others, and to take this into consideration to guide one's own behaviour (Kaczmarek & Hawryluk, 2014). However, although one study found that six-year-old children were better at identifying anger and fear in speech after one year of keyboard training than those who had no training and those who studied singing or drama (Thompson, Schellenberg, & Husain, 2004), subsequent research has reported no significant increase in emotional intelligence after musical training (Schellenberg, 2011). Glenn Schellenberg and Monika Mankarious (2012) did find differences between musically trained and untrained children on scores of emotional intelligence. However, the difference disappeared when IQ scores were held constant, suggesting that general intellectual ability is the primary factor. Thus, the evidence as to whether greater exposure to music or musical training can result in enhanced emotional intelligence is at this stage, inconclusive.

Thirdly, Levinson proposes that an additional reward enjoyed from listening to sad music is that of 'emotional communion', or the idea that we are sharing the emotional experience with another human being, even if an imaginary one. This, too, is a persuasive argument. As noted above, one of the primary functions of music throughout human history has been to enhance social bonding and promote group cohesion. From an evolutionary perspective cooperation between members of a group is important for survival because groups are more effective than individuals at defending against predators. A lone zebra, for example, is more likely to be caught by a lion than one that is in the middle of a large herd.

In primates, group cohesion is often promoted by grooming behaviours. Evolutionary anthropologist Robin Dunbar (1998) theorized that when social groups began to get too large for grooming to be an effective form of bonding, our ancestors therefore began to substitute vocalizations (or 'vocal grooming') for physical grooming. David Huron (2001) argued that this form of social bonding is one of the most plausible explanations for the development of music. He argues that it even offers several advantages over speech itself, in that singing is louder than speaking, and can be performed by a whole group of people at one time, thus coordinating motor activities or mobilizing a group to a particular activity by synchronizing their moods.

There is no doubt that one of the primary attractions of music is the sense of social connection to other people that it offers. Throughout human history, music has primarily been a group activity. Traditionally, in most cultures throughout the world, music was not the elitist profession that we know it as in the West today. Rather, every member of a tribe was a musician and music making was considered a part of the daily life of every member of the tribe. This understanding of music survives today in tribal cultures such as the Venda people of South Africa (Davidson & Emberly, 2012).

In the West, by contrast, the performance of music has largely become the domain of an elite group of trained professionals. In the twenty-first century technology now allows us to enjoy the sound of an entire symphony orchestra or rock concert in the comfort of our own home in complete solitude, without requiring the presence of a single other individual. Nevertheless, while the traditional meaning of music as a force for social cohesion may have been lost as its dominant function today, we do still retain a sense of connection to other people, even when entirely alone while listening to it. Where people are feeling otherwise alone, perhaps isolated by depression or loneliness, it is entirely plausible that sad music provides a sense of not being so alone in the experience of one's emotions. It may provide the sense that we are understood, whether by the singer, the composer or some unidentified imagined entity behind the music.

However, despite the persuasiveness of the functional explanations that Levinson lists and others, we still do not fully understand why we should be interested in experiencing it. Why should sad music hold equal or even greater attraction (for some) than music expressing happier emotions? Even if these benefits in some way mute the impact of the negative emotions there still does not seem any reason to actually enjoy them. If Levinson's proposals were true, the musical works would be even more enjoyable if the negative emotions were removed altogether. We could, presumably, enjoy a sense of emotional connection, or a sense of our own emotional potency by simply experiencing strong positive emotions which would not make it necessary for there to be any kind of 'compensation' for the negative emotions experienced. Again, these explanations all imply that the experience of sad music is somehow inherently unpleasant, but that we submit to for the ultimate benefits, failing to account for the fact that for some the experience is simply enjoyable in itself even when no benefits are obtained.

Organicist Explanations

Organicist explanations argue that listeners desire the whole gamut of emotional experiences involved in listening to music, which would include the experience of negative emotions. It is claimed that the negative emotions experienced when listening to music are but a small part of a larger experience, which is desirable in itself. Along these lines, Davies (1997) argues that the question of why we enjoy sad music is not really the issue at stake. It is merely part of the larger phenomenon that we enjoy music in general. He posits that since we do find enjoyment in listening to music, it is natural that we would want to explore the full range of musical experiences including sad music. Davies argues at length against Levinson's compensatory explanations described above, saying that most of Levinson's proposed benefits only show how the sad effect might be mitigated, but do not explain why we are attracted to it.

One limitation of Davies' hypothesis is that it still does not explain why people might at times be attracted to choose sad music over another kind of music. As Davies himself says, if he is right, "the listener should be as interested in the one kind of work as the other … negative responses are no more problematic than positive ones" (pp. 247, 249). In other words, they should be equally interested in both happy and sad music. Taking this line of argument even further, if Davies is right, people would also enjoy equally music that does not arouse them emotionally at all. The evidence indicates, however, that people tend to prefer music that evokes a strong emotional response (Schubert, 2007a).

In support of his reasoning, Davies argues that people who shun confrontation with pain and suffering miss out on the things that make life worthwhile, and that thus people seek the breadth of emotional experience that can be had when listening to music, whether positive or negative. However, if this were true, we would also expect people to seek out negative emotional experiences in real life. In reality, we know that, in general, people do avoid situations or events that induce negative emotions, although they may be willing to risk the experience of them in order to seek out other things that are important. This brings us back full circle to the compensatory explanations described by Levinson, which Davies worked so hard to argue against. In reality, Davies' argument merely broadens the problem rather than solving it.

Conversionary Explanations

Conversionary explanations maintain that the aesthetic context of musical experience transforms the experience into something agreeable. Levinson's (1990a, 1990b) argument that in aesthetic contexts the emotions aroused are not "full-fledged", but are very much like them (p. 308), is an example of a conversionary explanation. Levinson claims that when emotional affect is devoid of psychological and behavioural consequences it can be satisfying for its own sake. John Hospers (1969) made a similar argument when he explained that in music we get what he calls "the essence of sadness", which is different from "life-sadness" in that it is devoid of the usual causal conditions (p. 152). Colin Radford (1991) thus describes music as an "especially inviting way to experience the somber and tragic aspects of life" (p. 251).

Marcia Eaton (1982) argues that it is the element of control involved in aesthetic experiences which provides the essential difference to real-life experiences, making it possible to enjoy negative emotions. She draws a parallel with people who enjoy rollercoasters for the very fear that it arouses. Such an experience can be exhilarating, but only if the participant is in control of the situation, participates of their own free will, and believes that the risk is one that can be handled. Likewise, Eaton argues that people listen to sad music for the thrill of the emotional 'roller-coaster', knowing that they are in control of the situation, can terminate it at any time and are not in any real danger. Laurel Trainor and Louis Schmidt (2003) suggest that the extra control is cognitive, that music is somehow more subject to cognitive control than other emotions, and that this is what distinguishes it from emotions experienced in everyday life. Rather than providing an opportunity for a roller-coaster ride of emotions, Jourdain (1997) presents a contrary idea, suggesting that the artificial environment of listening to music imparts a dignity to emotions which are usually perceived as unpleasant, allowing the experience of deeper feelings that are usually encountered in everyday life.

While the emotions experienced in response to sad music may feel just as real to many of us as those in real life, most would probably admit that the sting of such emotions is probably not as acute as it would be were they accompanied by the knowledge that some long-term damage or loss had been afflicted on us. When we know that the emotions we are experiencing are triggered by a piece of music that we can switch off or walk away from at will, or that will come to an end in a relatively short period of time, on some level, the pain of the emotion is likely to be dulled. However, this again does not appear to provide a full explanation for why we are attracted to sad music. Even if the pain is somewhat lessened, why experience that pain at any level if more pleasant experiences in the form of happier music are readily available? Conversionary explanations again leave us with the difficulty that we still don't understand why people enjoy sad music or are attracted to it over and above happier music.

The Flaws in the Philosophical Arguments

Many of the explanations offered above have considered the paradox of tragedy from the point of view of a general philosophy of aesthetics. It is only in the last five years or so that anything other than theorizing and 'armchair' philosophizing has taken place. Little systematic research was undertaken to test the viability of these proposed explanations or any others until quite recently. The empirical research that has been conducted since then is the subject of much of the discussion in the rest of the volume.

Prior to the conduct of the empirical investigations that will be discussed in the subsequent chapters, many of the explanations offered by philosophers were largely based on their own personal experiences, generalizations about the observed behaviour of others or sometimes even speculation about the behaviour of a fictitious listener. Eaton's arguments, for example, (1982) draw largely on descriptions of her own film-watching experiences. Similarly, Levinson (1990b) begins his account with a description of a fictitious man sitting by a record player, an imaginary listener. Walton (1997) admits that his argument is at least partly based on his own phenomenological experience, as does Kivy (1989) who say "what I hear in music must be … the basic data for my theory" (p. 989).

These are, of course, valid approaches to philosophical discussion and a necessary stage to the finding of answers to any question about human behaviour. After all, no empirical testing is possible until the questions have been clearly defined, and this is often the domain of philosophers. However, the fact that the philosophical approach was the only approach taken to this question for hundreds of years meant that a plethora of *ideas* existed—some plausible and some less so—but little concrete evidence of how or why people are attracted to sad music.

Philosophical approaches also represent only one possible level of explanation. The 'level of explanation' of a hypothesis refers to the different ways a question can be explained, depending on who is explaining it. For example, a person eating may say that they are eating a piece of fruit because it feels good, whereas a biologist might explain the same behaviour by describing the chemical processes involved in cell metabolism and appetite stimulation. Neither explanation is wrong; they simply represent explanations of different levels. Daniel Dennett (1986) argues that the human mind can be discussed at "two levels of explanation" (p. 95): the personal and the subpersonal. The person eating in my earlier example was providing a personal level of explanation (sometimes referred to as phenomenological), whereas the biologist was applying a subpersonal level of explanation. A discussion at a personal level of explanation may examine a belief or the perception of the individual, while a sub-personal explanation might attempt to explain response in terms of mechanisms or processes of which the person may not be consciously aware.

Anecdotal evidence and personal explanations are, of course, not the most convincing forms of argument. There are certain paradoxes inherent in a situation where one attempts to observe the operation of one's own mind. The limitations of explaining psychological mechanisms by means of introspection are well documented (Leahey, 1992). Despite the certainty with which individuals may think they understand their own experience, abilities to explicitly characterize experience are often inadequate and can vary depending on circumstances (Schooler & Schreiber, 2004). In all, it is difficult to gauge how much we have conscious access to cognitive mechanisms and how much of what we perceive is a result of a personal (though fictional) understanding of reality that we have created in our mind (Churchland, 1988).

It is perhaps even more problematic to understand the mind of another. Even when speaking about the actual experiences of an individual our understanding is filtered through both the individual's own description of it and our own experiences. It is difficult to know whether one's understanding is the 'reality' of a situation, the person's own distorted reconstruction of their experience, or is, in fact, a projection of one's own personal viewpoint and experiences. This danger is well illustrated by the varying conclusions that philosophers such as Kivy and Levinson arrive at, both using their own individual experiences as the basis for their arguments. It may well be that it is this very failure to consider evidence outside of one's own experience that has led to such vastly divergent theories. As Manuel (2005) writes: "this lack of consensus may derive from limitations inherent to the scholarly approach of aestheticians" (para 53).

These limitations are nowhere more apparent than in considering a question on which the cognitivists and emotivists are passionately divided: the question over whether people do actually feel sad when listening to sad music. In Manuel's (2005) somewhat informal study, he reports that of the 50 people he polled, very few people claimed that listening to sad music actually made them experience sadness at all. Manuel argues that this is a fundamental flaw in the arguments of many theorists, who assume that sad music actually does make us sad. While Manuel's survey was not intended to be a robust scientific study, it does highlight the fact that individual experiences differ with regard to their reaction to sad music. Manuel admits that his findings do not strongly support either the cognitivist or the emotivist viewpoints, since there was support for each argument within the responses of his participants. Other studies reveal similar contradictions (see, for example, Konečni, Brown, & Wanic, 2008).

One solution to this conundrum may be to conclude that there is no single response that is experienced by every person when listening to sad music. There are obviously some people who do not enjoy sad music—who, in fact, avoid it. There may be others who listen to sad music and are made sadder, others who do not experience any emotional reaction to it whatsoever, and others who listen to sad music and find it pleasurable. In fact, even a single individual may experience a different reaction to a given piece of music at different listenings. Radford (1991) agrees that personal disposition may affect a person's response to music. He argues that our response to music is tied to our ultimate view of life as sad and tragic or otherwise.

Nevertheless, most writers on the subject of why we listen to sad music consider the topic primarily at a personal level. Few have addressed the issue of the mechanisms or subpersonal explanations underlying emotional response to music. However, as Dennett argues, a phenomenological experience has a physical basis. David Owens (1989) argues that physics is at the base of the hierarchy of levels of explanation; it is the fundamental science. Therefore, much of the conflict between cognitivists and emotivists and other writers on the topic likely arises because the paradox is being discussed at a personal level, and individual differences may underlie the phenomenological differences in the experiences of these writers.

This kind of bias has been found to happen in other areas, such as the imagery debate, where Pearson (2007) found that different theories from distinguished scholars about mental image processing seemed to be influenced by personal beliefs. Thus, it seems likely that rather than there being a single answer as to why we are attracted to sad music, there is in fact some truth to many of the philosophical explanations discussed above, and that they simply represent part of the variety of human experience in response to music. A key to understanding the paradox of pleasure from tragedy, therefore, may be to examine the issue at a sub-personal level, including looking at underlying mechanisms, and thereby identifying the factors that are the basis of the individual differences in response to sad music.

Individual differences in response to music will therefore form a large part of the investigations discussed in subsequent chapters (see Chap. 4). Before going on to discuss this, however, the next chapter will consider the evidence relating to the physiological effects of listening to sad music, much of which will help to resolve the philosophical debates over whether or not real emotions are experienced.

References

Churchland, P. M. (1988). *Matter and consciousness: A contemporary introduction to the Philosophy of Mind*. Cambridge, MA: MIT Press.

Cross, I. (2001). Music; cognition; culture; evolution. *Annals of the New York Academy of Science, 930*, 28–42.

Davidson, J. W., & Emberly, A. (2012). Singing, dancing and embodied communication: Research perspectives. In R. MacDonald, L. Mitchell, & G. Kreutz (Eds.), *Music, health and wellbeing* (pp. 136–152). Oxford: Oxford University Press.

Davies, S. (1997). Why listen to sad music if it makes one feel sad? In J. Robinson (Ed.), *Music and meaning*. New York: Cornell University Press.

Dennett, D. C. (1986). *Content and consciousness*. New York: Routledge.

Dissanayake, E. (2000). Antecedents of the temporal arts in early mother-infant interactions. In N. L. Wallin, B. Merker, & S. Brown (Eds.), *The origins of music*. Cambridge, MA: MIT Press.

Dunbar, R. (1998). *Grooming, gossip, and the evolution of language*. Cambridge, MA: Harvard University Press.

Eaton, M. (1982). A strange kind of sadness. *Journal of Aesthetics and Art Criticism, 41*(1), 51–63.

Hallam, S. (2010). The power of music: Its impact on the intellectual, social and personal development of children and young people. *International Journal of Music Education, 28*(3), 269–289. doi:10.1177/0255761410370658.

Hospers, J. (1969). The concept of artistic expression. In J. Hospers (Ed.), *Introductory readings in aesthetics*. New York: Palgrave Macmillan.

Huron, D. (2001). Is music an evolutionary adaptation? *Annals of the New York Academy of Sciences, 930*, 43–61.
Huron, D. (2011). Why is sad music pleasurable? A possible role for prolactin. *Musicae Scientiae, 15*(2), 146–158.
Jourdain, R. (1997). *Music, the brain and ecstasy*. New York: William Morrow.
Kaczmarek, L., & Hawryluk, M. (2014). Emotional intelligence. In W. Thompson (Ed.), *Music in the Social and Behavioral Sciences: An Encyclopedia*. Thousands Oaks, CA: Sage.
Kivy, P. (1989). *Sound sentiment*. Princeton: Princeton University Press.
Kivy, P. (2002). *Introduction to a philosophy of music*. Oxford: Clarendon Press.
Konečni, V. J., Brown, A., & Wanic, R. A. (2008). Comparative effects of music and recalled life-events on emotional state. *Psychology of Music, 36*, 289–308.
Leahey, T. H. (1992). The mythical revolutions of American psychology. *American Psychologist, 47*(2), 308–318.
Levinson, J. (1990a). The concept of music. *Music, art and metaphysics* (pp. 267–278). Ithaca, NY: Cornell University Press.
Levinson, J. (1990b). Music and negative emotions. In J. Levinson (Ed.), *Music, art and metaphysics: Essays in emotional aesthetics* (pp. 306–335). Ithaca: Cornell University Press.
Levinson, J. (1996a). Music and negative emotions. In J. Robinson (Ed.), *Music and meaning*. New York: Cornell University Press.
Levinson, J. (1996b). *Musical expressiveness the pleasures of aesthetics: Philosophical essays*. New York: Cornell University Press.
Livingstone, S. R., & Thompson, W. F. (2009). The emergence of music from the theory of mind. *Musicae Scientiae, 13*(2), 83–115.
Manuel, P. (2005). Does sad music make one sad? An ethnographic perspective. *Contemporary Aesthetics, 3*. Retrieved from http://www.contempaesthetics.org/newvolume/pages/article.php?articleID=286
Owens, D. (1989). Levels of explanation. *Mind, 98*(389), 59–79.
Patel, A. D. (2008). Music as a transformative technology of the mind. Paper presented at the *Music: Its Evolution, Cognitive Basis, and Spiritual Dimensions symposium*, Wolfson College, Cambridge University.
Pearson, D. C. (2007). Mental imagery and creative thought. In I. Roth (Ed.), *Imaginative minds* (pp. 187–212). Oxford: Oxford University Press.
Pinker, S. (1997). *How the mind works*. New York: W. W. Norton.
Radford, C. (1991). Muddy waters. *Journal of Aesthetics and Art Criticism, 49*(3), 247–252.
Rathus, S. A. (2002). *Psychology in the New Millenium* (8th ed.). Orlando: Harcourt College Publishers.

Reniscow, J. E., Salovey, P., & Repp, B. H. (2004). Is recognition of emotion in music performance an aspect of Emotional Intelligence? *Music Perception, 22*(1), 145–158.

Schellenberg, E. G. (2011). Music lessons, emotional intelligence, and IQ. *Music Perception, 29*(2), 185–194.

Schellenberg, E. G., & Mankarious, M. (2012). Music training and emotion comprehension in childhood. *Emotion, 12*(5), 887–891.

Schooler, J. W., & Schreiber, C. A. (2004). Experience, meta-consciousness, and the paradox of introspection. *Journal of Consciousness Studies, 11*(7-8), 17–39.

Schubert, E. (2007). The influence of emotion, locus of emotion and familiarity upon preferences in music. *Psychology of Music, 35*, 499–515.

Thompson, W. F., Schellenberg, E. G., & Husain, G. (2004). Decoding speech prosody: Do music lessons help? *Emotion, 4*, 46–64.

Trainor, L. J., & Schmidt, L. A. (2003). Processing emotions induced by music. In I. Peretz & R. J. Zatorre (Eds.), *The cognitive neuroscience of music* (pp. 310–324). Oxford: Oxford University Press.

Trehub, S. (2003). The developmental origins of musicality. *Nature Neuroscience, 6*(7), 669–673.

Walton, K. (1997). Listening with imagination: Is music representational? In J. Robinson (Ed.), *Music and meaning*. New York: Cornell University Press.

Zarco, W., Merchant, H., Prado, L., & Mendez, J. C. (2009). Subsecond timing in primates: Comparison of interval production between human subjects and rhesus monkeys. *Journal of Neurophysiology, 102*, 3191–3902.

4

Physiological Effects of Sad Music

Often the most startling aspects of an emotional experience are the physiological changes that occur in the body. For example, when a person feels nervous or apprehensive about something such as an approaching exam or an important meeting, their heart may begin to race, their palms sweat and they may feel unsettled in their stomach. These kinds of bodily reactions are physiological responses to an affective stimulus and reflect activity in our autonomic nervous system (ANS). Since physiological responses are a component of emotional response, they are of particular interest to us in relation to the question of whether we experience real emotions in response to music, and, for the purposes of this volume, whether we do in fact experience sadness when listening to sad music. This chapter will, therefore, firstly discuss the role that physiological reactions play in emotional responses generally before examining the evidence in relation to music and sad music more specifically.

S. Garrido, *Why Are We Attracted to Sad Music?*,
DOI 10.1007/978-3-319-39666-8_4

The Role of Physiological Responses in Emotions

The ANS is the part of our nervous system that regulates many of the body's systems over which we have no voluntary control, such as our blood pressure, our heart rate, and perspiration. The ANS is the seat of what is often called the 'fight-or-flight' response—that is, the rapid and instinctive preparation that our body makes to enable us to defend ourselves or to flee when our environment signals that there is danger about. Thus, in the face of perceived danger or unexpected events, hormones such as epinephrine (adrenalin) or cortisol are released, which are associated with increased heart rate, faster respiration and intensified sweat secretion. These physiological changes deliver a burst of energy to our muscles to enable a swift reaction to an immediate threat, or in the case of an exam or a meeting as is more often the case in modern-day life, to enable us to act with a heightened sense of alertness.

On the other hand, positive emotions involve the release of chemicals in the ANS such as dopamine and opioids that are involved in the reward pathways of the brain. These pathways are activated whenever we engage in something or encounter something that is pleasurable, such as eating, sexual intercourse or pleasant social interactions, and act so as to "reward" or motivate us to engage in the same behavior again.

Emotion theorists have not always agreed over the role that physiological responses play in an emotional reaction. For example, according to the James–Lange Theory of emotion, the physiological response is the primary element of an emotional response. William James and Carl Lange, who had developed this theory in the latter part of the nineteenth century, posited that the emotion experienced is a result of the individual's perception or recognition of the physiological symptoms they are experiencing. Emotions are thus the consequences rather than the precursors of the physiological symptoms. If a person is in a threatening situation and begins to experience elevated heart rates and rapid breathing, for example, then perceiving this physical response as a fear response the individual draws the conclusion that they are scared.

One criticism that has often been levelled at this theory is that it presupposes that each emotion has one specific physiological profile. A principal proponent of this idea of emotion-specific physiological profiles has been one of the most influential psychologists in the field of emotional expression, Paul Ekman (1992), who argued that each emotion had unique physiological features that are a product of their evolutionary function. Ekman and his team found some support for this in a study in which they looked at physiological responses to a directed facial action task and a task in which participants were asked to relive a past emotional experience (Ekman, Levenson, & Friesen, 1983). They found that several measures, including heart rate, finger temperature, skin resistance and forearm muscle tension, could be used to differentiate between positive and negative emotions, and to distinguish between fear, anger and sadness.

However, the idea of emotions being based solely on the perception of ANS activation is called into question by studies demonstrating that people with spinal cord injuries who have impaired levels of feedback for such physiological systems are still able to experience emotions (Chwalisz, Diener, & Gallagher, 1988). The overall evidence for emotion-specific physiological responses also remains inconclusive. In a meta-analysis John Cacioppo and colleagues (Cacioppo, Berntson, Larsen, Poehlmann, & Ito, 2000; Larsen, Poehlmann, Ito, & Cacioppo, 2008) found that although some reliable autonomic differentiation was achieved in several studies, the specific patterns of physiological responses were less clear. They concluded that while particular emotions such as sadness or anger could not be differentiated by physiological responses alone, it seemed that, overall, stronger ANS responses are usually associated with negative emotions. Thus, while it seems that there is no specific pattern of physiological responses associated with distinct emotions, it is possible to distinguish positive from negative emotions, and high arousal from low arousal responses.

In the 1920s Walter Bradford Cannon and Philip Bard developed an alternative view of the role of physiological responses in emotions. Known as the Cannon–Bard Theory, this theory argues that physiological changes occur simultaneously with, rather than prior to, the subjective experience of an emotion. Stanley Schachter and Jerome Singer

(1962) also attempted to overcome the limitations of the James–Lange Theory by proposing a mechanism by which the undifferentiated physiological responses might be distinguished by the person experiencing the emotion. They argued that the perception of physiological arousal creates an "evaluative need" which then motivates the individual to understand and label the state, and that the cognitive processes involved cause the individual to consider the particular situation they are in at the time in making this judgment. For example, the physiological effects of excitement and fear can be quite similar: racing heart, sweating palms, etc. However, according to Schachter and Singer, whether or not the individual experiences fear or excitement will depend to a large degree on whether or not they perceive the situation they are in to be one of danger.

Gary Berntson and colleagues (Berntson, Sarter, & Cacioppo, 1998) argue that the processes are even more complex. They proposed a neurobiological model that emphasizes the contribution of multiple systems, including cognitive processes and visceral reactivity. This is borne out by the neurobiological evidence available to date. It is known that activation of the ANS takes place in the brain, in particular the limbic system, which is sometimes called 'the emotional brain'. This network of structures in the brain includes the amygdala and the hippocampus, and is the part of the brain that regulates our emotions, and where long-term memories are encoded. It is the amygdala, in particular, that initiates the fight-or-flight response in reaction to a perceived threat, at times recruiting connections to the hippocampus to retrieve memories that can help in the decoding of the emotional content of cues from our environment. The prefrontal cortex, on the other hand, is where the cognitive part of our emotional response takes place. It is here that the appraisal of a situation occurs and the reactions of the amygdala may be mediated. It appears that these processes in the prefrontal cortex often occur well after the initial response of the amygdala to a stimulus, and that the successful moderation of emotional responses rely on connectivity between the amygdala and the prefrontal cortex (Banks, Eddy, Angstadt, Nathan, & Luan Phan, 2007). Klaus Scherer (2005) similarly proposes a component process model in which emotions are defined as consisting of synchronized responses across several or all organic subsystems that include physiological arousal, motor expression and subjective feelings, a cognitive element and action tendencies. Thus, emotional reactions involve a complex interplay between rapid and automatic responses and higher-level cognitive processes.

Physiological Changes in Response to Music and Sad Music

Since physiological responses to a stimulus are among the most noticeable and the most measurable indicators of emotions, the evidence in relation to the physiological effects of listening to sad music could offer a useful resolution to several of the philosophical questions discussed in previous chapters. If, for example, we feel real emotions when listening to music, we would expect that the physiological responses observed in listeners would be similar to that observed in people in non-aesthetic contexts. Similarly, if we do experience sadness when listening to sad music, we would expect that listeners would display physiological responses that are comparable to experiences of sadness experienced in real-life settings. On the other hand, if, as many cognitivists posit, the emotions we experience are not real then we would expect the physiological indicators of emotion to be absent or to differ in some way from that of 'everyday emotions'.

General Responses to Music

In general, it seems that our physiological responses to music are much the same as our response to other emotion-eliciting sounds in our environment. Our brains are biologically programmed to respond quickly and instinctively to particular sounds and then to analyze the source of the sound and evaluate the potential danger it signals. The arousal caused by the response of the ANS prompts us to attend to and assess the surrounding environment. While sensitivity to certain sounds appears to be instinctive, throughout our life other sounds also take on referential associations, thus expanding the subset of sounds that serve as auditory warnings (Petocz, Keller, & Stevens, 2008).

The first thing that becomes obvious when looking at the evidence in relation to biophysical responses to music is that when we listen to music we like, the same reward systems in the brain are activated that are triggered when engaging in other pleasurable activities (Blood & Zatorre, 2001; Menon & Levitin, 2005). These are often associated with intense physiological symptoms such as "chills", or shivers down the spine, and piloerection. However, listening to pleasurable music has been found to *de-activate* areas of the limbic system such as the amygdala and hippocampus that are involved in our response to stressful situations (Blood & Zatorre, 2001; Koelsch, Fritz, Yves v Cramon, Mueller, & Friederici, 2006). This appears to occur whether the music we listen to is happy or sad (Blood & Zatorre, 2001; Gabrielsson, 2001; Panksepp, 1995).

On the other hand, listening to unpleasant music such as dissonant music results in activation of the amygdala and many of the usual accompanying physiological manifestations. Psychoacoustic dissonance[1] is generally perceived as unpleasant by the vast majority of listeners across cultures, and appears to be the most primitive musical feature to trigger emotional responses, since even infants as young as two months old demonstrate a preference for consonance over dissonance (Trainor, Tsang, & Cheung, 2002). Several studies have found that areas of the limbic system are implicated in this response to dissonance. For example, Nathalie Gosselin and colleagues (2006) found that patients with damage to the parahippocampal cortex were less emotionally sensitive to dissonance, although they were still able to accurately perceive its presence and to distinguish between happy and sad music. The authors concluded that this part of the limbic system is specific to the emotional interpretation of dissonance, since such interpretations may be based largely on memories in which dissonant sounds have been paired with other emotional stimuli (see also Khalfa, Guye, et al., 2008). In other studies, increases in musical tension have also been found to result in activation in the amygdala (Lehne, Rohrmeier, & Koelsch, 2014).

[1] Psychoacoustic dissonance is sounds that are perceived as having an acoustic 'roughness' or a buzzing as a result of the physical properties of the inner ear. Cultural dissonance on the other hand, is based on aesthetic preferences that are developed through exposure to conventional musical harmonies of a particular culture.

What About Sad Music?

The evidence in relation to physiological responses to sad music paints a slightly more complex picture. As discussed in Chap. 2, listening to sad music often involves a high degree of cognitive modulation as the music may trigger memories or associations that are involved in the induction of emotion. It may also often involve a cognitive judgment that the situation invoking the emotion is fictional and therefore has few real-life consequences. Thus, listening to sad music likely involves less intense amygdala responses and more complex interactions with the prefrontal cortex, which may act so as to modulate physiological responses. Secondly, as alluded to frequently throughout this volume, unlike dissonance, sadness in the context of music is often experienced as pleasurable despite the common understanding of sadness as a negative emotion. However, when researchers look at biophysical responses to sad music they often fail to differentiate between experiences of sadness that are unpleasant and those sad experiences that are enjoyable, and typically use only mode and tempo to distinguish between happy and sad music. Thus, many of the complex responses that people have to sad music remain unaccounted for.

Even in terms of the perception of sadness in music, results are inconclusive. One of the earliest studies to use brain scan technology to look at emotion perception and music was by Stephanie Khalfa et al. (2005), who found that regions of the brain associated with introspection and self-referential evaluation were activated in response to music in a minor mode and a slow tempo. Gosselin and colleagues (2006) found that the amygdala was not critical for valence appraisal. In a later study, however, Khalfa and her team (2008a, 2008b) found that epileptics who have had brain resections involving the amygdala did demonstrate impaired recognition of sadness in music, suggesting that the amygdala is involved in our perception of sadness in music.

In relation to the actual emotions induced in the listener, it has been found that music that elicits both fear-like and sadness responses enhanced the reactivity of the amygdala and hippocampus to sad visual stimuli (Baumgartner, Lutz, Schmidt, & Jancke, 2006), suggesting that the amygdala and hippocampus are both involved in our emotional response to sad music. Similarly, researchers at King's College in London found increased activation in the hippocampus and amygdala as well as auditory processing areas of the brain when participants were played sad excerpts of classical music, in contrast to the presentation of neutral music, which activated only the auditory areas (Mitterschiffthaler, Fu, Dalton, Andrew, & Williams, 2007). However, the authors did not note whether the participants perceived the musical excerpts played as pleasant or not.

In contrast to these results, Elvira Brattico and colleagues at the University of Helsinki (2011) found that sad music induced activity within the right caudate head (activated during reward based learning and during highly pleasurable chill-inducing music) and the left thalamus, but that there was no activation of the amygdala and hippocampus. The contrast with the results in the study by Mitterschiffthaler and team may be due to the fact that the stimuli used by Brattico and colleagues was self-selected music rather than researcher-selected classical music. It is quite likely that participants selected music that they liked for both the happy and sad conditions and that the familiarity and subjective pleasure of the music contributed to the recruitment of different areas of the brain compared to the music used in Mitterschiffthaler's study.

Interestingly, Brattico's study also found that limbic system responses to sad music with lyrics were greater than to sad music without lyrics, while happy music was equally effective in inducing happy emotions whether it had lyrics or not. This is confirmed by behavioural studies that have also shown that instrumental music is effective in representing positive emotions, whereas sad emotions are reinforced by the presence of lyrics (Ali & Peynircioğlu, 2006).

It may be that it is the addition of the singing voice that increases the emotional intensity or that the presence of lyrics calls upon memory-based and contextual associations via the hippocampus. Thus, Sacha Früholz et al. (2014) suggest that, in fact, several neurological pathways may be implicated in processing musical emotions. They posit that a primary pathway that involves a direct route from the auditory system to the amygdala provides a speedy analysis of coarse acoustic information to facilitate immediate response. However, more complex acoustic information can activate other neural pathways that connect the higher-level auditory cortex, the amygdala and the hippocampus and that involve evaluations of social and contextual settings as well as the acoustic cues themselves. Thus, sad music can activate parts of the brain that both relate to instinctive and rapid physiological responses, and that relate to more complex auditory processing involving the retrieval of personal associations and memories as well as the semantic processing of lyrics.

David Huron's (2006) ITPRA theory, which was developed specifically in relation to how we perceive music, similarly suggests that a series of events are involved in our emotional responses to any kind of stimulus. Given that it is often surprising events that stimulate amygdalic activity, Huron's theory considers the role of expectation in our emotional response to music. He theorizes that there are five stages in our response: Imagination, Tension, Prediction, Reaction and Appraisal. It is from these that the theory takes its acronymic title.

As a first stage, Huron argues that we make predictions about an event or stimulus based on our knowledge of musical conventions (Imagination). The brain then increases its level of attention in order to be prepared for the expected outcome (Tension). The amygdala is involved in the Prediction response, particularly where expectations go unfulfilled. Huron thus argues that where the predictions are correct, the response will be positively valenced, while if the prediction is inaccurate the response will be negatively valenced. There is then an immediate and unconscious evaluation of the stimulus (Reaction), which is followed by a slower evaluation that takes place in the cerebral cortex (Appraisal). Where the outcome is more positive than is expected, however, the mismatch between the prediction and the outcome will result in an amplification of the effect, leading to an even greater positive evaluation.

As is evident from the above-cited studies a number of biological and neurological systems as well as cognitive processes are involved in our emotional response to music. It is likely this complex interplay of processes that makes studies of the physiological response to music so difficult to interpret.

Do We Experience Real Sadness in Response to Sad Music?

One of the primary difficulties with untangling the evidence from studies of physiological response to music goes right back to the fundamental differences between the James–Lange and later theories of emotion such as that of Schachter and Singer: the issue of whether particular emotions can be distinguished on the basis of physiological response, or whether what we see is a more generalized differentiation between valence or intensity. In one of the first studies to explore physiological response to music, Carol Krumhansl (1997) found significant changes to heart rate, blood pressure, skin conductance and skin temperature in response to sad excerpts. Ivan Nyklíček et al. (1997) also found that happy, sad, serene and agitated music could be distinguished from one another by measures of respiration and heart rate. More recent studies have also found distinct patterns of physiological activity in response to sad music as compared to other music conditions. For example, Joset Etzel et al. (2006) found that participant heart rates decelerated during sad music, but accelerated during the fear mood induction. Khalfa and colleagues (2008a, 2008b) also found that participants who listened to happy and sad music differed significantly on diastolic blood pressure, electrodermal activity, and zygomatic activity, while a control condition that was varied only according to tempo did not produce such differentiations. Lars-Olov Lundqvist and associates (Lundqvist, Carlsson, Hilmersson, & Juslin, 2009) also found decreased skin conductance, higher finger temperature, and decreased zygomatic activity in participants who listened to sad music.

However, other studies suggest that what is indicated by these physiological indices is the intensity of the emotion rather than any specific emotion or its valence. For example, physiological responses such as a racing heart, changes in body temperature, breathing or muscle tension have also been found, along with chill responses in relation to strong experiences of emotion both where participants reported being in a state of excitement and where they reported a state of deep relaxation (Gabrielsson, 2001). Nikki Rickard (2004) also found that physiological arousal as indicated by skin conductance increased with the intensity of the self-reported emotional response. Similarly, Kirk Olsen and Catherine Stevens (2013) found that longer increases in autonomic arousal as indicated by skin conductance were associated with higher ratings of emotional arousal.

The studies reported above in relation to the activation of brain regions and the physiological responses reported to music in general do suggest that the emotions we experience in response to music are real. Some emotion theorists do not regard fluctuations in peripheral arousal or changes in cerebral blood flow to be of themselves indicative of the presence of emotion. Konecni, Brown and Wanic (2008), for example, argue that one can be highly aroused by dynamics or rhythmic aspects of the music, without experiencing any emotion whatsoever. However, it is evident that key brain areas that are involved in the emotional responses to real-life situations are also activated in response to music, as are typical bio-physical indices of emotional response throughout the body, suggesting that the responses experienced are highly comparable to emotions experienced in real-life contexts.

As for differentiating between sadness and other emotions, this is complicated by the fact that physiological measures do not necessarily present a distinct pattern for specific emotions. It is further complicated by the fact that aesthetic situations such as music listening likely involve a higher degree of cognitive modulation of emotional responses than emotions such as fear, which require a more urgent and immediate response to the environment. It appears that at times this cognitive modulation can go so far as to make the experience of sadness pleasurable when listening to music, a concept that will be further discussed in Chap. 6. Thus, we do appear to see some slight differences between the way musical emotions are processed over emotions presented through other acoustic cues (Frühholz et al., 2014). However, these differences do not indicate that real emotions are absent, but merely that they are likely mitigated by cognitive appraisals of the situation.

It is possible that further investigations of the physiological response to sad music may begin to help us to further understand the phenomenon of how listening to sad music can be pleasurable. Several researchers are beginning to explore these questions. For example, in a study conducted at the National Taiwan University (Tsai, Chen, & Tsai, 2014), researchers played popular songs about heartbreak to their participants. They found that finger temperature responses exhibited a U-shaped response across the duration of a song. The authors concluded that these results reflected an increase in negative emotions at the beginning of a song that was subsequently resolved or released while listening to the song, suggesting that this provides evidence for the cathartic effects of sad music. However, participants were not asked about whether they were personally experiencing any form of negative emotions at the time, nor to what degree they were in need to some kind of cathartic release for these emotions. Thus, it is equally possible that no true catharsis was obtained, but rather the negative emotions aroused in the music were a response to the music itself, which subsequently stabilized through habituation to the music, or was resolved as the music progressed. While the results reported in this study suggest that the emotional reactions are real, it does not necessarily confirm that the opportunity for catharsis is the only psychological value that sad music offers, nor the primary reason we are attracted to it.

Another hypothesis proposed about how physiological responses could suggest mechanisms is made by David Huron (2011), who focuses on one of the most obvious physical manifestations of sadness: tears. Tears elicited by emotional arousal tend to contain high levels of the hormone prolactin (Frey, 1985), which is associated with lactation in females. However, prolactin also produces feelings of tranquility, calmness, wellbeing or comfort, one reason, perhaps, that people report feeling somewhat better after crying (Huron, 2011). It appears, however, that prolactin is released even when no actual tears are discharged and even in response to a fictional event such as a sad film scene (Turner et al., 2002). Huron (2011) thus suggests that this may be one reason why people enjoy listening to sad music. Prolactin, he argues, offers the same counteractive effect to psychic pain that endorphins offer for physical pain, and thus listening to sad music is a way to induce the sensation of wellbeing and calmness without actually experiencing real psychic pain.

The research discussed in this chapter tends to resolve some of the philosophical questions around whether we experience real emotions in response to sad music, putting an end to the view of many cognitivists that music-evoked emotions only involve aesthetic experiences, lacking motivational components and goal relevance. The similarities between the way we respond neurologically and physiologically to music and to other acoustic cues suggests that our emotional reactions are fundamentally the same no matter the source of the sounds in our environment. However, aesthetic situations involve cognitive appraisals that may tend to modify the more primitive physiological responses that we may otherwise experience. As to whether we experience sadness in response to sad music, the general pattern of physiological responses reported across the literature are consistent with real experiences of sadness, at least in some listeners. However, as will be discussed in later chapters in this volume, this is likely subject to a high degree of individual differences, a crucial component to the question of why we are attracted to sad music that makes the picture painted by physiological responses a complex one.

The evidence also sheds some light on the relative hierarchical importance of features of the music in evoking an emotional response in the listener, as discussed in Chap. 2. In this we see some distinction between sad music and other music, since lyrics appear to be critical for defining the sadness of a musical piece, whereas acoustic cues have a stronger role in determining the experience of happiness in music. The evidence from these studies also tend to confirm that no single musical features such as tempo is responsible for determining whether we perceive it as sad or experience sadness in response to it.

However, this review of studies relating to physiological responses to sad music also illuminates the fact that detecting psychophysiological correlates of emotional experiences is fraught with difficulty and easily confounded by complications such as how researchers define sad music, whether the participants are familiar with the music, and whether participants experience the music as pleasant or unpleasant. Differentiating specific emotions using physiological measures can also be difficult, since it can be difficult to distinguish sadness from physiological manifestations of other negative emotions such as fear, or to distinguish intense experiences of sadness from other high arousal emotions. Thus, future studies will benefit from triangulation of physiological measures with other indicators of emotional response.

One further issue that is important in studies that look at the effect of music on affective states is the investigation of not only the short-term emotional response to music, but also the longer-term impact of music on our moods and how music is used within strategies to regulate moods. This issue will be considered in the following two chapters.

References

Ali, S. O., & Peynircioğlu, Z. F. (2006). Songs and emotions: Are lyrics and melodies equal partners? *Psychology of Music, 34*(4), 511–534.

Banks, S. J., Eddy, K. T., Angstadt, M., Nathan, P. J., & Luan Phan, K. (2007). Amygdala-frontal connectivity during emotion regulation. *SCAN, 2*, 303–312.

Baumgartner, T., Lutz, K., Schmidt, C., & Jancke, L. (2006). The emotional power of music: How music enhances the feeling of affective pictures. *Brain Research, 1075*(1), 161–164.

Berntson, G. G., Sarter, M., & Cacioppo, J. T. (1998). Anxiety and cardiovascular reactivity: The basal forebrain cholinergic link. *Behavioural Brain Research, 94*, 225–248.

Blood, A. J., & Zatorre, R. J. (2001). Intensely pleasurable responses to music correlate with activity in brain regions implicated in reward and emotion. *Proceedings of the National Academy of Sciences, 98*, 11818–11823.

Brattico, E., Alluri, V., Bogert, B., Jacobsen, T., Nartiainen, N., Nieminen, S., & Tervaniemi, M. (2011). A functional MRI study of happy and sad emotions in music with and without lyrics. *Frontiers in Psychology, 2*, 308.

Cacioppo, J. T., Berntson, G. G., Larsen, J. T., Poehlmann, K. M., & Ito, T. A. (2000). The psychophysiology of emotion. In M. Lewis & J. M. Haviland-Jones (Eds.), *Handbook of emotions* (pp. 173–191). New York: Guilford Press.

Chwalisz, K., Diener, E., & Gallagher, D. (1988). Autonomic arousal feedback and emotional experience: Evidence from the spinal cord injured. *Journal of Personality and Social Psychology, 54*(5), 820–828.

Ekman, P. (1992). An argument for basic emotions. *Cognition & Emotion, 6*(3/4), 169–200.

Ekman, P., Levenson, R. W., & Friesen, W. V. (1983). Autonomic nervous sytem activity distinguishes among emotions. *Science, 221*(4616), 1208–1210.

Etzel, J. A., Johnsen, E. L., Dickerson, J., Tranel, D., & Adolphs, R. (2006). Cardiovascular and respiratory responses during musical mood induction. *International Journal of Psychophysiology, 61*, 57–69.

Frey II, W. H. (1985). *Crying: The mystery of tears*. Minneapolis, MN: Winston Press.

Frühholz, S., Trost, W., & Grandjean, D. (2014). The role of the medial temporal limbic system in processing emotions in voice and music. *Progress in Neurobiology, 123*, 1–17.

Gabrielsson, A. (2001). Emotions in strong experiences with music. In P. N. Juslin & J. A. Sloboda (Eds.), *Music and emotion: Theory and research* (pp. 431–449). Oxford: Oxford University Press.

Gosselin, N., Samson, S., Adolphs, R., Noulhiane, M., Roy, M., Hasboun, D., … Peretz, I. (2006). Emotional responses to unpleasant music correlates with damage to the parahippocampal cortex. *Brain, 129*, 2585–2592.

Huron, D. (2006). *Sweet anticipation: Music and the psychology of expectation*. Cambridge, MA: MIT Press.

Huron, D. (2011). Why is sad music pleasurable? A possible role for prolactin. *Musicae Scientiae, 15*(2), 146–158.

Khalfa, S., Guye, M., Peretz, I., Chapon, F., Girard, N., Chauvel, P., & Liegeois-Chauvel, C. (2008a). Evidence of lateralized anteromedial temporal structures involvement in musical emotion processing. *Neuropsychologia, 46*, 2485–2493.

Khalfa, S., Roy, M., Rainville, P., Dalla Bella, S., & Peretz, I. (2008b). Role of tempo entrainment in psychophysiological differentiation of happy and sad music? *International Journal of Psychophysiology, 68*, 17–26.

Khalfa, S., Schön, D., Anton, J. L., & Liegeois-Chauvel, C. (2005). Brain regions involved in the recognition of happiness and sadness in music. *Neuroreport, 16*, 1981–1984.

Koelsch, S., Fritz, T., v Cramon, D. Y., Mueller, K., & Friederici, A. D. (2006). Investigating emotion with music: An fMRI study. *Human Brain Mapping, 27*, 239–250.

Konečni, V. J., Brown, A., & Wanic, R. A. (2008). Comparative effects of music and recalled life-events on emotional state. *Psychology of Music, 36*, 289–308.

Krumhansl, C. L. (1997). An exploratory study of musical emotions and psychophysiology. *Canadian Journal of Experimental Psychology, 51*(4), 336–352.

Larsen, J. T., Berntson, G. G., Poehlmann, K. M., Ito, T. A., & Cacioppo, J. T. (2008). The psychophysiology of emotion. In M. Lewis, J. M. Haviland-Jones, & L. F. Barrett (Eds.), *Handbook of emotion* (2nd ed., pp. 180–195). New York: Guilford Press.

Lehne, M., Rohrmeier, M., & Koelsch, S. (2014). Tension-related activity in the orbitofrontal cortex and amygdala: An fMRI study with music. *Social Cognitive and Affective Neuroscience, 9*(10), 1515–1523.

Lundqvist, L.-O., Carlsson, F., Hilmersson, P., & Juslin, P. N. (2009). Emotional responses to music: Experience, expression and physiology. *Psychology of Music, 37*(1), 61–90.

Menon, V., & Levitin, D. J. (2005). The rewards of music listening: Response and physiological connectivity of the mesolimbic system. *Neuroimage, 28*(1), 175–184.

Mitterschiffthaler, M., Fu, C., Dalton, J., Andrew, C., & Williams, S. (2007). A functional MRI study of happy and sad affective states induced by classical music. *Human Brain Mapping, 28*(11), 1150–1162.

Nyklíček, I., Thayer, J. F., & Van Doomen, L. J. P. (1997). Cardiorespiratory differentiation of musically-induced emotions. *Journal of Psychophysiology, 11*(4), 304–321.

Olsen, K. N., & Stevens, C. J. (2013). Psychophysiological response to acoustic intensity change in a musical chord. *Journal of Psychophysiology, 27*(1), 16–26.

Panksepp, J. (1995). The emotional sources of "chills" induced by music. *Music Perception, 13*(2), 171–201.

Petocz, A., Keller, P. E., & Stevens, C. (2008). Auditory warnings, signal-referent relations, and natural indicators: Re-thinking theory and application. *Journal of Experimental Psychology: Applied, 14*(2), 165–178.

Rickard, N. S. (2004). Intense emotional responses to music: A test of the physiological arousal hypothesis. *Psychology of Music, 32*(4), 371–388.

Schacter, S., & Singer, J. E. (1962). Cognitive, social and psychological determinants of emotional state. *Psychological Review, 69*(5), 379–399.

Scherer, K. R. (2005). What are emotions? And how can they be measured? *Social Science Information, 44*(4), 696–729.

Trainor, L., Tsang, C. D., & Cheung, V. H. W. (2002). Preference for sensory consonance in 2- and 4-month old infants. *Music Perception, 20*(2), 187–194.

Tsai, C.-G., Chen, R.-S., & Tsai, T.-S. (2014). The arousing and cathartic effects of popular heartbreak songs as revealed in the physiological responses of listeners. *Musicae Scientiae, 18*(4), 410–422.

Turner, R., Altemus, M., Yip, D., Kupferman, E., Fletcher, D., Bostrom, A., … Amico, J. (2002). Effects of emotion on oxytocin, prolactin, and ACTH in women. *Stress, 5*(4), 269–276.

5

A Historical Overview of Music and Mood Regulation

One of the primary reasons that people report for listening to music is to improve or change their mood (Saarikallio, 2011). For example, people may use specific music to help them relax before sleeping, to help them stay motivated while exercising, or to create the right atmosphere for a romantic evening. Individuals do this instinctively as we go through our daily lives, with no need for musical training or any particular knowledge of psychology. However, for centuries music has been used as part of deliberate strategies to improve health and wellbeing, having been believed to be a crucial part of the training of medical practitioners throughout much of human history. Since many of the explanations for why we listen to sad music that have been proposed over the centuries relate to the effect it might have on our mood or psychological wellbeing, an in-depth discussion of the role of music in mood regulation is warranted in relation to the topic of this volume. In order to trace the origins of modern understandings of theories surrounding the role of music in health, we will begin with a historical overview before proceeding, in Chap. 6, to consider current theories.

S. Garrido, *Why Are We Attracted to Sad Music?*,
DOI 10.1007/978-3-319-39666-8_5

Music in Mood Regulation in Ancient Cultures

Music's influence on emotional and mental states is not a recent concept. Ancient cultures across the world believed in the power of music to alter the mind and influence moods, even those of unborn children (Davidson & Garrido, 2014; Garrido & Davidson, 2013). Over 4000 years ago in ancient China, for example, flute music was prescribed to calm an overexcited foetus (Brettingham-Smith, 1993). Music was also apparently being used for therapeutic purposes by the Egyptians as early as 1500 B.C. (Bunt, 1994). Another often-cited example of the use of music to improve mood in ancient times, is the biblical account of King Saul of Israel, who was soothed by the playing of David's harp. In fact, it was only during the seventeenth and eighteenth centuries, with the dichotomy between the arts and sciences that occurred during the scientific revolution, that music became of less interest to health scientists.

In Western cultures belief in the power of music to affect mood goes back to the ancient Greek philosophers such as Homer (*c.*eighth-century BC) and Pythagoras (*c.* 500 BC). Homer recommended music as an antidote to negative emotions such as anger, sorrow, fear and emotional fatigue (Bunt, 1994). Pythagoras was both a mystic and a serious scientist who studied the world around him. One of the tools he used for studying the effect of music on people was the monochord—a one-stringed instrument on which he apparently experimented with notes and intervals in order to test their effect on the listener (Wigram, Pedersen, & Bonde, 2002). Thus, Pythagoras and his followers developed a framework of guidelines for 'prescribing' music to address particular physical and mental imbalances.

In Pythagorean theory the scientific laws of tones and intervals were a reflection of the cosmic world. According to Pythagoras and his followers, the planets vibrate with the same frequencies and with the same ratios as the harmonics of notes. It was believed that the heavenly bodies in motion actually produced a series of tones like a scale (David, 1951). In fact, by the time of Plato (c. 428–348 B.C.) certain tones and tone series were even believed to correspond to particular planets. The moon, for example, was believed to produce the note 'A' and the notes of the

Mixolydian mode, and the sun, the note 'D' and the notes of the Dorian mode. This theory became known as the 'harmony of the spheres', and was one of three key theories about music and its power to influence mood that came from the Ancient Greeks.

A second influential theory stemming from Pythagoras was his belief that different musical modes or scales could influence mood in particular ways. This second key doctrine from Pythagoras became known as the 'doctrine of ethos'. It was believed that each mode or 'harmonia'—a one-line melody on which much Greek music was based—had a specific quality that would influence a person's mood in quite distinctive ways. In fact, the word 'mode' is etymologically related to the word 'mood', a further indication of the long-standing connection between music and mood (Stevenson, 1952). Pythagoras himself used music to treat patients with mental illnesses, and developed specific melodies to be used where people felt sad and others to be used to counteract anger (Mitchell & Zanker, 1948). Pythagoras and his followers themselves would listen to "paeans", a song form expressing triumph, in order to induce desirable mood states (Porphyry, 1920). In fact, Paeon also became known as the god of health, another etymology that attests to the strong connection between music and health during this period (Macurdy, 1930).

Specific anecdotes from classical literature illustrate how music was used in practice among the ancient Greeks to address undesirable mood states. For example, in his *Republic* (Book III), Plato recounts a dialogue between his brother Glaucon and Socrates, in which Socrates apparently encouraged the use of Dorian and Phrygian modes to inspire men to bravery while calling the Ionian and Lydian modes 'relaxed', and saying that its use would encourage drunkenness, softness and indolence. Lydian mode, in particular, was said to express sorrow. One of Plato's pupils, Xenocrates (d. 314 BC), is also said to have used harp music to cure hysterics, employing specific modes and rhythms to achieve the desired effect.

While the fragmentary evidence available limits our understanding of the exact notes used in ancient Greek modes,[1] the Dorian mode advocated

[1] The ancient Greek modes differed from the similarly named church modes that became dominant in the medieval period.

by Socrates to inspire bravery was the principal mode in the old Greek musical system and was believed to draw on the powers of the Sun. It likely consisted of the tones: C D E F# G# A# B C (Hamilton, 1953). With its relatively large interval sizes, this harmonia is more akin to our modern-day major scale than to a minor scale. Conversely, the Phrygian mode, similarly recommended by Socrates, is more closely related to our modern-day minor scales. The Lydian mode, which was believed to invoke the power of Mercury, involved smaller interval sizes and a flattened sixth note, and thus to the modern ear would likely seem more closely related to a minor scale than some other modes as well. Thus, the music that particularly expressed sorrow to the ancient Greeks does bear some similarity to the diatonic minor scale, which is often associated with expressions of sadness in present-day Western music. However, what is of particular interest here is the fact that music that was felt to convey sorrow was believed by Socrates to encourage undesirable affective states that should be counteracted by the use of alternative modes.

Another anecdote about the use of music to counteract undesirable mood states was recounted by Boethius (born *c.* 480 AD) in his treatise *De Institutione Musica*, where he relates a story about how Pythagoras calmed a young man who had become wrought up by the sound of the Phrygian mode. The young man had apparently discovered his 'harlot' in the house of another man and, with the added inducement of the music, was ready to burn down the man's house. The man reputedly responded to reason immediately upon the mode of the music being changed to the slow and rhythmic Spondaic mode, a rhythmic mode that involves long, sustained notes. This suggests that rhythm and tempo were strongly involved in both the perception of emotion in music and the inducement of specific mood states even from ancient times. Boethius also cites details of the expulsion of one Timotheus of Miletus from Lacedaemonia, who is said to have steered the youths of Sparta astray from virtue by altering the pitches in an octave so that they were closer together, like chromatics (Leach, 2006). Thus, to the ancient Greeks, both 'tonal' modes and rhythm could invoke undesirable mood states, and could likewise be harnessed to counteract undesirable mood states.

According to Aristotle, even a person's soul and disposition could be altered by listening to music. His descriptions of the qualities of modes agree with that of Socrates and Plato, as he argues that the Lydian mode causes grief while the Phrygian mode fills the soul with enthusiasm. Aristotle also commented on the specific effects of rhythms: "some fix the disposition, others occasion a change in it; some act more violently, others more liberally" (*Politics*, Book VIII, Chapter V).

Aristotle's observations regarding catharsis were amazingly astute given the other mystic sources to which music's powers were commonly attributed in his time, as were his observations about how individual differences affect the impact of music. He argued that people differ both in the extent to which they experience emotions that will need purging, and in the extent to which music may be the thing which will move them emotionally and allow them to vent their negative emotions. He writes:

> For feelings such as pity and fear, or again, enthusiasm, exist very strongly in some souls, and have more or less influence over all. Some persons fall into a religious frenzy, whom we see as a result of the sacred melodies—when they have used the melodies that excite the soul to mystic frenzy—restored as though they had found healing and purgation. Those who are influenced by pity or fear, and every emotional nature, must have a like experience, and others in so far as each is susceptible to such emotions, and all are in a manner purged and their souls lightened and delighted. The purgative melodies likewise give an innocent pleasure to mankind. (*Politics*, Book VIII, Part VII)

It is interesting to see here how Aristotle distinguishes the immediate emotional response of the listener, which might be one of 'excitement', from the long-term effect on mood, which is to leave them "purged", "lightened and delighted". This idea will be considered in more depth in Chap. 6.

A third doctrine on which much of the belief about the relationship between music and health became based was the idea of humoural medicine, which was in circulation around the time of Hippocrates (c. 400 BC). According to that theory, four bodily fluids or humours influence health: blood, phlegm, yellow bile and black bile. Good health was believed to reflect a balance between the humours while illness or disturbances of mood were believed to be caused by an imbalance. Music was considered to be capable of restoring the balance between the humours (Wigram et al., 2002).

These three key theories—the harmony of the spheres, the doctrine of ethos, and theories of humoural medicine—persevered over the centuries. Celsus, a second-century Greek philosopher, for instance, advocated soothing the sadness of melancholia by means of music (Cook, 1981). The second-century Greek physician Galen (or Galenus), in his treatise *On Temperaments*, expanded on theories about bodily humours by proposing that personalities could be characterized according to humoural imbalances as either phlegmatic, choleric, sanguine or melancholy. In line with this theory, medieval physicians would attempt to regulate the irritability of choleric patients by insisting on the use of tranquil music to accompany a particular diet. If, on the other hand, the patient was melancholic they would prescribe a milk diet with the accompaniment of sensuous, joyful melodies (Cosman, 1978). Again, music was deemed valuable for the purposes of restoring equilibrium between the humours, by the power of specific modes to draw on planetary influences (Godwin, 1993). Galen also wrote about the influence of music on the pulse (*De Pulsibus*).

An interesting aspect of this overview of music in mood regulation in ancient cultures is the importance put upon using music to rectify deeply rooted negative mood states and even temperament. Also of interest to the question of why people are attracted to sad music is the recognition in ancient cultures of the fact that particular types of music could exert either a positive or a negative effect on mood. This is a concept that we will return to later. We also see the emergence of some interesting psychological insights that are of relevance to the use of music in therapeutic contexts today, such as the importance of considering the temperament of the patient.

The Medieval Period

These ideas of the ancient Greeks were to continue to influence theory in the following centuries. During this period, Christianity and the liturgy were spreading, thus influencing the development of both music and the theory surrounding it. The ancient Greek ideas about the music of the spheres were applied to newer Christian thinking and were in turn shaped by Egyptian and Arabic philosophy, becoming known as Neo-Platonism (Gouk, 2004).

Two of the most notable medieval writers on music and its influence on mood were Boethius and Cassiodorus (480–573). Through their writings they transmitted the ancient Greek theories of Pythagoras, Plato and Aristotle into the Christian era. The treatise by Boethius, *De institutione musica*, was an important university text especially in medicine, which in some Italian universities was part of the 'faculty of arts and medicine' (Cosman, 1978).

Boethius, drawing on the earlier philosophies of the harmonies of the spheres, divided music into several categories: *Musica mundana* was the heavenly music of the motion of the spheres. Its reflection was found in *musica humana*, the rhythms and cycles of the human body. At the bottom of the hierarchy was *musica instrumentis,* which was the music made by humans with instruments of their creation. Neo-Platonists explained the connection between the spheres by analogy to a lyre: when one string on the instrument has been struck, another tuned to the same pitch will also vibrate (Gouk, 2004). Thus humanity could be induced to vibrate in harmony with each other and with the celestial bodies if they could be brought into 'tune'.

Cassiodorus was successor to Boethius. He gives an interesting description of the value of music to influence moods in a letter to Boethius (first published *c.* 538) requesting his assistance in finding a harp player for Clovis, King of the Franks. He asked Boethius to help him find a skilled musician who with his "sweet sound can tame the savage hearts of the barbarians". He wrote of music:

> Harmful melancholy he turns to pleasure; he weakens swelling rage; he makes bloodthirsty cruelty kindly, arouses sleepy sloth from its torpor, restores to the sleepless their wholesome rest, recalls lust-corrupted chastity to its moral resolve, and heals boredom of spirit which is always the enemy of good thoughts. (Cassiodorus, 1886)

He also repeated the Platonic theory that each mode has a particular 'ethos', stating:

> Phrygian arouses strife, and inflames the will to anger; the Aeolian calms the storms of the soul, and gives sleep to those who are already at peace; the Ionian sharpens the wits of the dull, and as a worker of good, gratifies the longing for heavenly things among those who are burdened by earthly desire. The Lydian was discovered as a remedy for excessive cares and weariness of the spirit: it restores it by relaxation, and refreshes it by pleasure. (Cassiodorus, 1886)

Boethius' words differ somewhat from that of both Socrates and Aristotle in that Boethius appears to believe that the Phrygian mode aroused undesirable mood states while Lydian could calm them, in contrast to the warning by Socrates that Lydian mode would encourage drunkenness and sloth. How much of these differences of opinion can be attributed to the differences between the modes used in the medieval period and those used by the Ancient Greeks is unclear. However, in the anecdote described above in which Boethius reports Pythagoras' use of music to calm a distressed young man, it is interesting to note that the very mode that Socrates and Aristotle recommended for inspiring bravery was reported as being responsible for the overwrought state of the young man. His state was 'treated' by the use of a slow and calming rhythm. It is possible that, in fact, Boethius' description only differs from Socrates and Aristotle since the situation in which music was called for differed. Boethius may simply have recognized that a mode that might in one situation inspire enthusiasm, could in other circumstances cause one to become overwrought. Similarly, a mode that might in one individual encourage sloth, could calm down a case of overexcited nerves in another.

Another important writer on music in the fifth century was Martianus Cappella, who reported the cure of the mentally ill by music (Paul & Staudt, 1958). His work, *De Nuptiis Philologiae et Mercurii* (On the Marriage of Philogy and Mercury), which was influential for almost all of the medieval period, was an allegorical tale in which seven maids representing the seven arts describe the arts they personify. The final one represents music (Harmony). This was an important work in ensuring the survival of the Pythagorean ideas about the harmony of the spheres through into the Renaissance.

These ideas were further disseminated in the eighth and ninth centuries when Europe began to achieve a degree of unity under Charlemagne. Charlemagne's conquests involved the acquisition of manuscripts including those of Boethius and Cappella, which began to be copied and dispersed throughout the empire, resulting in a revival of interest in Pythagorean ideas, particularly among monastic scholars. Monastic scholars, with their strong interest in the mathematics of musical pitch and ratios, basically dominated thinking on music until *c.* 1200 (Callahan, 2000). With the founding of universities following this, there was a returning interest in the teachings of Galen amongst medical practitioners. Physicians were encouraged to have a liberal education in the arts, including music, in order to enhance their understanding of the human rhythms and pulse.

One abbess and composer—Hildegard of Bingen (c. 1098–1179)—showed an interest in the practical use of music, writing two medical treatises, *Physica* and *Causae et Curae*. Her theories differed somewhat from the usual doctrine of humours, although she does employ the Galenic classification of personalities. While she does not specifically mention music as a treatment, we can make some interesting inferences from her theological discussion of mankind's 'fall' in which the humours play a part. Melancholia, in particular, is described as having come into existence when the Devil first attacked the nature of man resulting in his banishment from Eden. This banishment severed mankind from the heavenly choirs with which he had, until then, sung in harmony. Music came into being, she claims, through the prophets, which enabled humans to once again sing with joy. For Hildegard, therefore, music was a psychic force capable of countering the spiritual ill of melancholy (Callahan, 2000). Bruce Holsinger (1993) argues that this belief that music could imbue humans with the divine is embodied in her own compositions. Her musical 'prescriptions' for melancholia appeared to involve rapturous melodies that defied the simplicity of plainchant common at the time.

Other medieval physicians who wrote about music, mostly from Italy, include Peter of Abano (1257–1315), who gave extensive descriptions of musical theory based on the writings of Boethius and argued that this was essential knowledge for physicians. According to Gentile da Foligno (d. 1348), an Italian professor and doctor, both musical consonance and musical mathematical properties were to be found within the pulse. He argued that high and low pitches correspond to strength or weakness in the pulse, while the speed of the pulse corresponded to the measuring of time in music (Hatter, 2011). A healthy pulse was considered to be equal and steady, while irregularities were indications of illness.

Similarly, Jacopo da Forli (c. 1364–1414) argued that the variations of a pulse, like the different voices in a group of singers, could be either harmonious or dissonant. These variations could be caused by emotional state among other things. Da Forli argued that a person's pulse could be out of harmony with his nature even if 'well proportioned' in itself, just as funeral music would be inappropriate at a wedding.

Thus 'tactus', which originally referred to the keeping of time by beating with the hand, became an important concept in polyphonic music to help keep the separate voices synchronized (Hatter, 2011). Rhythmic modes—a medieval concept in which the relative duration of notes were determined by their position within a rhythmic series—were also utilized to modulate affective states. There were six such modes in which *ars antiqua* motets and other music were written at the time. Peter of Abano made direct application of the rhythmic modes of to the regulation of the pulse, recommending using particular modes to increase a sluggish pulse or adjust a rapid or erratic one (Callahan, 2000).

Other writers of the time discussed more directly the influence of music on melancholia. 'Melancholia' was a term coined by Hippocrates (460–370 BC), which he used to describe a condition where a person has suffered fear or distress for an ongoing period (*Aphorisms* VI:9). Today, the condition would likely be recognized as a mood disorder such as depression, although meanings of these terms have changed throughout history.

William of Auvergne, a French priest who served as Bishop of Paris from 1228 to 1249, dedicated a chapter to music in his treatise. While William disagreed with Plato's explanation of music's healing powers, he does agree with him as to its therapeutic value. In his *De Universo*, he described its usefulness in treating insanity, melancholia and other mental disturbances. Similarly, Franciscan monk Bartholeus Anglicus (*c.*

1203–1272) describes a condition akin to depression in his encyclopaedia, *De Proprietatibis Rerum*, suggesting that music would be of assistance in treating it. Twelfth-century Welsh chronicler Geraldus Cambrensis puts it with some poetry when he says:

> The sweet harmony of music not only affords pleasures but renders important services. It greatly cheers the drooping spirit, smooths the wrinkled brow, promotes hilarity. Nothing so enlivens the human heart, refreshes and delights the mind ... There are no sufferings which music will not mitigate, and there are some which it cures. (Cambrensis & Forester, 1894, Chapter XII)

Thus, in the medieval period we see the continual evolution of ancient Greek ideas including the music of the spheres, as well as the use of music to balance specific humoural temperaments and to regulate the pulse. The choice of both the correct melodic mode and rhythmic mode to create the desired balance was considered important.

The Renaissance and Elizabethan Era

Renaissance scholars, especially in Italy, also demonstrate the influence of the ancient Greeks. A direct line can be traced from the works of Boethius to some of the major writers on music in the Renaissance period, including Gentile da Foligno, Marsilio Ficino and H. Cornelius Agrippa. There was also a particular interest in melancholy in this period, with the subject becoming a characteristic feature in poetry, art and music in the Elizabethan period (Wells, 1985). Shakespeare himself commented on the power of music to alter affective states in *A Merchant of Venice*, saying of people who are full of rage: "But music for the time doth change his nature" (Act V, Scene I). A further synthesis would also be achieved in this period between the various threads of theory developed in previous centuries, fusing Pythagorean cosmology with Galenic medicine and monastic writings on church modes.

This synthesis is evident in the works of Ramis de Pareja. In his *Musica Practica* (1482), he lists the Pythagorean beliefs about the influence of the modes on the humours, drawing upon Islamic Neo-Platonist writings to attribute the power of the modes to particular planets to which they correspond. Like philosophers in earlier centuries, he gives specific musical prescriptions for altering certain mood states. For example, Dorian mode, according to de Pareja, had the power to dry 'watery phlegm' by imparting the power of the sun resulting in equanimity and calm. Hypophrygian mode could mitigate the effect of yellow bile and soothe the soul with the power of Mercury. Lydian mode was said to reinforce happiness by drawing on the power of Jupiter. Hypolydian and Mixolydian modes, on the other hand, were believed to cause sadness and melancholia, while Hypomixolydian could impart the power of the stars to suppress black bile resulting in happiness and bliss.

Another interesting figure in the history of music and mood regulation is the Italian priest, theologian, astrologer and physician Marsilio Ficino (1433–1499). His work *De Vita Libri Tres (Three Books on Life)* (1489) also suggested how music might be used deliberately to manipulate the emotions, seeking to unite Platonism with Christianity. Ficino does not prescribe the use of specific modes, but does give detailed descriptions of the musical characteristics of each planet. He also offers a complex set of techniques for creating songs to attract beneficial planetary emanations. However, Ficino's thoughts about melancholy were somewhat different from those of many physicians in the medieval period, since he believed that it could be beneficial in that it was conducive to contemplation and therefore spirituality.

Ficino's particular understanding of the mechanisms involved in music's effect on one's affective state were heavily influenced by Neo-Platonist interpretations of the harmony of the spheres. He believed that sound, by causing air to vibrate, could connect directly with the ear and thus convey those vibrations to the soul and spirit. Therefore, music, carefully selected, was the most effective path to physical and spiritual balance and harmony. Ficino's astrological model lasted until the end of the eighteenth century when it was superseded by neurological and mechanical theories (Wigram et al., 2002).

Johannes Tinctoris was a composer and music theorist born in Flanders around the 1440s, who also discussed the use of music to regulate mood. His work entitled *Complexus Effectuum Musices* (1475) includes a summary of the functions of music, giving 20 specific effects that music can produce, including: "to amplify the joy of the blessed", "to banish sadness", "to cause ecstasy", and "to make men happy". Rob Wegman (1995) writes that in the works of Tinctoris, "sweetness" was an important quality of music, capable of making men joyful. This quality of "sweetness" was, in Tinctoris' view, mostly related to consonance, but could also have to do with the quality of the instrument or voice. However, once again we see an awareness of the role of individual differences in response to music, since Tinctoris argued that whether or not joy is inspired in the listener depends on the degree to which the individual is capable of perceiving the nature of the music. De Pareja, Ficino and Tinctoris, along with other writers in the Renaissance and Elizabethan eras, thus continued the melding of ancient Greek astrological theories pertaining to music with Galenic theories about humoural temperament and emerging theories of composition and aesthetics.

Baroque Period, Classicism and the Enlightenment

This era saw major changes to the creative goals of composers and musicians. Music during this period was marked by an emphasis on the capacity of music to move the emotions, and the development of deliberate strategies by composers to imitate the "passions" or "affections". This concept became known as the "doctrine of affections", a theory that again drew on ideas of the ancient Greeks and Neo-Platonism in speculating about the affective states that could be represented by specific tonalities, rhythms and melodic motifs. This preoccupation with the passions was stimulated in part by a revival of interest in the treatises of Aristotle and Cicero, in particular Aristotle's *Poetics* (Palisca, 2001), and coincided with a strong interest in the application of narrative and dramatic techniques to music. It was also a product of an age of rationalism in which there was a desire to impose order on emotions (Nagley & Bujic, 2001). These developments culminated in the birth of opera in Florence in 1600, and the establishment of a set of formulaic musical devices and performance gestures designed to convey specific emotions.

An interesting example of this is found in the eighth book of madrigals by Claudio Monteverdi. In his foreword to the volume, Monteverdi (1929) states that the human mind has three principal passions or affections, including anger, temperance, and humility or supplication, which he correlates to the high, medium and low ranges of the human voice. Here Monteverdi appears to have been influenced by the thoughts of Italian humanist Girolamo Mei (1519–1594), who wrote a detailed study of Greek music theory. He also quotes from Plato's *Republic*,[2] where Plato recommends the use of music that is able to represent the bravery of men going into battle. Monteverdi then sets out to present a continual juxtaposition of love and war throughout the entire eighth book of madrigals, using specific musical techniques that adhere closely to Platonic philosophy to embody each distinct passion. Monteverdi's detailed explanation of his techniques provides a clear illustration of how the focus of music in this period became the exploration of the emotive powers of music.

However, the seventeenth and eighteenth centuries also saw an important change in the approach of theorists towards the usefulness of music in mood regulation and the treatment of melancholy. In this period, as the scientific revolution progressed, the emphasis on experimentation and observation in the scientific process grew. As the focus of composers became the power of music to touch the emotions, music began to be seen in scientific circles as belonging firmly in the realm of art rather than as a science that was the equal of mathematics or medicine. Much of the belief of previous centuries was categorized as superstition (Gouk, 2004), and the power of music to influence mood and mental health became of decreasing interest in the world of science.

Nevertheless, the 'doctrine of the passions' provided a basis for some medical theorists to begin to investigate the effects of music on mood using systematic empirical methods. A number of physicians in the period retained an interest in the effects of music on mood and disease, particularly melancholia. Dr Robert Burton, for example, wrote extensively about music largely based upon his own experiences with depression in *Anatomy of Melancholy* (1621). In it he recommends music as

[2] Monteverdi mistakenly says that the words he uses come from Plato's *On Rhetoric*.

"a sovereign remedy against despair and melancholy" (Memb VI, Subs III). Like others before him, Burton demonstrates an understanding of the varying influences music can have depending on the individual. He argues that in some cases music can "make such melancholy persons mad", citing Plato's warning that music be carefully used "lest one fire increase another" (Memb VI, Subs III). On the other hand, referring to Aristotle's doctrine of catharsis, Burton states that:

> Many men are melancholy by hearing music, but it is a pleasing melancholy that is causeth, and therefore to such as are discontent, in woe, fear, sorrow or dejected, it is a most present remedy: it expels care, alters their grieved minds and easeth in an instant. (Memb VI, Subs III)

Richard Browne's *Medicina Musica, or a Mechanical Essay on the Effects of Singing, Musick and Dancing* (1729), like Ficino's *De Vita* and Burton's book, was aimed at readers with tendencies towards melancholy. Music was again recommended as a cure for the spleen, vapours, melancholy and madness. It was particularly designed to appeal to the "fair sex", whose "tender and delicate constitutions" rendered them the most vulnerable to melancholy. Browne also discussed the causes of "spleen" (a condition similar to melancholy), arguing that it was caused by malfunctions in the secretion of 'animal spirits'. Music could be used to treat this, according to Browne, because it invigorated and increased the flow of spirits in the body.

Another work by a medical practitioner was Richard Brocklesby's *Reflections on Ancient and Modern Music with the Application to the Cure of Disease* (1749). He discusses at length how music an affect the mind, holding that it is necessary for the mind to be in a balanced state without undue influence from any particular emotion. Both Browne and Brocklesby noted that the same music could have differing effects on different people and that the wrong choice of music could actually worsen symptoms in some conditions.

One of the most famous accounts of the use of music for mood regulation in this period is the story of the male soprano Farinelli, who was engaged to perform in order to treat the depression of Philip V, King of Spain (Kamen, 2001). Princess Izabella Czartoryska of Poland similarly claimed to have been cured of melancholia by the power of music. After Benjamin Franklin invented his glass harmonica in 1761 he played it for the princess, who later wrote in a letter that this was the beginning of her recovery (Gallo & Finger, 2000). Franz Anton Mesmer, who believed that 'animal magnetism' was an actual fluid that could be strengthened by sound, also used the glass harmonica in his treatment sessions. Music was also reputedly used to treat the depression of George II of England and Kind Ludwig of Bavaria (Cook, 1981). Thus, the belief that music could be used to cure affective conditions such as melancholic continued to flourish in some circles despite the increasing separation between art and science during this period.

Evidence can also be found of the use of music to treat people in mental asylums and other health contexts during the 1800s, being mentioned, among others, by Florence Nightingale (2010), and several other medical practitioners (Cooke, Chaboyer, Schluter, & Hiratos, 2005; Paul & Staudt, 1958). The awareness that musical selections needed to be carefully designed to suit the particular patient was also evident in the writings of eighteenth-century English physician William Pargeter (1792), who wrote: "a considerable share of knowledge in music, then, will be requisite to select those compositions and instruments and that arrangement of the instrumental parts as may, with an exact correspondence with the *pathos animi*, attract and fascinate the attention, and influence the temper of the animal spirits. ... Whether it should be executed in the *allegro, andante, or dolce—largo* or *presto* time; and whether the tone should be *forte* or *fortissimo*—or *piano* or *pianissimo*. This must be regulated by the feelings of the patient" (pp. 107–108).

The Thread Throughout History

As can be seen from the above review, the power of music to produce specific mood effects as well as to treat psychological conditions such as melancholy or depression, has been recognized by philosophers and health practitioners alike since the time of the ancient Greeks. The effects of music were believed to be long-term, i.e., not limited to the specific emotions aroused by the music, but able to counteract dispositional imbalances and affective maladies such as melancholia or depression.

Theories as to the mechanisms inherent in music's ability to shape moods have ranged from belief in its power to exert planetary energies, to its capacity to balance bodily fluids and to regulate the pulse. Likewise, theories about the specific effects of particular modes have differed over the centuries. We have seen, for example, that whereas Socrates discouraged the use of the Mercurian Lydian mode, saying that it encouraged drunkenness and laziness, Boethius described it as a remedy for excessive cares, and Ramis de Pareja believed that it reinforced happiness by drawing on the power of Jupiter. The value of sad music was similarly the subject of contradictory recommendations by different people: while Aristotle spoke of the benefits of catharsis, proponents of Galenic theories of personality recommended joyful melodies to counteract a melancholic temperament. Robert Burton referred to the strange paradox of the "pleasing melancholy" that some experience when hearing sad music. These differing recommendations likely reflect the fact that different music was applied depending on the imbalance that was being addressed.

It seems that beliefs surrounding the effects of rhythm have been somewhat more stable over the centuries than those relating to mode, since from the time of the ancient Greeks it appears that slow rhythms have been encouraged as a calming remedy, much as they likely would be today. In any case, from the ancient Greeks such as Pythagoras and Plato to Italian Renaissance writers such as Ramis de Pareja and Marsilio Ficino, the common thread has been the link between music and its mood-altering qualities. Many of the theorists mentioned in this review were also composers, and their theories were reflected in their compositions. Thus, the very course of music has been shaped by this underlying belief.

Another common thread that is found in the reviewed literature across the centuries is the important fact that music can have distinctly different effects on the individual depending on their temperament and affective state. Although not based on empirical study, scholars and medical practitioners throughout the ages have recognized based on instinct and personal observation, that while music can be used effectively to promote healthy affective states, it also has the potential to promote unhealthy ones. As our review of the philosophical arguments about why people listen to sad music in Chap. 3 has revealed, a recognition of the role of individual differences has been largely lacking in the philosophical literature from the twentieth century. As I will now go on to demonstrate in Chap. 6, some of the more recent empirical research about music and mood regulation also uses a similar broad-brush approach, omitting the consideration of both the positive and negative effects that listening to sad music could have on different individuals.

References

Brettingham-Smith, J. (1993). The sick child and music. *Child's Nervous System, 9*(4), 193–196.

Bunt, L. (1994). *Music therapy: An art beyond words*. London: Routledge.

Burton, R. (1621). *Anatomy of melancholy*. Oxford: J. Lichfield & J. Short.

Callahan, C. (2000). Music in medieval medical practice: Speculations and certainties. *College Music Symposium, 40*, 151–164.

Cambrensis, G., & Forester, T. (1894). *The historical works of Giraldus Cambrensis: The topography of Ireland*. London, New York: George Bell & Sons.

Cassiodorus, M. A. (1886). *The letters of Cassiodorus: Being a condensed translation of the Variae Epistolae of Magnus Aurelius Cassiodorus Senator* (T. Hodgkin, Trans. Vol. II). London: Frowde.

Cook, J. D. (1981). The therapeutic use of music: A literature review. *Nursing Forum, 20*(3), 252–266.

Cooke, M., Chaboyer, W., Schluter, P., & Hiratos, M. (2005). The effect of music on preoperative anxiety in day surgery. *Journal of Advanced Nursing, 52*(1), 47–55.

Cosman, M. P. (1978). Marchaut's medical musical world. *Annals of the New York Academy of Sciences, 314*(1), 1–36.

David, H. T. (1951). The cultural functions of music. *Journal of the History of Ideas, 12*(3), 423–439.

Davidson, J., & Garrido, S. (2014). *My life as a playlist*. Perth: University of Western Australia Publishing.

Gallo, D. A., & Finger, S. (2000). The power of a musical instrument: Franklin, the Mozarts, Mesmer, and the glass armonica. *History of Psychology, 3*(4), 326–343.

Garrido, S., & Davidson, J. W. (2013). Music and mood regulation: A historical enquiry into individual differences and musical prescriptions through the ages. *Australian Journal of Music Therapy, 24*, 89.

Godwin, J. (1993). *The harmony of the spheres: A sourcebook of the Pythagorean tradition in music*. Rochester: Inner Traditions.

Gouk, P. (2004). Raising spirits and restoring souls: Early modern medical explanations for music's effects. In V. Erlmann (Ed.), *Hearing cultures: Essays on sound, listening and modernity* (pp. 87–105). Oxford: Berg.

Hamilton, E. (1953). *The modes of ancient Greece*. Retrieved January 27, 2016, from http://www.nakedlight.co.uk/pdf/articles/a-002.pdf

Hatter, J. (2011). Col tempo: Musical time, aging and sexuality in 16th-century Venetian paintings. *Early Music, 39*(1), 3–14.

Holsinger, B. W. (1993). The flesh of the voice: Embodiment and the homoerotics of devotion in the music of Hildegard of Bingen. *Signs, 19*(1), 92–125.

Kamen, H. (2001). *Philip V of Spain: The king who reigned twice*. New Haven: Yale University Press.

Leach, E. E. (2006). Gendering the semitone, sexing the leading tone: Fourteenth century music theory and the directed progression. *Music Theory Spectrum, 28*(1), 1–21.

Macurdy, G. H. (1930). The derivation of the Greek word Paean. *Language, 6*(4), 297–303.

Mitchell, S. D., & Zanker, A. (1948). The use of music in group therapy. *The British Journal of Psychiatry, 94*, 737–748.

Monteverdi, C. (1929). *Madrigals, book VIII: Madrigali guerrieri et amorosi* (S. Appelbaum, Trans.). New York: Dover.

Nagley, J., & Bujic, B. (2001). *Doctrine of affections*. Grove Music Online. Oxford Music Online. Retrieved from http://www.oxfordmusiconline.com/subscriber/article/opr/t114/e94

Nightingale, F. (2010). *Notes on nursing: What it is, and what it is not*. New York: D. Appleton and Company.

Palisca, C. V. (2001). Baroque. *Grove Music Online*. Oxford Music Online. Retrieved from http://www.oxfordmusiconline.com/subscriber/article/grove/music/02097

Pargeter, W. (1792). *Observations on maniacal disorders*: Printed for the author and sold by Smart and Cowslade, Reading, J. Murray, London, and J. Fletcher, Oxford.

Paul, R., & Staudt, V. M. (1958). Music therapy for the mentally ill: I. A historical sketch and a brief review of the literature on the physiological effects and on analysis of the elements of music. *Journal of General Psychology, 59*, 167–176.

Porphyry. (1920). *The life of Pythagoras*. English translation. Retrieved March 20, 2012, from http://www.ccel.org/.../files/porphyry_life_of_pythagoras_02_text.htm

Saarikallio, S. (2011). Music as emotional self-regulation throughout adulthood. *Psychology of Music, 39*, 307–332.

Stevenson, R. (1952). Thomas Morley's "Plaine and Easie" introduction to the modes. *Musica Disciplina, 6*, 4. Retrieved from http://www.jstor.org/stable/20531854

Wegman, R. C. (1995). Sense and sensibility in late-medieval music: Thoughts on aesthetics and 'authenticity'. *Early Music, 23*(2), 298–312.

Wells, R. H. (1985). John Dowland and Elizabethan melancholy. *Early Music, 13*(4), 514–528.

Wigram, T., Pedersen, I. N., & Bonde, L. O. (2002). *A comprehensive guide to music therapy: Theory, clinical practice, research and training* (Vol. 1). London: Jessica Kingsley Publishers.

6

The Role of Sad Music in Mood Regulation

Modern understandings about the way music works and its impact on the brain and the body have come a long way since the time of Plato. Although music and medicine became separated during the scientific revolution, in some ways we now appear to have come full circle, with music being increasingly used in health contexts once more. However, the interruption to the scientific consideration of music as an influence on health and wellbeing has meant that some of the threads of theory that were common in previous centuries have been lost. In particular, as will be argued in this and subsequent chapters, modern theories have tended to focus on the *benefits* of musical engagement without paying any consideration to the possible negative impact. A trend towards the *bulk* administration of musical interventions without regard for individual differences in response to music can also be observed. This chapter will therefore consider what we have gained and what may have been lost in our understanding of the impact of music on mood in the twenty-first century.

Before discussing this in more detail, it will first be useful to discuss some of the conceptual differences between moods and emotions. Many of the explanations for why we listen to sad music that have been discussed

S. Garrido, *Why Are We Attracted to Sad Music?*,
DOI 10.1007/978-3-319-39666-8_6

in this volume to date, including Aristotle's compensatory argument of catharsis, suggest that an emotional response of sadness while listening to music can ultimately result in an improvement in mood. Such arguments hold that people are willing to tolerate a short-term experience of sadness in order to obtain long-term benefits.

Compensatory explanations suggest, therefore, that the *mood* impact of the music may differ from the initial *emotional* response of the listener. For example, a person may listen to a piece of sad music, even being moved to the point of tears, but then walk away from the music, forgetting about it shortly afterwards. On the other hand, a person could listen to a fun, upbeat party song, but this may then lead them to start to think about how busy they are and how they no longer have any time for parties, and suddenly they find themselves in a depressed mood that could last for several hours or even days. Thus, the emotions we experience while actually listening to a piece of music can differ considerably from the effect the music has on our overall mood, suggesting that there are different mechanisms at work. It is therefore important to understand differences between emotions and moods more clearly before considering the role of sad music in mood regulation more generally.

In a useful study of both academic theories and popular beliefs, Beedie, Terry and Lane (2005) identified some of the key features that seem to distinguish emotions and moods. They argued that emotions are usually understood to be relatively intense and uncontrollable affective experiences that are linked to a specific triggering event, and which generally occur immediately after that event and are of relatively short duration. Moods, on the other hand, may be the result of several events rather than a specific event, or they may occur some time after a specific triggering event as a result of thoughts arising surrounding the event. While moods can be affected by emotions (Pieters & van Raaij, 1988), moods tend to be of longer duration, are more controllable and less intense than an emotion. Thus, in relation to listening to music, while a relatively short piece of music—perhaps only a few seconds in length—can arouse powerful and largely uncontrollable emotional responses, it would likely take a longer period of music listening to have a more enduring effect on our mood, and this long-term impact would probably involve a number of intervening cognitive processes (Garrido, 2014; Garrido, Schubert & Bangert, 2016).

If compensatory theories such as Aristotle's are correct, in addition to music having the capacity to change our mood, the mood we are in may also be an important influence on the music to which we choose to listen. In most individuals moods fluctuate from day to day. The strategies that people have developed in order to control their moods also differ from person to person. Based on one's prior experiences, an individual learns certain behaviours for responding to adverse events, and these usually become long-term patterns for dealing with emotional experiences (Moulds, Kandris, Starr, & Wong, 2007). Thus, whether or not a person will choose to listen to sad music as a way of coping with their own emotional state also depends on their learned mood regulation strategies. Such strategies can be either adaptive or maladaptive, healthy or unhealthy.

Mood Management Theories in the Modern Day

Researchers in the field of media and communications have developed several helpful theories that can begin to help us understand how people use media such as music in order to regulate their moods. One primary theory that has emerged is that of so-called 'mood management theory' (Zillmann, 1988). This theory proposes that people will select music and other media that will either diminish a negative mood (if they are in one), or that will help to perpetuate a previously good mood. The evidence suggests that, for the most part, this is what people do. For example, research indicates that when women are either premenstrual or menstruating, and hence likely to be in a lower mood than at other times in their cycle, they are more likely to choose to watch comedy programs (Meadowcroft & Zillmann, 1987). Likewise, females in a negative mood are also more likely to select to read positive news stories rather than negative ones (Biswas, Riffe, & Zillmann, 1994).

The research suggests that our consumption of music generally follows similar patterns. William Thompson, Glenn Schellenberg and Gabriela Hussain (2001), for example, found that after listening to classical music, enjoyment ratings are higher for an uptempo piece in a major key than they are for a slow tempo piece in a minor key. In a subsequent study (Husain et al., 2002), these researchers found that when listeners hear different versions of the same piece of music in which the tempo and mode have been altered, ratings of liking are highest for the happiest-sounding versions in fast tempos and major keys. These studies tend to support mood management theory in that they indicate that people generally do prefer to consume media including music that makes them feel happy.

However, mood management theory does not explain why people at times choose to listen to sad music or to watch sad films. Thus, alternative theories suggest that people select music that is congruent with their mood. This theory also enjoys considerable empirical support. Patrick Hunter and colleagues, for example, found that after inducing a sad mood, the typical preference for happy music disappeared (Hunter, Schellenberg, & Griffith, 2011). Other studies also suggest that when people are in a depressed mood they tend to be less attracted to energetic music and music that could improve their moods (Dillman Carpentier et al., 2008; Punkanen, Eerola, & Erkkila, 2011). Similarly, people report deliberately selecting sad music particularly when feeling lonely or distressed (Taruffi & Koelsch, 2014).

As a result, Randy Larsen (2000) suggested a modification of mood management theory, proposing that while the ultimate aim might be to achieve a pleasant mood state, people will postpone the immediate gratification of their hedonic desires in order to enjoy other benefits. This is similar to the 'compensatory benefits' proposed by Levinson that were discussed in Chap. 3, and suggests that people might be willing to tolerate a sad emotional response to music where the long-term result is mood improvement. A number of empirical studies have subsequently examined some of the possible reasons that people might select mood congruent music and some of the compensatory benefits that they might enjoy from postponing hedonic pleasure.

Robin Nabi et al. (2006), for example, found that people who were dealing with regret over personal decisions preferred to watch TV programs that were relevant to their situation. The authors proposed that the programs may have helped the viewer to process their feelings of regret.

Suvi Saarikallio (2010) has also found that although people sometimes listen to mood-incongruent music in order to distract themselves from their emotions, at other times they listen to mood-congruent music in order to reinforce their affective state. In adolescents, Saarikallio and Jaakko Erkkila (2007) reported that there were seven distinct strategies at work, several of which involved the selection of music to intensify or perpetuate a current negative mood: Revival (to relax or be rejuvenated); Mental Work (mental contemplation and reappraisal of emotions); Discharge (release and venting of emotions); Diversion (distraction); Solace (to obtain comfort, support and emotional validation); Strong Sensations (the seeking of intense emotional experiences); and Entertainment (to enhance or maintain a happy mood).

In my own research with Emery Schubert (Garrido & Schubert, 2011), in-depth interviews with our participants revealed similar results. Our participants described five specific mood regulation strategies that motivated their music-listening selections: to generate mental or emotional stimulation or arousal; to relax or calm down; to distract from negative emotions; as catharsis for negative emotions; or to reflect on and make sense of life events. Annemieke Van den Tol and Jane Edwards (2013) similarly report a number of rationales that people give for listening to mood-congruent music when in a negative mood, that suggest important mood regulation strategies that are being employed. They report that people listened to sad music in order to: re-experience affect, retrieve memories, feel connected to the music as if it were a friend, be distracted from negative emotions, and enhance their mood. Interestingly, other studies suggest that where the sad situation that has invoked the negative emotions is perceived to be unresolvable and therefore sadness is no longer useful for motivating change, study participants tend to prefer to listen to happy music (Tahlier, Miron, & Rauscher, 2013). This suggests the value of sad music in helping the listener to conduct the cognitive work necessary to resolve negative emotions.

Another important theory that is suggested by many of the mood regulation strategies reported by participants in the above studies is the 'optimal stimulation theory'. Since both under-stimulation and over-stimulation can be unpleasant, it has been argued that an individual will seek to *optimize* their level of arousal by either reducing or increasing it as necessary at a given point in time (Zentall & Zentall, 1983). This theory, based on the work of Berlyne (1971, 1972) and others (see, for example, Duffy, 1962; Fiske & Maddi, 1961), assumes that for each individual there is an ideal level of arousal that is most comfortable and productive. The level most comfortable to an individual and the type of stimuli they will choose to achieve this can vary depending on factors such as the intelligence of the individual, whether they are introverted or extroverted, and how much stimulation they are experiencing within their environment at the time of listening (Chamorro-Premuzic & Furnham, 2007; Rentfrow & Gosling, 2003).

With regards to music listening choices, therefore, this theory would predict that if an individual is in a state of arousal below their individual optimal level, they would choose more energetic music. Alternatively, if a person is feeling over-stimulated or over-emotional, they might choose calming and relaxing music in order to lower their state of arousal. As indicated in the studies reviewed above, the mood regulation strategies people use do variously involve either a deliberate reduction of physiological arousal in order to produce a more relaxed state, or the use of music to actually increase emotional arousal. This is a concept to which we will return in subsequent chapters. However, of interest at this point is the fact that this strongly suggests that people's individual level of optimal stimulation plays an important role in whether they would choose to listen to music that is slow and thus low in arousal like much sad music or whether they select something more energetic and upbeat. It is also possible that people in low arousal states, might choose music that causes them to experience emotional stimulation for the sake of the increased arousal that accompanies it.

The theories of mood management, mood congruency and optimal stimulation provide a useful theoretical framework for beginning to look at why people might listen to sad music, and the empirical evidence cited above supports these theories to various degrees. However, one of the most obvious differences between the above-cited research in relation to musical mood-regulation strategies and the historical viewpoints reviewed at the beginning of this chapter, is the omission in the empirical research of any possible negative impact of music. In fact, most of these studies focused solely on the strategies being employed by listeners or their motivations for music selection, and did not measure actual outcomes or whether listeners actually achieved their mood regulation goals. In contrast, many of the medical practitioners who have recorded their observations of patients throughout the centuries have noted the fact that in some situations, music can "make melancholy persons mad" (Burton, 1621, Memb VI, Subs III).

In fact, the idea that people gain some psychological benefits from listening to sad music not only presumes that people will only listen to sad music when they are experiencing some psychological distress, but is also based on the assumption that listening choices reflect adaptive strategies for emotion regulation. While the motivations of many, if not most listeners, may be to achieve some psychological advantage, there may also be some whose motivations are not quite so rational or who do not achieve the intended goals.

One particular habitual coping strategy may be closely related to a tendency to seek out sad music. The word 'rumination' in its original sense refers to the way cows and other animals regurgitate partially digested food in order to chew over it more thoroughly ("Rumination," 1989). In psychology, it refers to an involuntary focus on negative and pessimistic thoughts about one's self, the world and the future (Joorman, 2005) and is a stable response style that is strongly predictive of clinical depression (Nolen-Hoeksema, 1991; Smith & Alloy, 2009).

Rumination in this sense can be distinguished from 'reflection'—a distinction that was proposed by Paul Trapnell and Jennifer Campbell (1999). Trapnell and Campbell proposed this distinction as a solution to the 'self-absorption paradox'—the fact that a disposition to reflect and to examine the self is viewed as a highly adaptive and psychologically healthy trait, but that it is also associated with neuroticism, depression and poor self-esteem. They proposed that it is the ruminative rather than the reflective aspect of private self-focus that is maladaptive, since the latter allows the individual a chance to process and work through negative emotions, while the former tends to involve a pattern of cyclical thinking from which depression sufferers have difficulty in emerging.

Depression is, by definition, a disorder of affect dysregulation that tends to involve behaviour that prolongs negative affective states, and reduced motivation to engage in behaviour likely to improve mood (Forbes & Dahl, 2005). Rumination appears to keep depressogenic schemata active, simultaneously hindering more active and effective coping strategies (Spasojevic & Alloy, 2001), resulting in the prolongation of a depressed mood (Nolen-Hoeksema & Morrow, 1993).

Since the effects of rumination in this pathological sense are detrimental, the question remains as to why people engage in it. Brendan Bradley and colleagues (Bradley, Mogg, & Lee, 1997) suggest that ruminative behaviour is related to a difficulty in detaching from negative input once it has come to their attention. Empirical evidence tends to support this idea of a malfunction of inhibitory mechanisms resulting in a negative attentional bias. Dysphoric students, for example, are slower to name the colour of an ink when it spells a word of negative valence, suggesting that they are more distracted by the emotive content of the word than healthier controls (Gotlib et al., 2004). They similarly tend to form more negative sentences from scrambled words than healthier participants, even when no longer feeling dysphoric (Wenzlaff & Bates, 1998). Rumination is also associated with a tendency to interpret neutral facial expressions as conveying negative emotions (Raes et al., 2006) and with negatively biased memory recall (Lyubomirsky et al., 1998).

This attentional bias applies to musical stimuli, too, as demonstrated in a study by Ehud Bodner et al. (2007) in which depressed patients showed a heightened response to sad excerpts, selecting more descriptive labels in response to sad music than other excerpts, while the control group evinced the opposite response. Other studies have similarly shown that depressed participants tend to evaluate sad or angry music more negatively than healthy controls (Punkanen et al., 2011). Neurologically, depressed participants tend to show heightened responsivity in the amygdala when processing a negatively valenced stimulus, suggesting a reduced ability to modulate amygdalic activity through cognitive processes (Siegle, Steinhauer, Thase, Stenger, & Carter, 2002).

Dysphorics induced to engage in self-focused rumination also demonstrate reduced willingness to engage in pleasant, distracting activities that could lift their moods, even when they believe they would enjoy those activities (Lyubomirsky & Nolen-Hoeksema, 1993). Greg Siegle and colleagues (Siegle et al., 2002) also found that whereas non-depressed individuals displayed amygdala responses to all stimuli that quickly decayed after offset, depressed individuals displayed sustained amygdala responses to negative words, suggesting that the cognitive processes that often act so as to moderate immediate emotional responses are impaired in people with depression.

Alternatively, Michelle Moulds et al. (2007) propose that rumination may be an avoidance strategy that allows the individual to evade active engagement in problem-solving. Some researchers also suggest that depressed people tend to rationalize ruminative behaviour, arguing that it will help them to gain insight into their problems (Papageorgiou & Wells, 2001; Watkins, 2004). However, Jeannette Smith and Lauren Alloy (2009) argue that the concept of rumination as a conscious and controlled thinking process, rather than an unconscious or automatic one, is inaccurate. It seems highly likely that ruminative behaviour is not enacted volitionally in most depression sufferers (Silk, Steinberg, & Sheffield Morris, 2003), although various cognitive and behavioural therapies may be able to increase both awareness and control (Wright & Beck, 1983).

If ruminators find it difficult to disengage from negative stimuli, and indeed demonstrate an attentional bias towards it, it follows that this would be apparent in their listening choices. This effect is suggested in a study by Lei Chen and colleagues (Chen, Zhou, & Bryant, 2007). In that study, the authors predicted that most people in a sad mood would initially be attracted to negative media, but that after some time they would be motivated to decrease their negative mood. While this proved to be true of most participants, it was found that ruminators spent more time on distressing music than non-ruminators and that they also seemed to lack the desire to rid themselves of their negative mood contrary to the authors' hypothesis. Similarly, Rentfrow and Gosling (2003) reported that depressed people in their study chose music which sustained their melancholic mood (see also Miranda & Claes, 2009).

Thus, it seems likely that although a sad mood may motivate some people to choose music that will help repair that mood either immediately or through cognitive processes that ultimately result in psychological gain, rumination and the affect dysregulation that accompanies depression likely disrupts this process. Since people with tendencies to depression may have a propensity to view sad music as even more negative than other people, and may also find it difficult to disengage from the emotions aroused by sad music, it is possible that sadness evoked by music could have a particularly detrimental effect on their long-term moods. This is a consideration that was recognized by physicians of long ago such as Robert Burton and Aristotle, but that has been largely neglected in more recent discussions of why we listen to sad music.

We have here discussed at least one way in which individual differences may have an influence on our affective responses to sad music. However, several other personality traits may also be involved in why we listen to sad music and how we respond to it. The next chapter will, therefore, consider individual differences in rumination and other personality traits as predictors to an attraction to sad music.

References

Beedie, C. J., Terry, P. C., & Lane, A. M. (2005). Distinctions between emotion and mood. *Cognition and Emotion, 19*(6), 847–878.

Berlyne, D. E. (1971). *Aesthetics and psychobiology*. East Norwalk, CT: Appleton-Century-Crofts.

Berlyne, D. E. (1972). Experimental aesthetics. In P. C. Dodwell (Ed.), *New horizons in psychology* (pp. 107–125). Oxford: Penguin.

Biswas, R., Riffe, D., & Zillmann, D. (1994). Mood influence on the appeal of bad news. *Journalism & Mass Communication Quarterly, 71*(3), 689–696.

Bodner, E., Iancu, I., Gilboa, A., Sarel, A., Mazor, A., & Amir, D. (2007). Finding words for emotions: The reactions of patients with major depressive disorder towards various musical excerpts. *The Arts in Psychotherapy, 34*, 142–150.

Bradley, B. P., Mogg, K., & Lee, S. C. (1997). Attentional biases for negative information in induced and naturally occurring dysphoria. *Behaviour Research and Therapy, 35*(10), 911–927.

Burton, R. (1621). *Anatomy of melancholy*. Oxford: J. Lichfield & J. Short.

Chamorro-Premuzic, T., & Furnham, A. (2007). Personality and music: Can traits explain how people use music in everyday life? *British Journal of Psychology, 98*(2), 175–185.

Chen, L., Zhou, S., & Bryant, J. (2007). Temporal changes in mood repair through music consumption: Effects of mood, mood salience, and individual differences. *Media Psychology, 9*, 695–713.

Dillman Carpentier, F. R., Brown, J. D., Bertocci, M., Silk, J. S., Forbes, E. E., & Dahl, R. C. (2008). Sad kids, sad media? Applying mood management theory to depressed adolescents' use of media. *Media Psychology, 11*, 143–166.

Duffy, E. (1962). *Activation and behavior*. Oxford, England: Wiley.

Fiske, D. W., & Maddi, S. R. (1961). *Functions of varied experience*. Homewood, IL: Dorsey Press.

Forbes, E. E., & Dahl, R. C. (2005). Neural systems of positive affect: Relevance to understanding child and adolescent depression? *Development and Psychopathology, 17*, 827–850.

Garrido, S. (2014). A systematic review of the measurement of mood and emotion in music studies. *Psychomusicology, 24*(4), 316–327.

Garrido, S., Bangert, D., & Schubert, E. (2016). Musical prescriptions for mood improvements: An experimental study. *The Arts in Psychotherapy, 51*, 45–53. Retrieved from http://dx.doi.org/10.1016/j.aip.2016.09.002

Garrido, S., & Schubert, E. (2011). Negative emotion in music: What is the attraction? A qualitative study. *Empirical Musicology Review, 6*(4), 214–230.

Gotlib, I. H., Krasnoperova, E., Neubauer Yue, D., & Joormann, J. (2004). Attentional biases for negative interpersonal stimuli in clinical depression. *Journal of Abnormal Psychology, 113*(1), 127–135.

Hunter, P. G., Schellenberg, E. G., & Griffith, A. T. (2011). Misery loves company: Mood-congruent emotional responding to music. *Emotion, 11*(5), 1068–1072.

Husain, G., Thompson, W. F., & Schellenberg, E. G. (2002). Effects of musical tempo and mode on arousal, mood, and spatial abilities. *Music Perception, 20*(2), 151–171.

Joorman, J. (2005). Inhibition, rumination and mood regulation in depression. In R. W. Engle, G. Sedek, U. V. Hecker, & D. N. McIntosh (Eds.), *Cognitive limitations in aging and psychopathology: Attention, working memory, and executive functions* (pp. 275–312). New York: Cambridge University Press.

Larsen, R. J. (2000). Toward a science of mood regulation. *Psychological Inquiry, 11*, 129–141. doi:10.1207/S15327965PLI1103_01.

Lyubomirsky, S., Caldwell, N. D., & Nolen-Hoeksema, S. (1998). Effects of ruminative and distractive responses to depressed mood on retrieval of autobiographical memories. *Journal of Personality and Social Psychology, 75*(1), 166–177.

Lyubomirsky, S., & Nolen-Hoeksema, S. (1993). Self-perpetuating properties of dysphoric rumination. *Journal of Personality and Social Psychology, 65*(2), 339–349.

Meadowcroft, J. M., & Zillmann, D. (1987). Women's comedy preferences during the menstrual cycle. *Communication Research, 14*(2), 204–218.

Miranda, D., & Claes, M. (2009). Music listening, coping, peer affiliation and depression in adolescence. *Psychology of Music, 37*(2), 215–233.

Moulds, M. L., Kandris, E., Starr, S., & Wong, A. C. M. (2007). The relationship between rumination, avoidance and depression in a non-clinical sample. *Behaviour Research and Therapy, 45*, 251–261.

Nabi, R. L., Finnerty, K., Domschke, T., & Hul, S. (2006). Does misery love company? Exploring the therapeutic effects of TV viewing on regretted experiences. *Journal of Communication, 56*, 689–706.

Nolen-Hoeksema, S. (1991). Responses to depression and their effect on the duration of depressive episodes. *Journal of Abnormal Psychology, 100*(4), 569–582.

Nolen-Hoeksema, S., & Morrow, J. (1993). Effects of rumination and distraction on naturally occurring depressed mood. *Cognition & Emotion, 7*(6), 561–570.

Papageorgiou, C., & Wells, A. (2001). Metacognitive beliefs about rumination in recurrent major depression. *Cognitive and Behavioural Practice, 8*, 160–164.

Pieters, R. G. M., & van Raaij, F. (1988). Functions and management of affect: Applications to economic behavior. *Journal of Economic Psychology, 9*, 251–282.

Punkanen, M., Eerola, T., & Erkkila, J. (2011). Biased emotional preferences in depression: Decreased liking of angry and energetic music by depressed patients. *Music and Medicine, 3*(2), 114–120.

Raes, F., Hermans, D., & Williams, J. M. G. (2006). Negative bias in the perception of others' facial emotional expressions in major depression: The role of depressive rumination. *Journal of Nervous and Mental Disease, 194*(10), 796–799.

Rentfrow, P. J., & Gosling, S. D. (2003). The do re mi's of everyday life: The structure and personality correlates of music preferences. *Journal of Personality and Social Psychology, 84*(6), 1236–1256.

Rumination. (1989). *Oxford English Dictionary* (online). 2nd ed. Retrieved from http://dictionary.oed.com.viviena.library.unsw.edu.au/cgi/entry/50210526?single=1&query_type=word&queryword=rumination&first=1&max_to_show=10

Saarikallio, S. (2010). Music as emotional self-regulation through adulthood. *Pyschology of Music, 39*(3), 307–327.

Saarikallio, S., & Erkkila, J. (2007). The role of music in adolescents' mood regulation. *Psychology of Music, 35*(1), 88–109.

Siegle, G. J., Steinhauer, S. R., Thase, M. E., Stenger, A., & Carter, C. S. (2002). Can't shake that feeling: Event-related fMRI assessment of sustained amygdala activity in response to emotional information in depressed individuals. *Biological Psychiatry, 51*, 693–707.

Silk, J. S., Steinberg, L., & Sheffield Morris, A. (2003). Adolescents' emotion regulation in daily life: Links to depressive symptoms and problem behaviour. *Child Development, 74*(6), 1869–1880.

Smith, J. M., & Alloy, L. B. (2009). A roadmap to rumination: A review of the definition, assessment, and conceptualization of this multifaceted construct. *Clinical Psychology Review, 29*, 116–128.

Spasojevic, J., & Alloy, L. B. (2001). Rumination as a common mechanism relating depressive risk factors to depression. *Emotion, 1*(1), 25–37.

Tahlier, M., Miron, A. M., & Rauscher, F. H. (2013). Music choice as a sadness regulation strategy for resolved versus unresolved sad events. *Psychology of Music, 41*(6), 729–748.

Taruffi, L., & Koelsch, S. (2014). The paradox of music-evoked sadness: An online survey. *PLoS One, 9*(10), e11490. doi:10.1371/journal.pone.0110490.

Thompson, W. F., Schellenberg, E. G., & Husain, G. (2001). Arousal, mood and the Mozart effect. *Psychological Science, 12*, 248–251.

Trapnell, P. D., & Campbell, J. D. (1999). Private self-consciousness and the five-factor model of personality: Distinguishing rumination from reflection. *Journal of Personality and Social Psychology, 76*(2), 284–304.

Van den Tol, A. J. M., & Edwards, J. (2013). Exploring a rationale for choosing to listen to sad music when feeling sad. *Psychology of Music, 41*(4), 440–465.

Watkins, E. (2004). Appraisals and strategies associated with rumination and worry. *Personality and Individual Differences, 37*, 679–694.

Wenzlaff, R. M., & Bates, D. E. (1998). Unmasking a cognitive vulnerability to depression: How lapses in mental control reveal depressive thinking. *Journal of Personality and Social Psychology, 75*(6), 1559–1571.

Wright, J. H., & Beck, A. T. (1983). Cognitive therapy of depression: Theory and practice. *Hospital and Community Psychiatry, 34*(12), 1119–1127.

Zentall, S. S., & Zentall, T. R. (1983). Optimal stimulation: A model of disordered activity and performance in normal and deviant children. *Psychological Bulletin, 94*(3), 446–471.

Zillmann, D. (1988). Mood management through communication choices. *American Behavioral Scientist, 31*(3), 327–340.

7

Individual Differences in the Attraction to Sad Music

Individual Differences and Music

The study of individual differences, which encompasses personality, has been a significant part of psychology since ancient times (Hampson & Coleman, 1995). It can be defined as the science of describing how people differ (Westen, 2002). An important assumption in the individual differences perspective is that to understand the complexity of human behaviour and experiences it is necessary to study how they are different from person to person (Goldberg, 1993).

As we have seen in previous chapters, much of the discussion of the paradox of tragedy over the centuries has omitted consideration of the influence of individual differences. The explanations proposed by philosophers thus far about why people listen to sad music are persuasive and contain much logic, but each one seems inadequate in itself as a full explanation for the phenomenon. As discussed in Chap. 3, this may be because the philosophical approach by necessity is based on observations of the philosopher's own personal experiences and explanations are thus largely formed from a single perspective.

S. Garrido, *Why Are We Attracted to Sad Music?*,
DOI 10.1007/978-3-319-39666-8_7

However, individuals are different and we could therefore expect them to react differently to music just as they react differently to other things. Research on individual differences has already revealed numerous between-person differences to identical psychological tasks or situations. For example, Simon Baron-Cohen, Rebecca Knickmeyer and Matthew Belmonte (2005) present convincing evidence that females tend to be greater empathizers—able to infer the mental states of others and respond appropriately—while males are more often systemizers—tending to focus on the operation of systems and rules. Thus gender has a profound influence on how individuals respond to a stimulus or event.

Numerous studies have also been conducted on the influence of personality traits such as the 'Big Five'—five aspects of personality that Lew Goldberg (1993) proposed as encompassing all aspects of personality differences (see, e.g., Rentfrow, Goldberg, & Levitin, 2011). It has been found, for example, that people with high scores in the Big Five personality trait of openness to experience tend to be highly motivated to learn new skills and so tend to cope better than others in work situations that require training (Barrick & Mount, 1991). Temperament also influences how we respond to external events, with research demonstrating that people with high levels of surgency—a trait that is closely related to extraversion and that features cheerfulness, spontaneity and sociability—are less likely to internalize problems than others (Berdan, Keane, & Calkins, 2008).

Individual differences also affect the way we react to music and hence the music that we are attracted to. Research has shown that taste in music and listening habits are shaped by many factors including socioeconomic status (Peterson & Kern, 1996), and parental influence (Ter Bogt, Delsing, van Zalk, Christensen, & Meeus, 2011). Patrick Litle and Marvin Zuckerman (1986) found that individuals with high scores in the personality trait of sensation-seeking evidenced a preference for highly stimulating music such as rock. Other studies have found that extraversion is associated with attraction to music with high-arousal properties such as jazz, while openness to experience was correlated with an enjoyment of a variety of non-mainstream and complex genres (Dollinger, 1993), and that respondents with high scores of psychoticism or reactive rebelliousness enjoyed hard rock (Robinson, Weaver, & Zillmann, 1996). Similarly, a study by William McCown and colleagues (McCown,

Keiser, Shea, & Williamson, 1997) demonstrated an association between gender, the trait of extraversion and a tendency to psychoticism, and a preference for music with enhanced bass.

Eckart Altenmüller and colleagues (Altenmüller, Schurmann, Lim, & Parlitz, 2002) have also found important gender differences in how people respond to music. In their study females demonstrated greater valence-related variations in brain-activation patterns to the music they listened to, indicating that their emotional response to music may have greater variability than that of males. Günter Kreutz, Emery Schubert and Laura Mitchell (2008) also found that personality and gender had an important influence on one's cognitive style of listening. They applied the research of Baron-Cohen and colleagues cited above, to music, and found that some listeners were 'music empathizers'—tending to focus on the emotional aspects of the music, while others were 'music systemizers'—evincing a style of listening that centered on structural features of the music.

Other studies have examined the influence of personality variables on the ways people use music in daily life. Tomas Chamorro-Premuzic and Adrian Furnham (2007) reported that intellectually engaged individuals with higher IQs tended to use music in a different way from neurotic, introverted and non-conscientious individuals. Tom ter Bogt and colleagues (Ter Bogt, Mulder, Raaijmakers, & Gabhainn, 2010) identified three groups of music listeners, finding that 'high-involved' listeners liked a broad range of genres and most often used it for mood enhancement, coping with distress, identity construction and social identity formation, experiencing more intense affective responses to music, while music tended to be of less importance to low- and medium- involved listeners.

Given the broad range of ways in which people use music and respond to it, it seems highly likely that the way we utilize sad music is also influenced by a variety of personal differences. Could it be, therefore, that the philosophical explanations outlined in previous chapters are all, to some degree, correct and that the apparent conflict between them arises because the individual authors' experiences are different? Is it the case, perhaps, that a combination of these explanations might together provide a comprehensive theory about why we are attracted to sad music? Tied in with this, it may be that addressing a level of explanation above that of the phenomenological by looking at mechanistic explanations may begin to illuminate how and why people differ in their attraction to sad music. By addressing the question at a subpersonal level we can identify the processes taking place and investigate the degree to which they are present in various individuals. We will now discuss one such mechanistic theory before looking at other individual differences that could shed further light on the phenomenon in question.

The Dissociation Theory of Emotion in Aesthetic Contexts

Emery Schubert has proposed a theory that offers a useful mechanistic model of emotional response to music in aesthetic contexts. Schubert's theory, which I will refer to as the Dissociation Theory of Emotion in Aesthetic Contexts (DTEAC), proposes that when negative emotions are activated in aesthetic situations in which the stimulus is cognitively discounted as unreal, a "dissociation node" is triggered which inhibits the displeasure and pain units of the mind (Schubert, 1996, p. 25). Schubert's theory draws on the Cognitive Unit Activation Theory advanced by Colin Martindale (Martindale, 1988), which posits that the activation of cognitive units consisting of mental representations of various phenomena is more pleasurable than a state of non-activation. Schubert argued that when dissociation occurs and displeasure is deactivated, the remaining cognitive activation that is occurring as a result of the emotional arousal is inherently pleasurable (Schubert, 2013). The individual is thus able to enjoy the cognitive activation actuated by the emotional stimulation of the sad music without the sensation of displeasure that usually accompanies an experience of sadness.

Dissociation is defined by the American Psychiatric Association (1994) as "a disruption in the usually integrated functions of consciousness, memory, identity, or perception of the environment". In its extreme form, dissociation manifests itself in disorders in which victims of extremely traumatic events such as childhood abuse may detach themselves from reality in order to cope (Van Ijzendoorn & Schuengel, 1996). At a pathological level, dissociation may involve amnesia, identity disturbance or the experience of subpersonalities, and depersonalization or de-realization (the sense of not experiencing one's self as real) (Ray, June, Turaj, & Lundy, 1992). It is thought that these symptoms are differing manifestations of a single underlying process that exists along a continuum ranging from normative behaviours to major psychopathological conditions such as multiple personality disorder or fugue states (Bernstein & Putnam, 1986; Briere, Weathers, & Runtz, 2005).

That dissociation is also a part of normative behaviour is evinced by findings that dissociation can also occur during positive experiences such as sport, sex, prayer, contact with nature, acting and performing or listening to music (Pica & Beere, 1995). Non-pathological dissociation is most commonly manifested as absorption, an occurrence that is experienced by most people in daily life (Ross, 1996). Lisa Butler (2006) describes absorption as "the heart of the normative experience" (p. 46). Absorption, similar to daydreaming, is an experience in which attention is deeply narrowed and there is a lessening of awareness of internal states or external conditions as a result (Eisen & Lynn, 2001). Absorption enables a person to temporarily set aside reality while engaged in something else. This narrowing of attention differs from pathological dissociative disorders, in that certain areas of experience merely remain at the periphery of consciousness rather than being blocked altogether from conscious experience (Leavitt, 2001).

Cognitively, absorption is associated with the ability to create mental representations, an intense feeling of empathic identification with objects of attention, and a strong desire to experience such deep connection or engagement (Tellegen & Atkinson, 1974). Absorption is also positively correlated with participation in the arts, a tendency to use the arts to influence mood, and the importance of the arts in daily life (Wild, Kuiken, & Schopflocher, 1995). Similarly, there seems to be a positive correlation between absorption, dissociation and the occurrence of religious experiences, all of which may be linked to hyperactivity of the limbic system (Saver & Rabin, 1997). Some scholars thus hypothesize that the varying capacities for dissociation amongst individuals may be the crucial determinant of why some are attracted to religion and spirituality, with those who are highly dissociative naturally finding such experiences more rewarding (Seligman & Kirmayer, 2008).

Absorption is also discussed in the literature regarding mysticism and heightened states of consciousness. Some may experience an altered sense of self during an episode of absorbed concentration. It appears to be involved in the experience that many athletes and musicians know as 'flow', described as a state of consciousness in which people are so intensely absorbed in an activity that they are barely aware of the passage of time or of the things that are happening around them (Csikszentmihalyi, 1991). In addition, absorption and dissociation are consistently associated with susceptibility to hypnosis (Tellegen & Atkinson, 1974). Snodgrass and Lynn (1989) reported that highly hypnotizable subjects experienced greater absorption when listening to music than those who were less hypnotizable. Kreutz and colleagues (Kreutz, Ott, Teichmann, Osawa, & Vaitl, 2008) similarly found that participants scoring high on the absorption scale reported stronger emotions in general in response to music, with a significant correlation for sadness.

Ruth Herbert (2011) claims that it is these very processes of absorption and dissociation that make music so useful for both psychological and physiological self-regulation. She argues that people habitually use music to detach from unpleasant situations around them, such as travelling in an overcrowded train or waiting in a doctor's surgery, or even to block out their own negative thoughts. It may be that music is a particularly effective agent for inducing experiences of absorption because of the multiple ways in which it can engage the listener (Herbert, 2012).

Since dissociation involves a disconnection from pain or trauma at both a clinical and a normative level, it is possible that this psychological process is involved in Schubert's DTEAC model. As Schubert proposes that some people are able to deactivate or dissociate the displeasure often associated with experiences of sadness, it may be that this capacity is heightened in people with strong tendencies to non-pathological dissociation and absorption.

Schubert's theory is related to the idea that all emotional arousal stimulates neural activation which is prima facie pleasurable, while at the same time retaining the feeling tone of the emotion itself, i.e. the sadness of a sad emotion (Schubert, 2009–2010). It also involves the idea of appraisal. Many scholars have alluded to the fact that our perception of aesthetic situations as non-threatening is related to our enjoyment of sad music (see Chap. 2). However, what Schubert adds to the picture here, is a mechanistic model that goes some way towards explaining why it is *enjoyable*, rather than merely *tolerable*. As early as 1956, Leonard Meyer argued that the occurrence of unexpected events within the music generates emotional arousal. This arousal may be a key source of the pleasure that we find in listening to music. Thus, when the situation is one that is perceived to have no real-life implications such as when listening to music, Schubert proposes that displeasure is dissociated or de-activated. Since various personal factors cause individuals to evaluate situations differently, and since individual capacities for dissociation differ, we could therefore expect people to have different emotional reactions to and different levels of enjoyment of sadness in music (Silvia & Brown, 2007).

According to the dissociation model, sad music can evoke real emotions, but they "do not activate real-life fully fledged consequent actions of the emotion (such as avoidance behavior)" (Schubert, 2013, p. 20). Here Schubert refers to the argument made by Louis Charland (2005), who proposes that there is a demarcation between "affect valence" and "emotion valence" (p. 85). Affect valence, according to Charland, is related to how the experience as a whole feels subjectively, i.e. whether the experience is pleasurable or unpleasurable. On the other hand, the emotion valence relates to the positive or negative charge of the emotion experienced (see also Colombetti, 2005). Affect valence and emotion valence are often indistinguishable, since an experience of anger for example, (a negative emotion valence) is usually experienced as unpleasant (a negative affect valence). However, Schubert maintains that the experience of listening to sad music is a case in point of the differences. In this case, he argues, since dissociation occurs we can experience the *emotion valence* of sadness in response to the music, while the *affect valence* of the experience as a whole remains positive. In fact, two distinct cognitive processes may be occurring simultaneously making the experience one of genuine sadness and concurrent pleasure (Juslin, 2013; Schubert, 2016).

Researchers in the field of media and advertising have proposed similar processes. Murry and Dacin (1996) argued that the empathic responses elicited when viewing drama as opposed to comedy, for example, require more cognitive mediation and analysis of the situation than those which elicit positive emotions. The unpleasant effect of the emotions is then diminished by the assessment of the situation as not signaling a real threat to the individual.

Some evidence suggesting the existence of a neurological basis for these theories of appraisal and dissociation comes from a study by Anne Blood and Robert Zatorre (2001) in which the amygdala and the hippocampus was found to have received inhibitory presynaptic input when listening to sad music, suggesting that typical responses to negative affect were inhibited when listening to music. As suggested by brain studies indicating the activation of pleasure systems in the brain when listening to music (see Chap. 4), it is further possible that the shift in consciousness and temporary suspension of self-awareness involved in experiences of absorption may be a satisfying and desirable state in itself as is reported among elite athletes and musicians of their experiences of flow. Dissociative experiences and absorption may be rewarded by the brain since they enhance functioning or performance in certain activities while contributing to adaptation to the stresses of daily life. Seligman and Kirmayer (2008) further argue that dissociation is a highly adaptive state that allows people to express emotions or desires which may normally be socially unacceptable in a context in which normal reality has been suspended.

Since dissociation exists to varying degrees in individuals (Leavitt, 2001), the DTEAC model provides an interesting possibility for examining the differences between individual responses to sad music. Even in regards to pathological dissociation, individuals differ in the level of dissociation experienced in reaction to comparable trauma (Simeon, Guralnik, Knutelska, & Schmeidler, 2002). Younger people such as college students seem to have higher rates of dissociative experiences than older individuals (Seligman & Kirmayer, 2008). Interestingly, it is in this same age range that music often plays its most important role in emotional life (Campbell, Connell, & Beegle, 2007), while older people report lower levels of emotional strength in response to that of their younger counterparts (Schubert, 2007).

It is possible that there is also a strong connection between this mechanistic model proposed by Schubert and the role of empathy and imagination, which are often mentioned in the philosophical literature in connection with emotional response to music.

Imagination, Empathy and Openness to Experience

Absorption, as discussed above, is an experience much like daydreaming in which one becomes intensely focused on something and temporarily disconnected from the external environment. Imagination—described as the flow of thoughts from one idea to another and the ability to process one thing as if it were another (Nettle, 2007; Roth, 2007)—is also related to emotional sensitivity and to a propensity for dissociative experiences including absorption (Herbert, 2012; Merckelbah, Horselenberg, & Muris, 2001). For example, studies in virtual reality have demonstrated the role of dissociation in the capacity to become imaginatively engaged in a virtual scenario (Murray, Fox, & Pettifer, 2007). It is unsurprising, therefore, that imagination could be involved in the enjoyment of music. Studies show that imagination includes the formation of mental images including the auditory ones associated with music (Halpern, 2001).

Imagination is also linked to empathy. Empathy involves being able to imagine the experience of another, or to put oneself 'in their shoes'. It may be that these two processes—imagination and empathy—work closely together in our emotional response to music. Since music is often imitative of human expression of emotion, even in non-programmatic music some listeners may imaginatively create an object—the fictional person expressing the emotion perceived in the music—and experience an empathic response towards that object.

Even if the listener does not consciously imagine a character or scenario in the same detail that one might while reading fiction, they may still, at some level of consciousness, attribute the emotions expressed to some undefined, non-existent person. Kendall Walton (1997) argues that 'pure music' is not so easily distinguishable from programme music in any case. He states that "music stands ready to take on an explicit representational function at the slightest provocation" (p. 58). Kivy (1989) also makes the interesting suggestion that the tendency to attribute animate qualities to animate things may be part of our evolutionarily hard-wired survival mechanisms, such as when we instinctively perceive a stick to be a snake. Children also demonstrate this tendency to animate and personify

(Inagaki & Hatano, 1987). It is this adeptness at conjuring up powerful images and colouring our perceptions of characters or scenes in a film or story that makes music such a very useful tool in films and advertising. Thus, Ian Cross (2007) has suggested that engagement with music may in fact underlie the evolutionary development of imagination.

Empathy, however, may also be involved in our more instinctive reactions to music as well. Empathy entails a mirroring of emotion, and the development of parallel and reactive emotions in response to those perceived as being expressed by another (Vreeke & Van der Mark, 2003). The tendency to mimic facial expressions and other expressive behaviour more or less automatically is nearly universal. Studies indicate that these behavioural manifestations of emotional states can, at least to some extent, induce the very same state in the observer (Molnar-Szakacs & Overy, 2006). Thus aspects of the music to which our bodies automatically respond in a physiological sense through processes of motor mimicry, entrainment and autonomic arousal, may contribute toward actually inducing the same emotions in the listener. This is likely an important factor in emotional contagion (Darwall, 1997).

Cooke (1963) describes this well, when he argues that the way we respond to music is analogous to the way we may feel the very emotions of a friend as they tell us of their experiences. In a similar way, when we listen to music, we partake of the artists' experiences vicariously and empathically. Cooke claims that emotions conveyed through the arts are, in fact "more real" than emotions aroused in other circumstances, since music transmits "the naked feeling directly" (p. 21) without the need for words. Indeed, the extensive overlaps between the way the brain processes musical emotions and emotions encoded in speech does suggest a plausible connection between a propensity to empathize with the emotions expressed by others and a predilection for strong emotional engagement with music.

A more specialized form of empathy involved in response to music is "music empathizing", as described by Kreutz, Schubert and Mitchell (2008). This concept, based on the work of Baron-Cohen and colleagues (Baron-Cohen et al., 2005), relies on the premise that musicians and music lovers may have a specialized set of empathy skills that allow them to encode and decode emotion and related information in music-specific contexts. It is possible that this particular form of empathy may be even more closely related than general empathy to the capacity to imaginatively engage with aesthetic stimuli and be emotionally moved by them.

The mere involvement of empathy or imagination in emotional responses to music does not in itself explain why sad music holds comparable attraction for some people than music expressing happier emotions. The distance achieved by the knowledge that we are not ourselves threatened still does not reveal why we should be interested in experiencing it. In fact, it seems more likely that people who are highly empathic or imaginative would be particularly likely to avoid sad music because of their higher vulnerability to experience the emotions expressed (Oliver, 1993).

However, with the added involvement of absorption, itself an adaptive and therefore rewarding experience, we can begin to see how deep emotional responses to aesthetic stimuli that are enhanced by active propensities for empathy and imagination can enable even negative emotions to be experienced in a pleasurable way. It may be that highly imaginative, fantasy-prone people who have strong capacities for dissociation and absorption may be more likely to experience heightened, euphoric pleasure in listening to music, or even the altered states of consciousness and expanded awareness that is often associated with meditation or religious experiences. Individuals with these traits would thus be able to experience the strong emotional arousal evoked by sad music as pleasurable rather than disagreeable.

Like absorption and openness to experience, imagination and empathy are present to differing degrees in different individuals. Kivy (1989), for example, claims that he enjoys music without any "imaginative contortions" (p. 250). He admits that fictional works may arouse "garden-variety" emotions in us, but argues that absolute music with no programmatic content or lyrics, cannot. However, the fact that some people do not engage their imagination when listening to music does not disprove the arguments regarding the involvement of imagination. It merely further demonstrates the importance of considering individual differences. If individuals differ in their capacity to imaginatively engage with music and to experience empathy in response to expressed emotion, these may be key factors to understanding why some people are able to enjoy sad music.

Another personality trait that is closely associated with both absorption and imagination is the trait of openness to experience from the Big Five model of personality (Glisky & Kihlstrom, 1993; Wild et al., 1995). Openness to experience includes six aspects, including imaginativeness, aesthetic sensibility, attentiveness to inner feelings, enjoyment of variety, and intellectual curiosity (McCrae & Costa, 1985). Several studies report that people with high scores in openness to experience tend to enjoy sad music more than others. Jonna Vuoskoski and colleagues, for example (Vuoskoski, Thompson, McIllwain, & Eerola, 2012), found that participants in their sample with high scores in openness to experience both enjoyed sad music and were highly susceptible to intense responses to it. Similarly, Olivia Ladinig and Glenn Schellenberg (2012) found that people who liked music that made them feel sad tended to have high scores on openness to experience and low scores on extraversion.

These results suggest a relationship between personality and arousal levels as an additional factor in the enjoyment of sad music. As discussed in Chap. 5, personality contributes to determining what our individual optimal level of stimulation is. In general, introverts tend to have a rather low activation threshold for stimulation and therefore need less stimulation than other people (Geen, 1984). They may, therefore, be more likely to demonstrate a preference for low arousal sad music. On the other hand, in complex genres of music such as classical and jazz, music that is sad often contains a broader range of emotional expression (Schubert, 1999), a musical characteristic likely to be attractive to people with high scores in openness to experience since they perhaps require more complexity and variety in order to achieve increased arousal. Whether or not there are differences in the type of sad music or the arousing qualities of the music that introverts and people with high scores in openness to experience enjoyed would be an interesting question for future research. Alternatively, people with low scores in extraversion may be attracted to sad music because of the capacity of music to provide a sense of connection with other people in a relatively low arousal environment, allowing them to receive some sense of solace or social bonding without the need to interact directly with another person.

An Empirical Investigation of Individual Differences in Liking Sad Music

Since the literature discussed thus far has revealed a paucity of empirical investigations about why people listen to sad music and little consideration of the influence of individual differences, I set out to investigate some of these questions in a series of studies with Emery Schubert, who formulated the DTEAC model. An important aspect of individual differences psychology has been the development and use of psychometric tests to measure the differences and similarities between individuals in many different traits. Thus, these studies utilized standard psychometric tests for measuring propensities for dissociation, empathy and imagination, to explore the possible connection between individual capacities for absorption and other traits, and the tendency to enjoy sad music. In addition, given the question as to whether sad music may at times form part of a range of maladaptive mood regulation strategies, we also aimed to explore the influence of coping styles that could indicate a propensity for affect dysregulation, such as rumination.

In our first study (Garrido & Schubert, 2011), 59 student participants completed the music empathy scale that Kreutz and colleagues (2008a, 2008b) developed by adapting a general empathizing-systemizing measure to music. This scale was designed to investigate empathy as a cognitive style of processing music rather than as a general trait. Participants also completed two subscales of the Interpersonal Reactivity Index (IRI, Davis, 1983). The IRI was developed to assess the cognitive and emotional aspects of empathy on four separate aspects. Since the emotional facets seemed most pertinent to our central research question about the response to sad music, we focused on the empathic concern subscale rather than the subscales measuring the cognitive processes involved in empathy. This subscale was specifically designed to assess feelings of sympathy and concern for others (Davis, 1983). In addition we used a selection of items from the Fantasy-proneness subscale of the IRI as our indicator of imagination, a scale designed to measure the tendency to "imaginatively transpose oneself into fictional situations (e.g. books, movies, daydreams)" (Davis, 1980 p. 96).

Dissociation and absorption were both tested in this study so that we could explore the question of whether dissociation more generally is implicated in the attraction to sad music, or whether the more specific aspect of absorption is the primary aspect of dissociation involved. For general dissociation we used the Questionnaire of Experiences of Dissociation (QED; Riley, 1988), since it was developed using a normative sample. The items in the scale covered the broad spectrum of dissociative experiences, from daydreaming to pathological states such as dissociative fugue. The measure for absorption was a 12-item subscale drawn from Tellegen's Absorption Scale, one of the most commonly used measures of absorption from the Multidimensional Personality Questionnaire (Tellegen, 1982). After completing the RRQ (Trapnell & Campbell, 1999)[1] as measures of rumination and reflectiveness, participants were then questioned about their liking for sad music.

Our preliminary analysis showed that 30 of the 59 participants (50.8 percent) either agreed or strongly agreed that they liked music that made them feel sad. This is comparable to the figures reported by Schubert (2010) in which 10 out his 25 participants (40 percent) reported liking sad music, and also by David Huron (2011). Of the participants in our study who did like sad music, none claimed that they only liked it if it resolved happily. Thus, no support was found in our study for Levinson's (1996a) proposal that we listen to sad music in order to enjoy the reward of 'emotional resolution', or the sense of satisfaction that we get from a happy ending.

Interestingly, three of the psychometric measures of personality were correlated with a liking for sad music: absorption, empathic concern and music empathy. However, there was no significant correlation between dissociation as measured by the QED, or fantasy-proneness and a liking for sad music. This is in contrast to the study by researchers from Japan (Kawakami & Katahira, 2015) who found that fantasy-proneness significantly predicted a liking for sad music in a sample of 84 elementary schoolchildren. However, of the five possible sources of individual differences investigated in this study, absorption and empathy, whether general or music-specific, returned the most significant results.

[1] See Chap. 5 for more details.

This suggests that listening to sad music is primarily an adaptive behaviour, which is related to other healthy traits such as absorption and empathy. On the other hand, pathological dissociation and rumination were not related to a liking for sad music. It also offers some support for Schubert's DTEAC model, in that people with a propensity to experience states of absorption reported a greater liking for sad music than others, suggesting that where absorption or non-pathological dissociation is occurring, the experience of sadness can be enjoyable. This finding is consistent with previous studies that also report a connection between absorption and a high level of importance of the arts in daily life (Wild et al., 1995), and an emotional responsiveness to music more generally (Kreutz et al., 2008).

The association between general empathy and a liking for sad music was the statistically weakest result of the three significant predictors. The stronger correlation between music empathy and a liking for sad music indicates that a particular form of context-specific imaginativeness and empathy—distinct from what Fantasy Proneness or Empathic Concern were able to predict—is more closely involved in emotional response to music. This implies that a specialized ability to connect to music and to empathically decrypt musical expressions of emotion is necessary before an enjoyment of sad music is possible. The current study thus confirmed the importance of considering individual differences, since the correlations between certain personality traits and a liking for sad music adds further weight to the argument that not all people will be attracted to sad music in equal degrees or for the same reasons.

Are We Attracted to Sad Music Even When We Don't 'Like' It?

While no positive association was found in the study reported above between rumination and a liking for sad music, we argued that ruminators may still find themselves attracted to it, although not actually enjoying the experience of listening to it because of the negative effect on their mood. While more than half of our sample reported enjoying sad music, the possibility remained that for other listeners, whether ruminators or not, some ultimate psychological benefit might be gained by listening to sad music despite the fact that the experience was not pleasurable. It was also possible that while some individuals might be capable of taking pleasure from listening to sad music they might not necessarily demonstrate any particular bias toward it in their listening choices, suggesting that they valued it equally to happy music. Thus, the distinction between being attracted to sad music, enjoying listening to it and valuing it equally to other kinds of music, was something we intended to explore further.

Our second study attempted to replicate our previous results in a broader sample, as well as to tease out the differing ways that people may use sad music in more detail. The 152 participants of this second phase of research (Garrido & Schubert, 2013), included 72 undergraduate students, as well as members of the general public who were recruited through an association for depression sufferers, a music appreciation society and a meditation school. It was thought that members of such organizations might provide an interesting angle to the picture given the likelihood of their high levels of rumination (members of the association for depression sufferers), music empathy (the music appreciation society), and absorption (the meditation school).

In addition to using the same personality measures as we had used in the previous study, we developed a scale that we called the Like Sad Music Scale (LSMS), based largely on Mary Beth Oliver's Sad Film Scale (1993). Oliver's scale was developed specifically to test a tendency to experience sadness when watching sad films and the enjoyment of such sadness. In addition to seven items from Oliver's scale which were modified so as to reflect a liking for sad music rather than films, we constructed an additional four items that explored the possible use of sad music for the purpose of grieving, as well as the possibility that valence might have been of no importance in music selections for some listeners. It was expected that the resulting scale would provide a measure of liking for sad music whether the motive was hedonic pleasure, catharsis or some other psychological benefit.

To supplement the LSMS, which was designed to measure a *liking* for sad music, we also included a measure of listening *habits*, hypothesizing that some listeners might have a pattern of listening to sad music despite their deriving little or no pleasure from it. Previous studies have asked participants to estimate the amount of time in minutes that they spend listening to music per day as an indicator of the importance of music in daily life (North, Hargreaves, & O'Neill, 2000; Schwartz & Fouts, 2003). We added to that a question asking participants to estimate how much time they spent listening to sad music, so as to facilitate the calculation of the relative importance of sad music within that person's overall listening time. Thus, in combination with this LSMS we were able to obtain scores that reflected a *liking* for sad music—both because it was enjoyable or believed to be psychologically *beneficial*—and a score relating to the habit of listening to sad music.

Analysis of the data disclosed that people with high scores on the LSMS—suggesting an overall strong liking for sad music—tended to have high scores in absorption as in the previous study, and also in reflectiveness as measured by the RRQ. This suggested that the LSMS did encompass both people who found listening to sad music enjoyable (people with high scores in absorption), and people who were attracted to it for the potential psychological benefit it could confer (people with high scores in reflectiveness), as predicted. This was further confirmed by looking at the alignment of specific items of the LSMS with the personality scores. In particular, absorption was especially strongly associated with an item within the LSMS stating that the individual enjoyed "feeling strong emotions in response to music", while reflectiveness was most strongly correlated with the item relating to the use of sad music to grieve. Thus, we began to see a picture of distinct ways of using sad music emerging in people with different personality profiles: the use of sad music for hedonic reasons in people with high scores in absorption and the use of sad music to process negative emotions or grief in people with high scores in reflectiveness.

A regression model also revealed that rumination was a predictor of a liking for sad music, although the relationship was much weaker than for absorption or reflectiveness. In particular, rumination was positively correlated with LSMS items in which people agreed that listening to sad music helped them to "release the sadness" they were experiencing, or that they liked listening to sad music because they could "relate to the feelings and emotions being expressed". In addition, ruminators tended to demonstrate a higher percentage of sad music listening than people with low scores in rumination. This implied that people with a tendency to ruminate do tend to listen to sad music more than others, and that they do so because of the negative emotions they are experiencing and a belief that they obtain some cathartic relief from these negative emotions by listening to the music. Similar results have been demonstrated in a later study by John Hogue, Andrea Crimmins and Jeffrey Kahn (2015) in which they found that liking for sad music increased as depression increased.

It appeared that there were also some gender differences in the way people were reporting using sad music. While a regression model of the overall sample showed that reflectiveness, absorption and rumination were all predictors of a liking for sad music, when we conducted regression analyses on males and females separately, these variables appeared to be split between the groups. Absorption was the only significant predictor for the males in our sample, while a liking for sad music among females was predicted by both reflectiveness and rumination. This suggests that male participants were more likely to listen to sad music if they were absorbed by it, while females tended to use sad music in order to cope with negative emotions, both in healthy ways (reflection) and in unhealthy ways (rumination).

Interestingly, in this sample, dissociation also displayed some correlation with the percentage of sad music listening scores, although not with an overall liking for it. These findings in relation to both dissociation and rumination imply that people with pathological tendencies seem attracted to listening to sad music although they do not necessarily enjoy it. What remains unclear from the present study, however, is the direction of the relationship, i.e., whether or not they listen to sad music because they experience more negative emotions than other people, or whether the sad music contributes to the high degree of negative emotions they experience. This important question will be considered further in the studies reported in the next chapter.

As in the previous study a weak relationship existed between a liking for sad music and general empathy. However, in contrast to our previous results no significant result was obtained in this sample for the more specific form of music empathy. Similarly, no significant differences were found between student and non-student portions of the sample.

A Summary of the Empirical Evidence Thus Far

While the connection between a liking for sad music and empathy was relatively weak in both the studies summarized in this chapter, other researchers have found more significant associations (Vuoskoski et al., 2012), suggesting that some relationship exists—although perhaps with less strength than the relationship with absorption. It may be, in fact, that different facets of empathy are associated with different responses to sad music. Vuoskoski and colleagues found that fantasy proneness and empathic concern, which were only weakly related in our studies, were predictive of both a liking for sad music and the intensity of the emotional response. Other studies, however, have found a stronger relationship between sad music and perspective taking, a facet of empathy related to the ability to imagine how other people feel (Kawakami & Katahira, 2015).

Theoretically, the argument for a relationship between a liking for sad music and empathy is strong. Compassion and the ability to feel the emotions of others are adaptive traits, and therefore ones that are rewarded in the brain. As noted by Vuoskoski (2015), "it may be that empathic people find it intrinsically pleasurable to engage in vicarious experiences, especially in aesthetic contexts" (pp. 100–1). This may also help explain why people tend to prefer a matching between the emotion expressed in the music and the emotions they feel, since it is likely to create a sense of empathic connection between the music (or fictional object behind the music) and the listener (Evans & Schubert, 2008).

The results of the research overall suggest that feelings of sadness elicited when listening to music are enjoyable to many listeners. Others, however, appear to be attracted to it for alternative reasons. The finding that absorption was strongly correlated with a liking for sad music, a finding which was replicated across both studies, provides substantiation for Schubert's DTEAC model, in that it appears that absorption allows some people to dissociate or disengage the displeasure that might usually arise from an experience of sadness, and to just enjoy the strong emotions they are experiencing. These findings are also in harmony with studies relating to strong emotional experiences with music in which participants report that such experiences are both pleasurable and desirable, even when they involve sad music (Gabrielsson, 2001; Grewe, Nagel, Kopiez, & Altenmüller, 2007).

However, this is likely just one piece of the picture. The results also suggest that whether or not the experience is enjoyable, people with inclinations toward reflectiveness tend to use music listening as an opportunity to process and come to terms with events in their own lives, such as grief. It seems that this is particularly true in relation to females. The fact that reflectiveness is also related to openness to experience suggests that this may account for findings that people with high scores in openness to experience report a liking for sad music.

On the other hand, people with high scores in rumination do not necessarily enjoy sad music but they are nevertheless attracted to it because of the perceived opportunity for catharsis and because they can relate to the sad emotions being expressed. Although they do not necessarily *like* it, their listening habits nevertheless indicate an *attraction* to it. This proved to be the same with dissociation. Since high scores in rumination and dissociation both indicate the presence of abnormal psychology, the relatively higher percentage of sad music they listen to may be a manifestation of maladaptive mood regulation strategies. Ruminators may be predominantly attracted to sad music because of their own negative frame of mind.

However, whether or not these participants are obtaining the benefits that they believe they are attaining is a question that remains unanswered in the studies discussed in this chapter. Ruminative behaviour in general has the effect of perpetuating feelings of dysphoria (Nolen-Hoeksema, 1991). Nevertheless, the literature suggests that depressed people tend to justify their maladaptive behaviour and profess strong beliefs that they are benefiting from it. For example, several studies have shown that ruminators hold metacognitive beliefs that rumination is a useful coping strategy that can help them to avoid similar problems in the future (Barnhofer, Kuehn, de Jong-Meyer, & Williams, 2006; Papageorgiou &

Wells, 2001), and that in general people tend to lack insight into the causes of their affective states (Lehrer, 2009).

It is highly likely, therefore, that listening to sad music could, for people with tendencies to rumination, exacerbate cycles of negative thinking leading to negative mood outcomes, while the listener remains convinced that they are benefiting from doing so. In effect, it may be that people with tendencies towards rumination set out to listen to sad music with the same rational mood regulation goals that a reflective individual may have. However, while a reflective person is able to use the music as a tool for cognitive processing and to facilitate a shift to a more positive mood, ruminators may find themselves unable to disengage from the emotions invoked and thus find their negative thought cycles perpetuated.

These differing results between the personality traits offer an intriguing picture of the individual differences at play in the paradox of sad music listening. The two studies presented here thus support the presence of four broad groups of listeners:

1. People with strong propensities to absorption who are able to enjoy the purely hedonistic pleasure of emotional arousal that sad music provides them.
2. Those with reflective personality traits who derive psychological benefits from listening to sad music when life circumstances make it necessary to deal with negative emotions.
3. Those whose attraction to sad music is a manifestation of maladaptive mood regulation strategies, who may be drawn to sad music despite its limited value or detrimental influence on their mood-state.
4. Although not directly tested in the studies reported here, it seems likely that people who do not fit any of the above categories, would likely experience sad music as unpleasant and unhelpful and would therefore avoid it.

It seems possible, since people with strong empathic tendencies demonstrate a greater responsiveness to sad music, that empathic traits in combination with absorption, reflectiveness or rumination, would only augment the effects of the sad music. A person with tendencies to absorption who is also highly empathic would likely find themselves particularly susceptible to being drawn into the emotional journey of a sad song. Likewise a reflective person who is prone to strong empathic responses may find that their enhanced sensitivity to emotional expressions makes sad music a particularly accessible tool for reflecting on and processing their own emotional experiences. Where an individual has an inclination towards rumination, a highly compassionate person may similarly find that the likelihood of negative thoughts and feelings being elicited by sad music is high.

Matthew Sachs and colleagues (Sachs, Damasio, & Habibi, 2015), after a review of the literature about sad music listening, agree that the various personality traits implicated in the literature cause people to interact with sad music in widely diverse ways. They make the interesting argument that these personality traits cause people to use sad music in order to achieve a state of homeostatic equilibrium. It is likely here that individual optimal arousal levels come into play (see Chap. 5). Personality, as discussed earlier in this chapter, has an impact on the level of stimulation that an individual needs in order to reach a state of optimal functioning. This, in combination with the above personality traits, appears to interact with environmental factors to create a need for homeostasis, which the individual then seeks to attain using sad music in the various ways discussed above. Just how these factors interact is an area that future research will likely look at in more detail.

The fact that many listeners select sad music for a range of psychological functions has interesting implications for the use of music in therapeutic contexts, and indeed for maximizing the effectiveness of music use by people in everyday life to successfully regulate their moods. However, as has been alluded to several times already throughout the volume, there is some question as to whether listeners actually obtain the psychological benefits that they set out to attain, particularly where mood disorders are involved. It is to this question that the next chapter turns in more detail.

References

Altenmüller, E., Schurmann, K., Lim, V. K., & Parlitz, D. (2002). Hits to the left, flops to the right: Different emotions during listening to music are reflected in cortical laterisation patterns. *Neuropsychologia, 40*, 2242–2256.

American Psychiatric Association. (1994). *Diagnostic and statistical manual of mental disorders (DSM-IV)* (4th ed.). Washington, DC: American Psychiatric Press.

Barnhofer, T., Kuehn, E.-M., de Jong-Meyer, R., & Williams, J. M. G. (2006). Beliefs about the benefits of rumination in depressed men and women with and without a history of assault. *Behavioral and Cognitive Psychotherapy, 35*, 317–324.

Baron-Cohen, S., Knickmeyer, R. C., & Belmonte, M. K. (2005). Sex differences in the brain: Implications for explaining autism. *Science, 310*, 819–823.

Barrick, M. R., & Mount, M. K. (1991). The Big Five personality dimensions and job performance: A meta-analysis. *Personnel Psychology, 44*, 1–26.

Berdan, L. E., Keane, S. P., & Calkins, S. D. (2008). Temperament and externalizing behvior: Social preference and perceived acceptance as protective factors. *Developmental Psychology, 44*(4), 957–968.

Bernstein, E. M., & Putnam, F. W. (1986). Development, reliability, and validity of a dissociation scale. *The Journal of Nervous and Mental Disease, 174*(12), 727–735.

Blood, A. J., & Zatorre, R. J. (2001). Intensely pleasurable responses to music correlate with activity in brain regions implicated in reward and emotion. *Proceedings of the National Academy of Sciences, 98*, 11818–11823.

Briere, J., Weathers, F. W., & Runtz, M. (2005). Is dissociation a multidimensional construct? Data from the multiscale dissociation inventory. *Journal of Traumatic Stress, 18*(3), 221–231.

Butler, L. D. (2006). Normative dissociation. *Psychiatric Clinics of North America, 29*, 45–62.

Campbell, P. S., Connell, C., & Beegle, A. (2007). Adolescents' expressed meanings of music in and out of school. *Journal of Research in Music Education, 55*(3), 220–236.

Chamorro-Premuzic, T., & Furnham, A. (2007). Personality and music: Can traits explain how people use music in everyday life? *British Journal of Psychology, 98*(2), 175–185.

Charland, L. C. (2005). The heat of emotion: Valence and the demarcation problem. *Journal of Consciousness Studies, 12*(8–10), 82–102.

Colombetti, G. (2005). Appraising valence. *Journal of Consciousness Studies, 12*(8), 103–126.

Cooke, D. (1963). *Language of music*. Oxford: Oxford University Press.

Cross, I. (2007). Music, science and culture. In I. Roth (Ed.), *Imaginative minds*. Oxford: Oxford University Press.

Csikszentmihalyi, M. (1991). *Flow: The psychology of optimal experience.* New York: HarperCollins.
Darwall, S. (1997). Empathy, sympathy, care. *Philosophical Studies, 89*, 261–282.
Davis, M. H. (1980). A multidimensional approach to individual differences in empathy. *JSAS Catalog of Selected Documents in Psychology, 10*, 85.
Davis, M. H. (1983). Measuring individual differences in empathy: Evidence for a multidimensional approach. *Journal of Personality and Social Psychology, 44*(1), 113–126.
Dollinger, S. J. (1993). Research note: Personality and music preference: Extraversion and excitement seeking or openness to experience? *Psychology of Music, 21*(1), 73–77.
Eisen, M. L., & Lynn, S. J. (2001). Dissociation, memory and suggestibility in adults and children. *Applied Cognitive Psychology, 15*, S49–S73.
Evans, P., & Schubert, E. (2008). Relationships between expressed and felt emotions in music. *Musicae Scientiae, 12*, 75–99.
Gabrielsson, A. (2001). Emotions in strong experiences with music. In P. N. Juslin & J. A. Sloboda (Eds.), *Music and emotion: Theory and research* (pp. 431–449). Oxford: Oxford University Press.
Garrido, S., & Schubert, E. (2011). Individual differences in the enjoyment of negative emotion in music: A literature review and experiment. *Music Perception, 28*(3), 279–295.
Garrido, S., & Schubert, E. (2013). Adaptive and maladaptive attraction to negative emotion in music. *Musicae Scientiae, 17*(2), 145–164. doi:10.1177/1029864913478305.
Geen, R. G. (1984). Preferred stimulation levels in introverts and extroverts: Effects on arousal and performance. *Journal of Personality and Social Psychology, 46*(6), 1303–1312.
Glisky, M. L., & Kihlstrom, J. F. (1993). Hypnotizability and facets of openness. *International Journal of Clinical and Experimental Hypnosis, 41*, 112–123.
Goldberg, L. R. (1993). The structure of phenotypic personality traits. *American Psychologist, 48*, 26–34.
Grewe, O., Nagel, F., Kopiez, R., & Altenmüller, E. (2007). Listening to music as a re-creative process: Physiological, psychological, and psychoacoustical correlates of chills and strong emotions. *Music Perception, 24*, 297–314.
Halpern, A. R. (2001). Cerebral substrates of musical imagery. *Annals of the New York Academy of Science, 930*(1), 179–192.
Hampson, S. E., & Coleman, A. M. (Eds.). (1995). *Individual differences and personality.* London and New York: Longman.

Herbert, R. (2011). *Everyday music listening: Absorption, dissociation, and trancing*. Surrey, UK: Ashgate.
Herbert, R. (2012). Musical and non-musical involvement in daily life: The case of absorption. *Musicae Scientiae, 16*(1), 41–66.
Hogue, J. D., Crimmins, A. M., & Kahn, J. H. (2015). "So sad and slow, so why can't I turn off the radio": The effects of gender, depression, and absorption on liking music that induces sadness and music that induces happiness. *Psychology of Music*. doi:10.1177/0305735615594489.
Huron, D. (2011). Why is sad music pleasurable? A possible role for prolactin. *Musicae Scientiae, 15*(2), 146–158.
Inagaki, K., & Hatano, G. (1987). Young childrens spontaneous personification as analogy. *Child Development, 58*(4), 1013–1020.
Juslin, P. N. (2013). From everyday emotions to aesthetic emotions: Towards a unified theory of musical emotions. *Physics of Life Reviews, 10*, 235–266.
Kawakami, A., & Katahira, K. (2015). Influence of trait empahty on the emotion evoked by sad music and on the preference for it. *Frontiers in Psychology, 6*, 1541. doi:10.3389/fpsyg.2015.01541.
Kivy, P. (1989). *Sound sentiment*. Princeton: Princeton University Press.
Kreutz, G., Ott, U., Teichmann, D., Osawa, P., & Vaitl, D. (2008a). Using music to induce emotion: Influences of musical preference and absorption. *Psychology of Music, 36*, 101–121.
Kreutz, G., Schubert, E., & Mitchell, L. A. (2008b). Cognitive styles of music listening. *Music Perception, 26*(1), 57–73.
Ladinig, O., & Schellenberg, E. G. (2012). Liking unfamiliar music: Effects of felt emotion and individual differences. *Psychology of Aesthetics, Creativity and the Arts, 6*(2), 146–154.
Leavitt, F. (2001). MMPI profile characteristics of women with varying levels of normal dissociation. *Journal of Clinical Psychology, 51*(12), 1469–1477.
Lehrer, J. (2009). *How we decide*. Boston, MA: Houghton Mifflin Harcourt.
Levinson, J. (1996a). Music and negative emotions. In J. Robinson (Ed.), *Music and meaning*. New York: Cornell University Press.
Litle, P., & Zuckerman, M. (1986). Sensation seeking and music preferences. *Personality and Individual Differences, 7*(4), 575–578.
Martindale, C. (1988). Aesthetics, psychobiology, and cognition. In F. H. Harley & R. W. Neperud (Eds.), *The foundations of aesthetics, art and art education* (pp. 7–42). New York: Praeger.
McCown, W., Keiser, R., Shea, M., & Williamson, D. (1997). The role of personality and gender in preference for exaggerated bass in music. *Personality and Individual Differences, 23*(4), 543–547.

McCrae, R. R., & Costa Jr., P. T. (1985). Openness to experience. *Perspectives in Personality, 1*, 145–172.

Merckelbah, H., Horselenberg, R., & Muris, P. (2001). The Creative Experiences Questionnaire (CEQ): A brief self-report measure of fantasy proneness. *Personality and Individual Differences, 31*, 987–995.

Molnar-Szakacs, I., & Overy, K. (2006). Music and mirror neurons: From motion to 'e'motion. *SCAN, 1*, 235–241.

Murray, C. D., Fox, J., & Pettifer, S. (2007). Absorption, dissociation, locus of control and presence in virtual reality. *Computers in Human Behavior, 23*(3), 1347–1354.

Murry, J. P., & Dacin, P. A. (1996). Cognitive moderators of negative-emotion effects: Implications for understanding media context. *Journal of Consumer Research, 22*, 439–442.

Nettle, D. (2007). A module for metaphor? The site of imagination in the architecture of the mind. In I. Roth (Ed.), *Imaginative minds*. Oxford: Oxford University Press.

Nolen-Hoeksema, S. (1991). Responses to depression and their effect on the duration of depressive episodes. *Journal of Abnormal Psychology, 100*(4), 569–582.

North, A. C., Hargreaves, D. J., & O'Neill, S. A. (2000). The importance of music to adolescents. *British Journal of Educational Psychology, 70*, 255–272.

Oliver, M. B. (1993). Exploring the paradox of the enjoyment of sad films. *Human Communication Research, 19*(3), 315–342.

Papageorgiou, C., & Wells, A. (2001). Metacognitive beliefs about rumination in recurrent major depression. *Cognitive and Behavioural Practice, 8*, 160–164.

Peterson, R. A., & Kern, R. M. (1996). Changing highbrow taste: From snob to omnivore. *American Sociological Review, 61*(5), 900–907.

Pica, M., & Beere, D. (1995). Dissociation during positive situations. *Dissociation, VIII*(4), 241–246.

Ray, W. J., June, K., Turaj, K., & Lundy, R. (1992). Dissociative experiences in a college age population: A factor analytic study of two dissociation scales. *Personality and Individual Differences, 13*(4), 417–424.

Rentfrow, P. J., Goldberg, L. R., & Levitin, D. J. (2011). The structure of musical preferences: A five-factor model. *Journal of Personality and Social Psychology, 100*(6), 1139–1157.

Riley, K. C. (1988). Measurement of dissociation. *The Journal of Nervous and Mental Disease, 176*(7), 449–450.

Robinson, T. O., Weaver, J. B., & Zillmann, D. (1996). Exploring the relation between personality and the appreciation of rock music. *Psychology Report, 78*(1), 259–269.

Ross, C. A. (1996). History, phenomenology, and epidemiology of dissociation. In L. K. Michelson & W. J. Ray (Eds.), *Handbook of dissociation: Theoretical, empirical and clinical perspectives.* New York: Plenum Press.

Roth, I. (2007). Introduction: Imaginative minds: Concepts, controversies and themes. In I. Roth (Ed.), *Imaginative minds.* Oxford: Oxford University Press.

Sachs, M. E., Damasio, A., & Habibi, A. (2015). The pleasures of sad music: A systematic review. *Frontiers in Human Neuroscience, 9*, 404. doi:10.3389/fnhum.2015.00404.

Saver, J. L., & Rabin, J. (1997). The neural substrates of religious experiences. *Journal of Neuropsychiatry and Clinical Neurosience, 9*, 498–510.

Schubert, E. (1996). Enjoyment of negative emotions in music: An associative network explanation. *Psychology of Music, 24*, 18–28.

Schubert, E. (1999). Measuring emotion continuously: Validity and reliability of the two-dimensional emotion-space. *Australian Journal of Psychology, 51*(3), 154–165.

Schubert, E. (2007). Locus of emotion: The effect of task order and age on emotion perceived and emotion felt in response to music. *Journal of Music Therapy, 44*(4), 344–368.

Schubert, E. (2009–2010). The fundamental function of music. *Musicae Scientiae*, Special Issue, 63–81.

Schubert, E. (2010). Affective, evaluative, and collative responses to hated and loved music. *Psychology of Aesthetics, Creativity and the Arts, 4*(1), 36–46.

Schubert, E. (2013). Loved music can make a listener feel negative emotions. *Musicae Scientiae, 17*(1), 11–26.

Schubert, E. (2016). Enjoying sad music: Paradox or parallel processes? *Frontiers in Human Neuroscience, 10*, 312. doi:10.3389/fnhum.2016.00312.

Schwartz, K. D., & Fouts, G. T. (2003). Music preferences, personality style, and developmental issues of adolescents. *Journal of Youth and Adolescence., 32*(3), 205–213.

Seligman, R., & Kirmayer, L. J. (2008). Dissociative experience and cultural neuroscience: Narrative, metaphor and mechanism. *Cultural Medical Psychiatry, 32*, 31–64.

Silvia, P. J., & Brown, E. M. (2007). Anger, disgust and the negative aesthetic emotions: Expanding an appraisal model of aesthetic experience. *Psychology of Aesthetics, Creativity and the Arts, 1*(2), 100–106.

Simeon, D., Guralnik, O., Knutelska, M., & Schmeidler, J. (2002). Personality factors associated with dissociation: Temperament, defense and cognitive schemata. *American Journal of Psychology, 159*, 489–491.

Snodgrass, M., & Lynn, S. J. (1989). Music, absorption and hypnotisability. *International Journal of Clinical and Experimental Hypnosis, 37*(1), 41–54.

Tellegen, A. (1982). *Brief manual for the multidimensional personality questionnaire.* Minneapolis: University of Minnesota.

Tellegen, A., & Atkinson, G. (1974). Openness to absorbing and self-altering experiences ('absorption'), a trait related to hypnotic susceptibility. *Journal of Abnormal Psychology, 83*, 268–277.

Ter Bogt, T. F. M., Delsing, M. J. M. H., van Zalk, M., Christensen, P. G., & Meeus, W. H. J. (2011). Intergenerational continuity of taste: Parental and adolescent music preferences. *Social Forces, 90*(1), 297–320.

Ter Bogt, T. F. M., Mulder, J., Raaijmakers, Q. A. W., & Gabhainn, S. N. (2010). Moved by music: A typology of music listeners. *Psychology of Music, 39*(2), 147–163.

Trapnell, P. D., & Campbell, J. D. (1999). Private self-consciousness and the five-factor model of personality: Distinguishing rumination from reflection. *Journal of Personality and Social Psychology, 76*(2), 284–304.

Van Ijzendoorn, M. H., & Schuengel, V. (1996). The measurement of dissociation in normal and clinical populations: Meta-analytic validation of the Dissociative Experiences Scale (DES). *Clinical Psychology Review, 16*(5), 365–362.

Vreeke, G. J., & Van der Mark, I. L. (2003). Empathy, an integrative model. *New Ideas in Psychology, 21*(3), 177–207.

Vuoskoski, J. K. (2015). Music, empathy and affiliation: Commentary on Greenberg, Rentfrow, and Baron-Cohen. *Empirical Musicology Review, 10*(1), 99–103.

Vuoskoski, J. K., Thompson, W. F., McIlwain, D., & Eerola, T. (2012). Who enjoys listening to sad music and why? *Music Perception, 29*(3), 311–317.

Walton, K. (1997). Listening with imagination: Is music representational? In J. Robinson (Ed.), *Music and meaning.* New York: Cornell University Press.

Westen, D. (2002). *Psychology: Brain, behaviour and culture* (3rd. ed.). New York: Wiley.

Wild, T. C., Kuiken, D., & Schopflocher, D. (1995). The role of absorption in experimental involvement. *Journal of Personality and Social Psychology, 69*(3), 569–579.

8

Mood Regulation Disorders: An Exception to Mood Management Theory?

Listening to sad music is associated with a number of healthy and adaptive behaviours. As the studies discussed in the previous chapter indicate, people with tendencies to absorption are strongly attracted to sad music. Absorption is an adaptive trait that enables the maximization of performance and the effective reduction of stress. Also attracted to sad music are people with high measures of reflectiveness—a trait that enables an individual to engage in cognitive processing of negative emotions, motivating the development of strategies for changing the situations that caused the negative emotions, and ultimately leading to mood improvements.

Much of the research discussed in the previous chapter aligns with the predictions of mood management theory (Zillmann, 1988). The reader may remember that mood management theory predicts that people will listen to music that either improves their mood or helps them to maintain an already existing good mood. Previous research confirms that much of the time we do display a preference for happy music. In addition, where absorption enables some people to dissociate or disable the displeasure usually associated with sadness they are able to actually *enjoy* the sad music, and, by extension, to experience the desired prolongation of a good mood or mood improvement. Our finding that reflective

S. Garrido, *Why Are We Attracted to Sad Music?*,
DOI 10.1007/978-3-319-39666-8_8

people are motivated to delay the immediate gratification in favour of the longer-term effects of listening to sad music also tends to support a modified version of mood management theory. In this case, where a negative emotional response is experienced at the initial music listening, this is tolerated in order to ultimately obtain the desired mood benefits through a variety of cognitive and psychological processes that may take place while listening to the music.

However, there were some indications in the research presented previously, that people with tendencies to rumination habitually listen to sad music even where they are not enjoying it and likely not experiencing the same psychological benefits as others either. Does this suggest an exception to mood management theory? It is to this question that we now turn.

A Breakdown in Mood Regulation Processes

The first indication that I had in my research that listening to sad music may not have such positive functions for all listeners came during an interview with one particular study participant (Garrido & Schubert, 2011b). This was a 46-year-old male who I will call Peter.[1] Peter had migrated to Australia as a teenager and in recent years had been diagnosed with clinical depression and anxiety. Of interest to me was the music that Peter liked to listen to. He explained that he was particularly attracted to a form of tragic love song that was popular in his native country. He described this music as “romantic and melancholy … dark”.

Being intrigued about the psychological functions that were served for Peter by listening to this music, I asked him if it made him feel better when he was depressed. Peter answered in the negative, stating that sometimes it actually made him feel worse. However, the music gave him a sense of connection to his native land and, in his words, “it gives me a reason to be sad”.

Peter’s case immediately piqued my interest because this participant appeared to have good reasons for listening to the music: the nostalgic feelings triggered by the music increased his sense of connection to his

[1] All participants’ names have been changed to protect their anonymity.

country of birth, and it provided an expressive outlet for his own sadness. However, despite these rational reasons, listening to it did not result in an improved mood. Nevertheless, he evinced an attraction to it that seemed to contain many of the hallmarks of addiction, saying: "I listen to this kind of music as much as I can ... I'm always looking for the feeling that it gives me. But it does make me a little bit blue and maybe sometimes I'd rather not do it, but I want to do it. It's almost addictive ... but I need to, so I can kind of revisit that space and time ... almost bring back that time." Thus, Peter demonstrated ambivalent feelings toward the music: while he was aware on some level that the music was not making him feel any better, he nevertheless craved the emotions that it aroused in him.

It is not altogether surprising that Peter would crave the feelings of sadness that were aroused in him by the music, particularly given his depression. Sadness itself, as distinct from depression, is considered by many to be an adaptive emotion (Horwitz & Wakefield, 2007; Keedwell, 2008). Just as any unpleasant sensation or feeling of distress, sadness motivates us to consider our environment and to make changes in order to avoid things that may be detrimental to us. There is also some evidence that when we feel sad we are more inclined towards a cognitive style that focuses on details, and show improved memory performance on various dimensions (Clore & Huntsinger, 2007), suggesting the adaptive function of sadness in promoting re-evaluation of personal circumstances and strategizing for change.

However, depression, in this regard, is a system gone wrong. Whereas a healthy individual will experience sadness in response to an event, may withdraw socially for a time in order to reflect and strategize, and will begin then to feel better due to practical steps taken or a process of cognitive reframing, depression makes an individual oversensitized to negative stimuli, causing them to experience levels of sadness that may at times be disproportionate to the stimuli (Kincaid & Sullivan, 2014). In addition, rather than motivating them to take action to improve their circumstances, depression often has a paralyzing effect on the sufferer, causing diminished motivation to take actions that may benefit them (Forbes & Dahl, 2005). Furthermore, rather than enhancing cognitive performance, people who are depressed suffer cognitive dysfunctions, including reduced concentration, deficits in episodic memory and impaired executive functioning (Austin, Mitchell, & Goodwin, 2001; Murrough, Iacoviello, Neumeister, Charney, & Iosifescu, 2011). Thus, people with mood disorders tend to experience less post-crying mood improvement than healthy non-patient groups (Rottenberg, Cevaal, & Vingerhoets, 2008). While sadness serves adaptive purposes, there is a clear malfunctioning of these processes in clinical depression.

Peter's case seemed a plain illustration of the breakdown of adaptive responses that occur in emotional pathologies such as depression, since he continued to be strongly attracted to music despite the lack of positive outcomes. Another participant from the same study, however, illustrated a different capacity to use music for mood regulation. This participant, a 40-year-old female who I will call Sharon, had also experienced ongoing problems with depression. However, in contrast to Peter, she appeared to have developed an understanding of how music could either perpetuate her low moods or help her to shift out of them: "You can sort of go two ways with it. Either put on something that is depressing and can perpetuate the mood that you're in. And sometimes depending on the issue, you do want a time for grieving and feeling miserable. And then there reaches a point where you know … its time to move on, get over it, whatever." Although the music that Sharon reported being very attracted to was rather slow and calm, the positive messages that she gained from listening to it helped her to cope: "don't worry about the small stuff and try to be happy".

Peter and Sharon's cases illustrate the fact that although listening to sad music may serve beneficial psychological functions for most people, motivations for listening to it may not always be rational, nor are the outcomes always positive. They further reveal that people with tendencies to depression may have differing levels of awareness of the effect that music can have on their moods.

The evidence from some studies suggests that cognitive and behavioural therapies can have a moderating influence on the effect of sad music on depression. In a study by Zindel Segal et al. (2006), patients with a major depressive disorder who were in remission were played a piece of sad music and asked to try to recall a time in their lives when they felt sad. Patients who had received cognitive behavioural therapy showed less reactivity to the sad music than people who had been treated solely with antidepressants. This reactivity was a significant predictor of a depressive relapse at the 18-month follow-up. The authors showed that the likelihood of a relapse was also related to the expression of dysfunctional attitudes, such as the belief that one's value depends on the opinions of others, in response to the sad mood induction. This illustrates that the effect of listening to sad music on the listener are likely closely related to the thoughts that the music triggers in the individual and to the strategies the individual has developed to deal with adversity, and less to do with any particular feature of the music itself, or the mood of the individual.

The reader may recall, however, that Peter reported feeling that the music gave him a greater sense of connection with his homeland. Furthermore, in one of the studies reported in Chap. 7 (Garrido & Schubert, 2013), we found that participants who had high scores in rumination reported that they listened to sad music because of the opportunity for catharsis it provided and because they could relate to the emotions being expressed. While Peter's case seems to indicate that despite these good reasons the music did not actually make him feel any better, the question of whether or not people were achieving the mood regulation goals they set out to accomplish was something that was not yet clear. One review of the literature about music use in adolescent depression suggested that researchers who study the benefits of music generally omit any consideration of the question of whether outcomes match the aims of music listening (McFerran, Garrido, & Saarikallio, 2013). This was something that we therefore set out to investigate in a further two studies.

Experimental Evidence of the Effect of Sad Music on Mood

In the first study (Garrido & Schubert, 2015a), 335 participants self-selected one piece of sad music and one piece of happy music which they listened to in the context of the experiment. Before and after measures of depression were taken on the Profile of Mood States (POMS: McNair, Lorr, & Droppleman, 1971) at three time points: baseline; after the sad listening condition; and after the happy music condition. The POMS is a measure of current mood that contains six subscales including one for depression. It does not measure clinical depression. Trapnell and Campbell's (1999) Rumination Reflectiveness Questionnaire (RRQ) was therefore included as a measure of coping style with rumination which could also indicate tendencies towards depression (see Chap. 6 for more information). We also included measures of the Big Five personality traits of neuroticism and openness to experience from the Big Five Aspect Scale (BFAS: DeYoung, Quilty, & Peterson, 2007), a scale which looks at two distinct aspects of each trait: withdrawal and volatility (neuroticism), compassion and politeness (agreeableness), industriousness and orderliness (conscientiousness), enthusiasm and assertiveness (extraversion), and, intellect and openness (openness to experience).

The results showed that participants with high scores in rumination and neuroticism generally tended to be in a more depressed mood at the outset of the experiment than those with low scores in those traits, as can be seen from Fig. 8.1. Interestingly, both low and high ruminators experienced significant increases in depression after listening to their self-selected sad music. For non-ruminators this was likely a minor setback. However, for high ruminators who were already more depressed

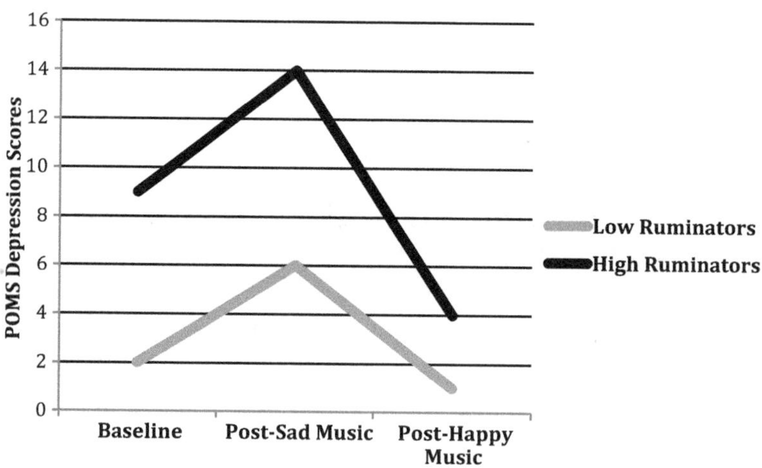

Fig. 8.1 Changes in POMS depression scores for low and high ruminators

than their happier counterparts and who have more difficulty disengaging from negative thoughts and emotions, this could have been a more serious problem.

However, after listening to their happy music selection, the high ruminators experienced significantly greater mood improvements than did the low ruminators, reaching levels of depression that were much lower than their baseline scores and that were even approaching the low depression levels of the non-ruminators. This suggests that for both people with tendencies to clinical depression and those without any such traits, listening to sad music can result in an initial increase in a depressed mood. However, the benefits of listening to happy music appears to be appreciably greater for people who do have tendencies to depression, resulting in the near eradication of an initially depressed mood.

The question remains then: why don't people listen to happy music when they are feeling depressed? In order to begin to answer this question we also considered the degree of perception that participants had about the effect of the music on their mood, particularly people with high scores in rumination. The results suggested that the high ruminators differed in their level of awareness about the impact of the sad music. People with elevated scores in rumination rated items relating to feeling sadder after listening to the music significantly higher than people with low scores in rumination. However, despite reporting increased depression levels on the POMS, many ruminators also reported feeling more peaceful and relieved as well as glad to know that other people felt the same as them. Thus, it appeared that some people either remained unaware of the effect of the music on their mood as measured by the POMS, or were experiencing some perceived benefits but ultimately a negative outcome like Peter. It was fascinating to see, however, that while reporting a worsening of depression, some participants still believed that they had benefited.

The benefits perceived as being achieved by these participants were similar to those by participants in our earlier studies (described in Chap. 7), in which they claimed they listened to sad music for its cathartic value and because of being able to relate to the emotions expressed. However, this reasoning is also reminiscent of beliefs that are held by ruminators in general about their ruminative behavior (Papageorgiou & Wells, 2001), despite the clear evidence that rumination results in a worsening or prolongation of a depressed state (Nolen-Hoeksema, 1991).

Thus, it seems plausible that these results depict the malfunction of the mood regulation systems that are involved in depression. Individuals who are in a sad or a depressed mood may tend to be attracted to sad music for rational motivations, and with the intention of making themselves feel better through processes of catharsis or by gaining a sense of validation or connection through the music. However, while these processes may be effective in people with healthy patterns of thinking who are able to use the music to engage in beneficial cognitive processes, the process may well break down in the case of people with tendencies to clinical depression, causing them to become stuck in cycles of negative thinking while continuing to believe that the behavior is helping them to deal with their negative emotions. Thus, it may be that one reason why people continue to listen to sad music, despite the fact that listening to happy music may have a more positive impact on their mood, is because of a limited level of consciousness of the processes that are occurring and their effects.

Levels of Awareness of the Effect of Sad Music on Mood

Such individual differences in degrees of cognitive insight have been demonstrated in other areas of mental health as well. For example, individual differences in levels of cognitive insight have been found to predict how responsive people with symptoms of psychosis will be to cognitive behavioural therapy (Perivoliotis et al., 2010). Although depression is generally associated with higher levels of cognitive insight than psychotic disorders such as schizophrenia, individuals with a diagnosis of a major depressive disorder do evince differing levels (Colis, Steer, & Beck, 2006). Thus, the degree of awareness that individuals have of the effect that music has on their mood was something requiring further investigation.

In order to look at this more closely, we conducted a second study that replicated the first, although with some differences (Garrido & Schubert, 2015b). In this second study we also asked participants to listen to self-selected sad and happy music while taking before and after measures on the POMS. Our results again showed that all participants, both high and low ruminators, reported increased levels of depression after listening to their selection of sad music. However, in contrast to our previous findings, in this sample the increase in depression levels was significantly greater for the ruminators, suggesting that the sad music had a particularly negative effect on people with tendencies to depression in this group of participants. This is in harmony with the literature demonstrating that the threshold for negative affect can be much lower for ruminators and people with clinical levels of depression. Once again, in this study, these depression levels dropped significantly after participants listened to their self-selected happy music.

In this second study, rather than merely asking participants about their perception of the impact of the sad music *after* they listened to it, we also asked them *prior* to listening to predict how the sad music would make them feel so that we could see whether the outcomes matched their predictions. Our results showed that people with high scores in rumination made both positive and negative predictions about how the sad music would make them feel. High ruminators rated an item predicting that the music would cause them to remember sad times and thus feel sadder significantly higher than low ruminators. However, they also gave significantly higher ratings to items predicting that they would gain a sense of relief from crying, and that it would feel good to know that other people felt like them, demonstrating a pattern of beliefs about the benefits of listening to sad music that fits those of our earlier studies. In addition, several items that indicated an ambivalent relationship with sad music also received significantly higher ratings from ruminators, with many participants strongly agreeing that they would "feel sad but enjoy being immersed in the emotions", or "feel sad, but somehow more alive". This seems similar to the experience of Peter, described earlier in this chapter, who seemed to crave the emotional experience that the sad music gave him—seeming almost addicted to it—despite recognizing that the ultimate effect on his mood was not positive.

In fact, depression and addiction commonly co-occur in many patients, with around one-third of people with a major depressive disorder having co-morbid substance abuse disorders (Davis, Uezato, Newell, & Frazier,

2008). A quick perusal of online sources revealed that reference to depression as a form of addiction among sufferers is similarly not uncommon. One anonymous blogger, for example, says: "I am drawn towards my depression. I love listening to hyper depressing songs, for how it makes me feel, it's like a friend visiting, a familiar feeling, a blanket that covers me. Intellectually I can see that its stupid, but it takes a lot not to return to the drinking fountains I used to feed my pain bodies" ("I feel drawn back into depression, is it like an addiction?," 2010).

Another online author adeptly described the way adaptive mood regulation strategies can develop into depression: "I believe depression is an addiction. It manifests itself as an assistant, (in the low mood stage) 'oh, I'm going to help you to regain yourself, rest for an extra five minutes, stay in bed'. It becomes a habit, although you believe those extra five minutes are necessary and then an addiction is born" (Wronowski, 2015). Another member of a public discussion board on mental health issues expresses similar observations: "Being depressed almost all my life I have come to realize that the behavior associated with it is very addictive" ("Is depression addictive?," 2009). This type of motivational ambivalence is not uncommon in depression, where opposing goals and beliefs may exist at the same time (Fauerbach, Lawrence, Bryant, & Sith, 2002).

Interestingly, in a study relating to the consumption of horror movies, Eduardo Andrade and Joel Cohen (2007) found that positive emotions appeared to be co-activated along with negative emotions in viewers who enjoyed the films, rather than entirely replacing the negative emotions. People who have an ongoing struggle with depression may in fact experience something similar with conflicting internal messages of reward and discomfort being activated by their behavior. Thus, in an article in *Psychology Today*, David Sack (2014) suggests that for some people there is a "comfortable familiarity with being dissatisfied". He argues that there are several reasons why people may have developed a sense of complacency or even snugness in being unhappy, including the fact that repeated experiences of trauma may simply have made sadness the state that is most familiar to them, and the fact that it is sometimes easier to avoid the work needed to address particular problems. Michelle Moulds and colleagues

(2007) similarly argue that ruminative behavior is reinforced because it allows the ruminator to evade active engagement in problem-solving.

Similar arguments may apply to some of the participants in the two large-scale experiments that have just been described. It may be that while listening to sad music does not result in a mood improvement or recovery in people with tendencies to depression, it does activate reward systems of some kind in the brain. This was also suggested by some of the additional results from the second experiment described in this chapter. In contrast to our findings in previous studies (Garrido & Schubert, 2013),[2] in this study rumination was predictive of a liking for sad music on our Like Sad Music Scale. Readers who have been following the thread of the research discussed in this volume may recall that in a previous study we found that there was no association between a *liking* for sad music and rumination, although ruminators did demonstrate a *habit* of listening to sad music. Those findings supported our theory that ruminators would listen to it despite not enjoying it. Thus, we were puzzled in the current study to find that ruminators *did* score strongly on the scale measuring a liking for sad music. However, when we controlled for absorption, the relationship disappeared. Thus it was evident that the relationship between rumination and a liking for sad music was mediated by absorption.

Absorption has been shown consistently throughout the multiple studies I have conducted with Emery Schubert and in studies by others (Garrido & Schubert, 2011a, 2013; Herbert, 2012; Kreutz, et al., 2008), to be associated with a capacity to *enjoy* sad music. However, readers may remember from Chap. 5, that rumination is a form of 'self-absorption' (Joireman, 2004; Joireman, Parrott, & Hammersla, 2002; Trapnell & Campbell, 1999), a tendency to become absorbed by negative thoughts about oneself, one's actions and one's circumstances. While absorption is normally considered an adaptive capacity, when accompanied by rumination (self-absorption), the two traits may have a synergistic effect, exacerbating tendencies to become immersed in negative thoughts and emotions. It is possible that people with high scores in both absorption and rumination may be simultaneously engaging in both an adaptive coping style (absorption) and a maladaptive one (rumination), resulting

[2] See Chap. 7.

in an ambivalent, 'bittersweet' relationship with sad music, as seemed to be occurring in the case of Peter.

This idea of an ambivalent relationship with sad music and the possible parallel operations of both adaptive and maladaptive coping styles is similar to what occurs in cases of addiction: the brain rewards the consumption of a substance that ultimately causes harm to the user, because of the pleasure that it activates. Thus, the user may continue to consume the substance despite an understanding of the detrimental effects involved.

Further Exploring Individual Differences in Awareness

In order to explore this phenomenon in relation to the attraction to sad music somewhat further, I conducted some additional interviews, focusing on participants who had experienced some degree of depression in the past.[3] The first participant, Sarah,[4] was a female in her thirties for whom music was an important part of daily life. She liked a diverse range of music, but her preferred style appeared to be something involving solo singers playing acoustic instruments. Of particular importance to this participant were the lyrics of the songs: "I also like the sort of music that has interesting lyrics. And so I can't listen to a song that's just complete nonsense."

Most of her preferred music was, by Sarah's description, quite sad. She explained that she never really listened to music to help calm herself down or to try to change her mood. Rather she listened to music designed to mirror her current mood. The fact that this had the effect of intensifying the emotions she was experiencing was something Sarah freely acknowledged. For example, she stated: "If I'm feeling sad I'll get out the really suicidal, Elliott Smith sort of stuff. That's my favourite depressive music and it is so grim and so gloomy and it's just such a downer." Her knowledge of the personal circumstances of the musician, particularly the fact

[3] Unpublished.

[4] Names have been changed to protect participants' anonymity.

that he himself committed suicide, added to the depressing effect of the music for her: "I think that all those things combined just make the whole situation seem so … it's just so sad … I just kind of think, 'Oh, God, this is just so sad and so depressing'. I kind of sit there and think 'Oh, woe is me' for a while". Sarah identified closely with the musicians, spending time reading about their lives on the internet, and reported strongly connecting with music that tells a story with which she could relate.

However, like Peter, Sarah displayed quite a bit of ambivalence in her statements about the effects of the music. Despite describing the depressing effect of the music she still maintained that listening to it provided some benefits: "I don't know why that's beneficial but I think it is." One possible benefit that Sarah suggested was that hearing the more extreme manifestations of sadness in the music made her feel better about herself. However, this contradicted her previous statements indicating that it made her think more about her own misery. Notwithstanding these perceived benefits, Sarah also stated that in the past she had decided to stop listening to those songs because she was getting too depressed. This experience with the music in the past did not seem to have resulted in any changed listening habits since Sarah still reported pulling out the same music whenever she felt depressed. Thus, again we see some level of awareness of the negative effect of the music alongside an unwavering belief that she was benefiting from listening to it.

In order to gauge more closely Sarah's consciousness of the processes occurring when listening to the sad music, towards the end of the interview I gently introduced the idea that for some people sad music seems to increase their depression. Although she had previously admitted to the same, at this point in the interview, Sarah became quite defensive about her listening choices. For Sarah, the kind of music she listened to appeared to be closely tied to her identity. She identified herself as someone who was able to appreciate alternative music, music that is original and outside the mainstream, and that clearly demonstrates the talent of the musician as opposed to the "mass commercial stuff" (Sarah). Happy music, in Sarah's opinion, could all be described as "overproduced, and the people who are making it have no talent". Thus, she felt that listening to happy music would be to violate her own sense of musical identity:

"for me to listen to happy music it would probably be one that goes against what are my preferences for the sort of music that I like". She demonstrated a strong resistance to the idea that different music might be more beneficial for her mental health.

In contrast to this was an interview I conducted with an undergraduate student who I will call Jennifer. Jennifer had experienced a severe bout of depression during her senior high school years. It was evident during this interview that through her experience, Jennifer had developed a clear sense of how music could be either a help or a hindrance in improving her mood. Her preferences were mostly classical and other forms of instrumental music, and she described listening to music that was slow and meaningful when she was feeling low. However, while Jennifer was more likely to listen to slower music when in a sad mood, she described avoiding music that she found depressing:

> I try not to listen to kind of like depressing music if I'm already feeling down because it's not going to do anything to help really. Sometimes I kind of need it to know that other people feel the same way, but a lot of time it's just going to make me feel worse and so then I don't want to do that … there comes a point when you are feeling bad enough and then that would make you feel worse and its something you have to stay away from. (Jennifer)

Thus, Jennifer's comments revealed a high degree of awareness and consciousness in her music selection, showing alertness to the value of validating the emotions she was experiencing, but also of moving on from that at an appropriate time.

In Sarah's case it had been clear that when she was in a depressed mood, music that was upbeat and happy would be far too irritating to be of any benefit to her. Jennifer was able to provide some insight into how this could be overcome without resorting to music that is likely to exacerbate a depressed mood. She said: "I think if something was too upbeat it would bother me. But if its just a moderate amount that's OK, and I think that helps more than it would bother me … I would listen to more negative music, but not always to bring me down, but more just kind of at a level that is just a little bit above what I'm feeling, to maybe bring me up a little bit but not so much that it would bother me."

Here Jennifer describes a deliberate strategy that she has developed for managing her own moods. Jennifer intentionally selects music that is only mildly different from her current mood, but that, in her words, "has a more positive feel to it", in order to shift her mood into a more positive one. Thus, she makes an interesting distinction between the relative helpfulness of music that is slow, and music that is depressing. Jennifer still seems to prefer music that matches her low arousal level when in a sad mood, but avoids music with negative content, as opposed to Sarah or Peter who seek out music that intensifies their state, likely triggering negative thoughts about their own situation. Here Jennifer demonstrates a similar process in her own mood regulation strategies as that utilized in some music therapy interventions, known as the "Iso principle". This approach, developed by American psychiatrist Ira Altshuler (Bunt & Stige, 2014), involves playing music that matches a patient's current mood and then gradually changing the music in the direction of the desired therapeutic outcome. On the other hand, both Sharon and Jennifer had discovered that sad music could be useful for a limited period of time, but that ultimately, if listened to for too long it could result in increased depression. The lyrics appeared to be the crucial point that could make music either depressing or positive to several of these participants.

Same Intentions, Different Outcomes

The interviews and experiments summarized in this chapter demonstrate that listening to sad music can have unfavorable effects on people with tendencies to depression, resulting in an increase of depression levels that may be greater than that experienced by the average listener. Ruminators reveal varying levels of awareness of this, with many arguing that they are benefiting from it or displaying an ambivalent relationship with the music. This suggests that despite the detrimental effects, listening to sad music is a behavior that has been reinforced in many people with depression for one reason or another. It may be that music listening falls within general behavior associated with depression that has become reinforced because of the fact that it allows the individual to evade responsibility, or to enjoy the comfortable familiarity of a depressed state, for example. Others reasons may relate more closely to the specific situation of listening to music, such as the reward systems activated by experiencing deep levels of absorption. In such cases it may be that parallel cognitive processes are occurring which both reward the behavior and intensify negative affective states. Alternatively, it may be that although the motivations for listening to sad music are rational, the mechanisms through which mood improvement would normally occur are distorted in cases of depression due to the negative thought cycles associated with the condition.

Thus, although it may at first seem that rumination and depression provide an exception to mood management theory since listeners in this case seek out music that can prolong or worsen their depressed mood; in actual fact, many may be listening to this music with a sincere belief in its ability to help them. The intentions with which sad music is sought when feeling depressed are likely the same whether an individual is a person with a generally healthy coping style who is experiencing a temporarily depressed mood, or a person prone to rumination who is likely to experience depression at clinical levels. However, the outcomes appear to be different, possibly because of both the content of the music selected—sad music with hopeful messages versus sad music with negative messages—as well as the thought patterns that are triggered in the individual. These findings are in harmony with studies that find that people with mood disorders tend to experience less mood benefits from crying in general than healthier participants, likely due to their reduced capacity to achieve new cognitive perspectives on events through the process (Rottenberg, Bylsma, & Vingerhoets, 2008).

Thus, rather than being an exception to mood management theory, ruminators and people with depression at a conscious level at least, may often intend to ultimately improve their mood by listening to sad music. While some may have firm beliefs that they are obtaining some psychological benefits from ruminating with music, others may be seeking the rewards associated with absorption or rewards pertaining to ruminative behaviour in general, while retaining minimal levels of awareness of the actual impact.

This conclusion would account for the numerous studies in which people report positive reasons for listening to sad music (e.g. Saarikallio

& Erkkila, 2007; Van den Tol & Edwards, 2013). Since these studies questioned the *goals* of their participants in selecting sad music rather than the *outcomes*, they report only the positive benefits believed to be derived from listening to sad music. However, the studies reported in this chapter demonstrate that outcomes may differ from goals and that individuals reflect differing levels of cognitive insight into the cognitive processes being triggered by the music and the ultimate effect it is having on their moods and mental health. As previous studies have shown, people are often prone to "affective misforecasting" or the tendency to misjudge the effect of events on future affective states (Gilbert, Pinel, Wilson, Blumberg, & Wheatley, 1998). Thus, it is likely that some of the participants in the studies cited in this paragraph might not have actually achieved the mood-regulation goals they reported having.

In contrast to the effect of listening to sad music demonstrated in the studies reported in this chapter, these studies show that 'happy' music can have positive mood effects on people with tendencies to depression. It also appears that some individuals with a propensity for depression are able to develop an awareness of the potential for music to have a negative effect and to modify their listening habits accordingly. Jennifer and Sharon, for example, had both modified their listening habits through learning from their experiences during previous bouts of depression. While cognitive and behavioural therapy and some forms of music therapy are effective methods for raising awareness of how thoughts and musical behaviors influence mood, what is the potential for people to develop such awareness in everyday music listening situations? Should people who are depressed simply listen to happy music in order to improve their mood? These are questions that were explored through a further study that is reported in Chap. 9.

References

Andrade, E. B., & Cohen, J. B. (2007). On the consumption of negative feelings. *Journal of Consumer Research, 34*(3), 283–300.

Austin, M.-P., Mitchell, P., & Goodwin, G. M. (2001). Cognitive deficits in depression: Possible implications for functional neuropathology. *The British Journal of Psychiatry, 178*(3), 200–206.

Bunt, L., & Stige, B. (2014). *Music therapy: An art beyond words* (2nd ed.). London: Routledge.
Clore, G. L., & Huntsinger, J. R. (2007). How emotions inform judgment and regulate thought. *Trends in Cognitive Science, 11*(9), 393–399.
Colis, M. J., Steer, R. A., & Beck, A. T. (2006). Cognitive insight in inpatients with psychotic, bipolar, and major depressive disorders. *Journal of Psychopathology and Behavioural Assessment, 28*(4), 242–249.
Davis, L., Uezato, A., Newell, J. M., & Frazier, E. (2008). Major depression and comorbid substance use disorders. *Current Opinion in Psychiatry, 21*(1), 14–18.
DeYoung, C. G., Quilty, L. C., & Peterson, J. B. (2007). Between facets and domains: 10 aspects of the Big Five. *Journal of Personality and Social Psychology, 93*(5), 880–896.
Fauerbach, J. A., Lawrence, J. W., Bryant, A. G., & Sith, J. H. (2002). The relationship of ambivalent coping to depression symptoms and adjustment. *Rehabilitation Psychology, 47*(4), 387–401.
Forbes, E. E., & Dahl, R. C. (2005). Neural systems of positive affect: Relevance to understanding child and adolescent depression? *Development and Psychopathology, 17*, 827–850.
Garrido, S., & Schubert, E. (2011a). Individual differences in the enjoyment of negative emotion in music: A literature review and experiment. *Music Perception, 28*(3), 279–295.
Garrido, S., & Schubert, E. (2011b). Negative emotion in music: What is the attraction? A qualitative study. *Empirical Musicology Review, 6*(4), 214–230.
Garrido, S., & Schubert, E. (2013). Adaptive and maladaptive attraction to negative emotion in music. *Musicae Scientiae, 17*(2), 145–164. doi:10.1177/1029864913478305.
Garrido, S., & Schubert, E. (2015a). Moody melodies: Do they cheer us up? A study of the effect of sad music on mood. *Psychology of Music, 43*(2), 244–261. doi:10.1177/0305735613501938.
Garrido, S., & Schubert, E. (2015b). Music and people with tendencies to depression. *Music Perception, 32*(4), 313–321. doi:10.1525/MP.2015.32.4.313.
Gilbert, D. T., Pinel, E. C., Wilson, T. D., Blumberg, S. J., & Wheatley, T. P. (1998). Immune neglect: A source of durability bias in affective forecasting. *Journal of Personality and Social Psychology, 75*(3), 617–638.
Herbert, R. (2012). Musical and non-musical involvement in daily life: The case of absorption. *Musicae Scientiae, 16*(1), 41–66.
Horwitz, A. V., & Wakefield, J. C. (2007). *The loss of sadness: How psychiatry transformed normal sorrow into depressive disorder*. New York: Oxford University Press.

I feel drawn back into depression, is it like an addiction? (2010). Retrieved from http://ask.metafilter.com/153063/I-feel-drawn-back-into-depression-is-it-like-an-addiction

Is depression addictive? (2009). Retrieved from http://www.healthboards.com/boards/depression/699414-depression-addictive.html

Joireman, J. A. (2004). Empathy and the self-absorption paradox II: Self-rumination and self-reflection as mediators between shame, guilt and empathy. *Self and Identity, 3*(3), 225–238.

Joireman, J. A., Parrott, L., & Hammersla, J. (2002). Empathy and the self-absorption paradox: Support for the distinction between self-rumination and self-reflection. *Self and Identity, 1*(1), 53–65.

Keedwell, P. (2008). *How sadness survived: The evolutionary basis of depression.* Oxford and New York: Radcliffe Publishing.

Kincaid, H., & Sullivan, J. A. (2014). *Classifying psychopathology: Mental kinds and natural kinds.* Boston: MIT Press.

Kreutz, G., Ott, U., Teichmann, D., Osawa, P., & Vaitl, D. (2008a). Using music to induce emotion: Influences of musical preference and absorption. *Psychology of Music, 36*, 101–121.

McFerran, K., Garrido, S., & Saarikallio, S. (2013). A critical interpretive synthesis of the literature linking music and adolescent mental health. *Youth & Society*. doi:10.1177/0044118X13501343.

McNair, D. M., Lorr, M., & Droppleman, I. F. (1971). *Manual for the profile of mood states.* San Diego, CA: Educational and Industrial Testing Service.

Moulds, M. L., Kandris, E., Starr, S., & Wong, A. C. M. (2007). The relationship between rumination, avoidance and depression in a non-clinical sample. *Behaviour Research and Therapy, 45*, 251–261.

Murrough, J. W., Iacoviello, B., Neumeister, A., Charney, D. S., & Iosifescu, D. V. (2011). Cognitive dysfunction in depression: Neurocircuitry and new therapeutic strategies. *Neurobiology of Learning and Memory, 96*(4), 553–565.

Nolen-Hoeksema, S. (1991). Responses to depression and their effect on the duration of depressive episodes. *Journal of Abnormal Psychology, 100*(4), 569–582.

Papageorgiou, C., & Wells, A. (2001). Metacognitive beliefs about rumination in recurrent major depression. *Cognitive and Behavioural Practice, 8*, 160–164.

Perivoliotis, D., Grant, P. M., Peters, E. R., Ison, R., Kulpers, E., & Beck, A. T. (2010). Cognitive insight predicts favorable outcome in cognitive behavioural therapy for psychosis. *Psychosis: Psychological, Social and Integrative Approaches, 2*(1), 23–33.

Rottenberg, J., Bylsma, L. M., & Vingerhoets, A. J. J. M. (2008a). Is crying beneficial? *Current Directions in Psychological Science, 17*(6), 400–404.

Rottenberg, J., Cevaal, A., & Vingerhoets, J. J. M. (2008b). Do mood disorders alter crying? A pilot investigation. *Depression and Anxiety, 25*(5), E9–E15.

Saarikallio, S., & Erkkila, J. (2007). The role of music in adolescents' mood regulation. *Psychology of Music, 35*(1), 88–109.

Sack, D. (2014). *Are you addicted to unhappiness?* Retrieved from https://www.psychologytoday.com/blog/where-science-meets-the-steps/201403/are-you-addicted-unhappiness

Segal, Z. V., Kennedy, S., Gemar, M., Hood, K., Pedersen, R., & Buis, T. (2006). Cognitive reactivity to sad mood provocation and the prediction of depressive relapse. *Archives of General Psychiatry, 63*, 749–755.

Trapnell, P. D., & Campbell, J. D. (1999). Private self-consciousness and the five-factor model of personality: Distinguishing rumination from reflection. *Journal of Personality and Social Psychology, 76*(2), 284–304.

Van den Tol, A. J. M., & Edwards, J. (2013). Exploring a rationale for choosing to listen to sad music when feeling sad. *Psychology of Music, 41*(4), 440–465.

Wronowski, D. (2015). *Depression, an addiction?* Retrieved from http://www.devilishlydisabled.co.uk/depression-addiction/-sthash.0fWw1ot3.dpbs

Zillmann, D. (1988). Mood management through communication choices. *American Behavioral Scientist, 31*(3), 327–340.

9

Musical Prescriptions: Do They Work?

The Precedents for Musical Prescriptions

Music has been prescribed by physicians along with other treatments for physical and mental disorders since the time of the ancient Greeks. As discussed in Chap. 5, Pythagoras himself developed specific music to address different physical and emotional maladies, believing that music could draw on the powers of the planets to bring about a state of internal balance and harmony. These theories became increasingly developed over the centuries, so that by the Renaissance detailed theses were produced by people such as Ramis de Pareja, outlining specific harmonic modes and rhythmic modes that could be employed to regulate moods and physical imbalances. Numerous accounts exist throughout the subsequent centuries of the use of music in the treatment of mood disorders and other mental health conditions.

In the modern day, too, music is used in a variety of health and mental health contexts for the purpose of mood regulation. It has been used, for example, to calm agitated patients in residential aged-care settings (Nair et al., 2011), to reduce stress among nurses caring for cancer patients (Lai, Li, & Lee, 2012), to reduce anxiety in pre-surgical patients (Cooke

S. Garrido, *Why Are We Attracted to Sad Music?*,
DOI 10.1007/978-3-319-39666-8_9

et al., 2005), to reduce depression in palliative care settings (Gallagher, Lagman, Walsh, Davis, & LeGrand, 2006), and to improve the mood of birthing mothers (Browning, 2000).

While there is convincing evidence that active forms of musical engagement, such as song-writing, improvisation or group music therapy, can be effective in addressing depression and anxiety (Cooke, Moyle, Shum, Harrison, & Murfield, 2010; Erkkila et al., 2011), these effects are often limited only to the immediate period in which the activity takes place (Nair, Browne, Marley, & Heim, 2013). Furthermore, the accessibility of forms of musical engagement that require the presence of a trained therapist or professional performer is limited by cost and other logistical factors.

In any case, relatively few people who suffer from mental health issues such as depression actually access professional health care services in relation to their disorder, with some studies estimating the number to be as small as 25–35 percent of people affected (Sawyer et al., 2000). These low rates may be due to various factors including perceptions of stigma, a lack of motivation and energy to seek appropriate treatment, denial or a lack of awareness. Adolescents and young adults seem to be particularly unlikely to seek professional help for mental and emotional problems (Rickwood, Deane, & Wilson, 2007). Thus, the potential for traditional therapeutic programs to assist people with mental illness is limited by these low compliance rates.

On the other hand, while resistant to the idea of obtaining professional help, people with depression tend to increase their search for self-help or web-based solutions (Jorm, Medway, & Christensen, 2000; Rice et al., 2014), preferring isolation and spending increased time in solitary pursuits. They also tend to increase their consumption of media such as music (Block et al., 2014). Given the ease with which a wide variety of pre-recorded music can be accessed from the privacy of one's own home, the frequency with which it is used during periods of isolation and depression, along with its demonstrated power to impact mood, music has the potential to play an important role in the self-management of depression. Music could, therefore, provide an important complementary role to talk-based therapies, or a form of self-help that might attract depressed people who resist professional assistance.

However, as demonstrated by the studies discussed in the previous chapters of this book, people with depression display varying levels of awareness of how music influences their moods. While our studies indicated that listening to happy music has a markedly positive effect on people with tendencies to depression, a number of studies show that the natural inclination of many people who feel sad or depressed is to seek out sad music (Garrido & Schubert, 2013; Van den Tol & Edwards, 2013). In people with clinical levels of depression or ruminative tendencies this can have the effect of exacerbating negative patterns of thinking and perpetuating a depressed mood.

This presents a dilemma for researchers and health practitioners interested in utilizing music to help people with depression: numerous studies have indicated that musical interventions are generally more successful when the music is self-selected (Nair et al., 2013; Schubert, 2010). However, depressed people may lack the requisite awareness to select music that is effective for improving their moods. Nevertheless, most of the programs that focus on music listening rather than active forms of musical engagement or formal music therapy in health contexts tend to involve either playing researcher-selected music to groups of participants, or allowing patients free rein to select their own music. Interventions that involve researcher-selected music often obtain mixed results because of the failure to account for individual differences in emotional response to music and music taste. On the other hand, interventions that involve completely self-selected music run the risk of facilitating the use of music in such a way as to aggravate existing mental health issues.

The Search for A Methodological Compromise

Along with my colleagues, Emery Schubert and Daniel Bangert, I attempted to see whether a viable approach to this quandary would be to create pre-selected music playlists that included a variety of styles and genres, but that fell within the general guidelines of music that we thought might benefit people with depression (Garrido, Schubert & Bangert, 2016). From our previous studies we had gathered a large database of songs that participants had nominated as making them sad, and another database of happy songs. Drawing on these databases we created two musical playlists of about six songs, or around 29 minutes each—a 'happy' playlist and a 'sad' playlist. The music on the playlists included jazz, classical, soundtrack, pop, rock and electronic. It was hoped that by including a variety of genres and by using songs that had been popular with previous participants of similar demographics, we would have a set of stimuli that would be of broad appeal to participants in a new study.

Our sample in this new study consisted of 176 undergraduate students with a mean age of 20.6 years (Garrido, et al., 2016). Participants were randomly assigned to either the happy or the sad music listening group, and listened to their assigned playlist in an initial listening session and then at least twice a week for the next four weeks. At the initial listening session we also rook rumination and reflectiveness scores using the Rumination–Reflectiveness Questionnaire (Trapnell & Campbell, 1999), and asked participants to report how familiar they were with the music on their playlist and how much they liked it.

We took mood measures on the short form of the Profile of Mood States (Curran, Andrykowski, & Studts, 1995) at four different time periods: before and after the four-week experiment as a whole, and before and after an initial listening session. The measures taken before and after the experiment as a whole were worded so as to capture long-term mood by asking participants how they had been feeling over the past week. The measures taken before and after the initial listening session, however, were worded so as to assess their current mood. The rationale for this was so that we could compare the short-term affective impact of listening to the playlist with the long-term effect on the general mood of participants. This would enable us to determine whether sad music was perhaps having some long-term benefits for listeners even where it initially intensified a depressed mood.

Although participants listened to the whole playlist during the initial session, we gave them some latitude in choosing whether to listen to all the songs on the playlist or only some for their regular listening sessions since we wanted to avoid them feeling obliged to regularly listen to music that they particularly disliked or that caused an unpleasant affective reaction.[1] Rather, participants were asked to keep a diary of when they listened to the music, which tracks they chose and why, as well as what impact it had on their affective state so that we could assess how effective the playlists were in regulating mood when used in the context of the participants' daily lives.

The Effects of Listening to Researcher-'Prescribed' Music

In general, participants indicated a relatively high liking for the music on the playlists they were assigned to and a moderate level of familiarity. Our analysis of changes in mood scores showed that at the initial listening session, both the happy and the sad playlists resulted in *decreased* depression and general mood disturbance scores in the sample as a whole, although a general (non-significant) trend in the data suggested that reductions in depression were greater for those assigned to the happy listening group than for the group that listened to sad music. This was true whether or not participants were ruminators or non-ruminators.

This was a noteworthy difference to our previous two studies described in Chap. 8, in which sad music listening resulted in *increased* depression. The differences possibly arose because of the way the playlists were selected. In our previous two studies, participants were asked to select music that they knew made them sad and then listen to it in the context of the experiment. They likely associated their self-selected songs with a sad event in their lives or chose music that had lyrics to which they could relate. In the current study, however, the music presented was researcher-selected, and therefore less likely to be music that held particular significance for the participant. It seemed that this researcher-selected music, lacking the personal significance of self-selected sad music, held less affective potency for the listeners. Thus it had a more positive effect on the

[1] This latitude was particularly important due to the potential for some participants to become further depressed by the music they were listening to. In order to further deal with this possibility, participants were advised that they were free to withdraw from the study at any time, and systems for professional counseling were in place to deal with any adverse effects.

mood of our current sample of participants compared to the self-selected music chosen by participants in our previous studies.

When we looked at the overall changes in mood scores over the four-week period, however, the results looked very different. In addition to the POMS mood scores, we also looked at what participants had recorded in their diaries about the affective impact of the music at each listening, and developed a system for quantifying this. From the diaries, we were thus able to derive a semi-weekly numerical rating of mood impact as well as a cumulative mood impact score obtained by aggregating reports of mood impact over the four-week period. Analysis of both the POMS and the diary entries of the sample as a whole revealed no statistically significant changes over time, although scores indicated a trend towards a positive mood impact particularly for the happy listening group. Thus, the music listening did not have a major effect on long-term mood no matter which playlist participants were assigned to.

However, when we split the participants according to their rumination scores a different picture began to emerge. As can be seen from Fig. 9.1, the happy listening group reported more positive mood impacts overall during the four-week period, whether they were high or low ruminators. Both high and low ruminators experienced similar mood impacts as others in their listening group in the first week of listening as evidenced by

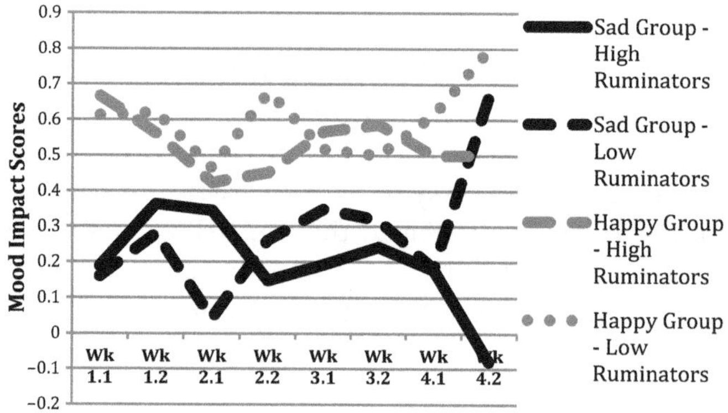

Fig. 9.1 Mood impact of happy and sad playlists on high and low ruminators

the close starting points on the graph in Fig. 9.1. However, for the high ruminators that impact deteriorated over time, particularly for the sad listening group, so that by the end of the four-week experiment, high ruminators in the sad listening group were reporting a negative impact from their assigned playlist. Conversely, the low ruminators reported increasingly positive impacts from their assigned playlist, whether happy or sad. These results suggest that happy music tends to have more positive effects on all listeners, but that rumination scores moderate the effects. High ruminators experience less positive effects from music listening over time, particularly when listening to sad music.

The Mechanisms of Affective Impact

In order to find out more about what was happening for our listeners and why these mood effects were occurring we conducted some detailed analysis of the diary entries. A deductive–inductive approach was used to enable us to draw on both existing theory and the data itself in our analysis (Srnka & Koeszegi, 2007). Thematic analysis was performed by coding the data according to over thirty fine-grained categories that were then assimilated into broader themes, and this was cross-validated by automated investigations of word frequencies and patterns of word use using both NVivo[2] and Linguistic Inquiry and Word Count software packages (LIWC: Tausczik & Pennebaker, 2010). LIWC provides a useful tool for content analysis because it calculates the percentages of the text that belong to specific word categories such as affect words and words relating to particular topics such as motion or death, for example. Previous studies have revealed that the frequent use of particular word categories can be indicative of coping style (Pennebaker, Mayne, & Francis, 1997), rates of recovery from trauma (Pennebaker, 1993), as well as personality traits such as social integration (Pennebaker & Graybeal, 2001) or deceptiveness (Newman, Pennebaker, Berry, & Richards, 2003). Thus, we also used it here in order to discern whether particular patterns of word use

[2] NVivo qualitative data analysis Software; QSR International Pty Ltd. Version 10, 2014.

might suggest how the music was working within participants' overall coping style.

The results of a keyword query run in NVivo revealed that the words most frequently used in the diary entries by people in the happy music group included words such as 'relaxed', 'friends', 'loving', and 'danced'. On the other hand, the words most frequently used by people assigned to the sad music playlist were words such as 'alone', 'memories' and 'thoughts'. This suggested that the music on each playlist triggered very different thoughts and memories. The music in the happy playlist seemed to be prompting thoughts related to good times spent with friends, while the music in the sad playlist seemed to activate pensive and solitary reflection on times past. Similarly, word patterns, as analysed in LIWC, demonstrated that the happy music group used significantly more words in the present tense, words expressing positive emotions, inclusive words (such as 'and', 'with' and 'include'), as well as words relating to motion. On the other hand the sad music group was more likely to use words expressing anger and sadness, or words related to death.

Patterns of word use as analysed using LIWC were also associated with coping style and the overall affective impact of the music listening. Significant correlations were found between the use of words about death and rumination scores, while high scores in reflectiveness were correlated with overall mood impact scores, as derived from the diary entries. This suggests that people who took a reflective approach to the music were more likely to experience positive mood effects from listening to it over the long-term, while people with tendencies to rumination were more likely to contemplate morbid themes in response to the music.

Positive mood impact scores were also associated with the use of positive affect words, inclusive words, and words relating to motion, achievement, and religion. The use of words relating to motion could be suggestive of an active coping style which is generally believed to be associated with the healthiest outcomes (McWilliams, Cox, & Enns, 2003). Similarly, the use of inclusive words could suggest a feeling of being supported by a strong social network, something that is also associated with positive mental health (Carver, Scheier, & Weintraub, 1989). Religious coping is likewise associated with healthy outcomes (Anderson, Marwit, Vandenberg, & Chibnall, 2005). Conversely, the use of sad words was negatively correlated with positive mood impact indicating that the more frequently sad words were recorded in the diaries, the less helpful the reported mood effects of the music.

These findings suggest that where the music triggered an adaptive coping style such as reflectiveness, an active coping style, social coping or religious coping, the outcome of the music listening was positive. Conversely, where the music generated thoughts related to death or loneliness, negative emotions, or ruminative patterns of thinking the mood impact was less likely to be positive.

This relationship between music, coping style, and the thoughts triggered when listening to the music was further illuminated in the more detailed thematic analysis of the diary entries that we conducted. One of the most important factors in whether the music had a potent affective impact on the listener was the personal relevance of the lyrics. Participants were often able to find personal meaning in the music, even where they had not themselves experienced the particular situation being described. At times, this response to the lyrics was quite powerful, causing participants to picture themselves in imaginary situations:

> The message, ideas and emotions portrayed in this song make me feel so much despair and loneliness, even though nothing even close to this is happening to me in my life. It makes my mind wander to a place where I am alone and I find myself putting my own thoughts and actions into the situation she is portraying. I would not call these memories as it is not something that has occurred to me in the past, but almost sad fantasies. (Female, aged 24)

The tendency to imagine themselves in the story being told by the music even where it is not something they have personally experienced may be something similar to the 'Forer effect' or 'Barnum effect'. Demonstrated across several studies by psychologist Bertram R. Forer (1949), the Forer effect is the tendency of people to believe in the personal application of vaguely written descriptions such as astrological predictions or personality assessments. In a comparable way, a vaguely worded song such as a love song or a song about heartbreak can find resonance with many people, even causing them to imagine themselves in a fictional situation or to imagine that the music is telling the story of their own experiences.

Where participants were unable to draw personal meaning from a song, the affective impact of the music tended to be less powerful:

> When I reflect this back to myself, and my relevant lack of recent personal tragedy, I think that might be why these tracks aren't really connecting with me. I know what it's like to get hit by a song out of the blue which will amplify whatever emotional process your mind is going through—perhaps it's just that I'm not really trying to process any complex emotions at the moment. (Male, aged 21)

Another powerful trigger of affective responses to the music was the beat or 'danceability' of the music. Participants described themselves as feeling "stronger and faster", "lively", "pumped", "energized", "rejuvenated", and "refreshed" after listening to the music, particularly music from the happy playlist. Descriptions of involuntary foot tapping or other physical compulsions, such as the impulse to get up and dance, were commonly reported. At times, the result lasted well beyond the duration of the song: "This kept me in an upbeat happy mood until the end of the day" (Female, aged 20). The slow music from the sad playlist often had the opposite effect on arousal levels, causing participants to relax and calm down, an effect that was sometimes desirable, but sometimes caused participants to feel 'sleepier' than they would have liked at the time.

It was also evident from the diaries that the music often triggered habitual patterns of thinking and coping styles. In some participants, the music prompted negative thoughts, tending to lead to a report of a negative affective outcome. Sometimes this appeared to be a deliberate goal of the listener: "Since I'm feeling homesick, I knew that listening to this song would keep me in a sad mood or even make me more sad, so I listened to it … After listening to this sad song, I will probably continue to listen to other sad songs" (Female, aged 20). For others, the negative content of the music appeared to have a gradual effect on the participant's thinking as the listening progressed. For example, one 36-year-old female began her diary entry describing her excitement about a date she was going on that night. She then listened to a song about heartbreak from the sad playlist while transcribing her thoughts and responses. By the end of the diary entry her mental state had changed from one of excitement to one of pessimistic rumination on past failed relationships.

The effect of the ruminative thinking patterns triggered by the music could be quite pronounced. As one participant experienced: "I found that the bad mood I was in became a distinct sadness and I was moving through a number of sad memories that were making me irritable and depressed. Yet, I had no desire to stop listening to the song" (Male, aged 20).

How Listeners Adapt the Music to Suit Desired Outcomes

Another fascinating process that was observed frequently throughout the diary entries was the way participants devised ways to resist the intended mood effect of their assigned playlist when it did not match their desired mood outcome at the time. One strategy that participants used was selectively listening to music from their assigned playlist that they thought most likely to relax, motivate or uplift them, or avoiding songs on the playlist that would trigger sad memories, or that would prove too distracting or arousing. Other participants listened to the entire playlist in a particular order so that they would hear preferred music or music that matched their desired mood outcome last, so as to end the listening activity in the affective state that they sought. Some counteracted their assigned playlist by listening to their own chosen music after listening to the playlist. As one participant described: "I shocked myself by getting somewhat emotional after listening to the song repeatedly and felt a great deal of nostalgia. I felt so moved and emotional by the experience that I quickly changed the album I was listening to" (Female, aged 20).

Some participants deliberately created a mental resistance to the emotional tone of the music. For example, one participant said: "I listened to 'Someone Like You' by Adele. It sounds like depressive wallowing but I didn't let the expression enter my energy field. I was on a good roll and wasn't going to let anything break my flow" (Male, aged 34). Or as another participant put it: "I am not in the mood for so many slow, sad songs. I am building a wall and staying happy" (Male, aged 24). Participants also attempted to minimize undesirable mood effects by listening to the music in situations designed to dilute the effect or distract them from the music. For example, some participants deliberately put the music on when there were other people around or while engaging in other tasks such as housework, cooking or studying so that they would avoid getting too absorbed in the emotional content of the music.

Prescribed Music or Consciousness-Raising Tasks?

As had been indicated by the POMS mood measures, the assigned music listening had only a minimal impact on general mood over the long term. The diaries gave us some indication as to why that may have been the case. Firstly, participants reported becoming somewhat overfamiliar and bored with the music: "I am finding it hard to listen to these pieces now because I have listened to them so much" (Female, aged 21). Others commented that toward the end of the study listening became a "chore". In general, despite our efforts to find music that was likely to appeal to a variety of people and also despite the relatively high liking of the music on the playlists that participants reported, they would still have preferred to listen to their own freely selected music: "If I need to be uplifted, I'm going to find something within the genres I prefer that will uplift me, rather than a piece I would not usually listen to just to be uplifted" (Female, aged 22).

It was further evident that for many participants the affective impact of the music was insufficient to counteract the stress of everyday life. As one participant described it: "If this track was having any influence on my mood, I would say it was just a little. I became more excited after listening to this track but still stressed and worried" (Female, aged 21). Others noted that the effect of the music listening was temporary: "listening to these songs did make me a bit sadder but only for the duration of the song. They didn't have a significant effect on my overall mood after listening" (Male, aged 21). In contrast, for a small number of participants particular songs had more intense and lasting effects: "I sort of rode this feeling throughout the whole day" (Female, aged 22); "I was shocked and overwhelmed by the extent to which it affected me" (Female, aged 20).

Participants found that while the music was at times a welcome distraction from stress, they were less engaged in the music listening when undergoing a stressful period. One participant put it this way: "The music did not sound as good as it did last week, and it didn't change my mood because I wasn't in a neutral state while listening to the songs. When I am in a stressed, high focused state of mind music doesn't penetrate my soul as much" (Male, aged 20).

While many participants stated that overall they would have preferred to listen to their own music, a number of participants reported that the task of listening to the prescribed music and recording their responses to it had raised their awareness of the influence of music on their moods. One participant said: "It was amazing to see how simple it is to control our moods simply by selecting an appropriate list of songs to listen to" (Female, aged 21). Another stated: "I realized I don't normally think too much about how my mood is affected by the music I listen to, but these diaries are definitely making me more aware" (Female, aged 20).

Participants were able to examine their listening habits in a certain amount of depth and to compare the effects of the prescribed music to the music they usually listen to. For example, one participant said: "My selective listening to a certain type of music according to my situation made me question my goals for listening to music" (Female, aged 22). Another revealed her growing awareness of how music was affecting her this way: "I believe this to be why upon more listening to the positive and fast tempo songs my mood rose. If I continued to listen to only smooth and somewhat sad music I believe I wouldn't have had a change in mood during the week" (Female, aged 21).

Several participants came to the realization that their previous listening choices had not always had a positive impact on their mood: "I realized the music I had put on had slow tempo and the lyrics were sad. I noticed I was feeling worse and decided to put on some music that I normally listen to when I am cheerful. After a few songs I noticed I was no longer wallowing and had actually improved my mood! The realization that I was making myself more sad highlighted the power music can have" (Female, aged 22). Another participant stated: "I think that occasionally [listening to sad music] can be fairly cathartic, though sometimes it does backfire and I only feel worse than before" (Female, aged 20). As another put it:

> I'm glad that I did choose those songs to listen instead of turning to slow and sad music that I usually am inclined to listen to when I'm feeling down … The more I listened to the songs mentioned the more I began to forget the painful feelings that I had harboured earlier today. It just made me realise that the situation I was in wasn't as bad as I thought, and that wallowing in negative emotions just makes it worse. Tomorrow is another day filled with endless possibilities. (Female, aged 24)

For some participants the music had a direct influence on their self-perception or their perception of events around them. One participant described it this way: "As I listen to different songs I find my mood changing and who I see myself as changing … This realization was very powerful for me" (Female, aged 24). Another reported specific effects of one song on her body image. She says:

> To be honest, I have a very low level of confidence in myself because I regard myself as fat, ugly and not attractive at all. I am always comparing my life and situation with those of others who are better than me and it made me feel even smaller. However, I was so consoled with the lyrics of this song especially with 'being the way you are is enough' and 'you don't know you're beautiful'. It seems like this song is going to be one of my favourite songs. (Female, aged 22)

In addition to increased awareness, several participants reported changed music-listening behavior, reporting increased deliberateness in their choice of music to achieve certain effects. For example, one participant who has done a lot of singing reported: "I now realize that the songs with the most positive memories for me are the ones that I have sung either on my own or with someone else and that by vocalizing my emotions by singing, I can experience more positivity in the moment and in day to day life" (Female, aged 22). Another came to the realization that she could make her mornings go better by using upbeat music to give her the energy to start the day. She reports:

> Like I had already done once, I set this song as my alarm clock for the early morning on Saturday. I did this again because I loved how quick I got out of bed the first time I did this and how awake I was when I did so. It amazes me because I am the hardest person to get out of bed most mornings! … I love these effects and will continue to do this with my mornings—or at least with music like this so I can have a big energy boost. (Female, aged 21)

Other participants deliberately experimented with the tracks from their assigned playlists, using them in a variety of situations or mood states in order to gauge their differing effects. The participants themselves were at times surprised by the results.

For some participants, the prescribed music presented an opportunity for them to listen to, and become accustomed to, music in styles or genres to which they would not normally listen. For several, this resulted in an increased appreciation of both individual songs and of unfamiliar styles, which they reported would influence their future listening. For example, one participant said: "This song obviously cheered me up. I think I would listen to this genre more" (Female, aged 21). With regard to one song, another participant reported: "I had never listened to this song before, and it has now become one of my favourites" (Female, aged 22).

As this volume has progressed, numerous studies have been presented that have demonstrated how sad music can be a useful tool for processing negative emotions in people experiencing distressing real-life events. It has also been demonstrated that sad music can be an enjoyable experience for other people, regardless of their current emotional state. However, questions still remained around the degree to which listening to sad music is helpful for people with tendencies to depression and whether or not listening to happier music is more useful. The mixed methods study discussed in this chapter has illuminated several important aspects of this question that have valuable implications for the use of music in therapeutic contexts.

Our previous studies (see Chap. 8) showed that listening to sad music resulted in a significant worsening of depressive symptoms in people with high scores in rumination, while listening to happy music could result in substantial reductions in depression levels. However, the current study demonstrated that when the sad music is researcher-selected and therefore likely to have less personal significance as distinct from the self-selected sad music used in our previous experiments, it can have a positive mood effect on listeners. This suggests that music listening in general—whether happy or sad—can have positive mood effects, even in people with tendencies to depression, when it is novel and has minimal personal relevance. However, again, our results showed that the impact of happy music was even greater.

Our finding that the personal relevance of the lyrics increased the potency of the affective impact tends to support this idea, since it points towards the fact that drawing parallels between the story told in the lyrics and personal experience plays an important role in the affective response. Nevertheless, some listeners proved to be adept at imagining themselves in the situation depicted in the lyrics, even when it did not portray something they had personally experienced. Thus, the personal relevance of the story told in the music, or one's capacity to imaginatively place oneself in the story can compound the sadness experienced in response to the music.

Whether or not the sadness experienced in response to sad music will then have a negative effect on mood also depends on several factors, most particularly the thoughts and memories that are triggered by the music. In general, for our participants the long-term impact of the music over the four-week period was minimal. Many of them reported effects that were temporary and rarely powerful enough to make a difference to their general mood. However, some participants reported effects that were more intense and that lasted for a whole day, or even several days, compounding negative moods where the music had triggered negative thoughts, or putting the participant in a positive state where positive thoughts were activated. Such positive thoughts were more likely to be activated by music from the happy playlist, with memories and thoughts of being with friends, parties, dancing, holidays and other relaxing and joyful occasions being activated. On the other hand, music from the sad playlist tended to stimulate thoughts about loneliness or sad memories of loved ones, even of death.

The fact that the lyrics again play an important role here is confirmed by multiple studies. Craig Anderson and colleagues, for example

(Anderson, Carnagey, & Eubanks, 2003), found that aggressive lyrics tended to increase aggressive and hostile thoughts, while humorous lyrics could have a positive impact on mood. Similarly, other studies have shown that songs with misogynistic lyrics can increase negative attitudes towards women, while songs with pro-equality lyrics promote positive behaviours towards women. Thus, while some people may focus more on the music itself rather than the lyrics, there is extensive evidence that song lyrics are an important factor in the thinking patterns that are triggered when listening to music, and, indeed, even in shaping attitudes and beliefs.

The thinking patterns set in motion by the music in our study were related, in turn, to the habitual coping style of the individual. Where adaptive coping styles such as reflectiveness, active coping, seeking social support, or religious coping were already in place or were triggered by the music, the outcome of the music listening, whether happy or sad, was generally positive. This accords with the literature, which indicates the general effectiveness of such coping styles. However, where less helpful coping styles such as rumination or social withdrawal were in action in the individual or were stimulated by the music, this resulted in less positive mood outcomes, with high ruminators who listened to sad music having particularly negative mood outcomes.

It was interesting to observe how participants absorbed their assigned music into their habitual ways of using music in order to achieve their personal mood goals. Where the music matched the mood regulation goals of the listener, the music was used as part of an overall strategy to achieve a particular mood, whether positive or negative. Where the music did not match the desired mood outcome, participants found ways to counteract or resist the effect of the music so as to still obtain their desired mood. This suggests that the music itself is less important in creating specific mood effects than are the individual's own mood regulation strategies and that prescribed music will be of limited effectiveness where the individual is not receptive to the affective tone of the music.

What does this research suggest about the utility of 'musical prescriptions' for helping people with depression in the modern day? This study confirmed that happy music is more effective than sad music in creating positive mood outcomes in people with tendencies to depression.

In fact, listening to sad music can hold particular dangers for people with strong propensities for rumination since it may tend to trigger patterns of negative thinking from which it is difficult for such people to escape. These results also suggest that researcher-selected music, whether happy or sad, can have positive mood effects when prescribed for a single listening session. Particularly where the music has limited personal significance, the mere enjoyment of listening to music can have a positive affective outcome. However, long-term mood listening programs would need to involve a greater variety of musical choice than provided to our sample, enabling more freedom of choice. Taken together, these results demonstrate that in order for music to have a positive affective impact on the listener, the music needs to match their current arousal needs, and to trigger positive thoughts or memories.

While some participants seemed to have a high level of awareness about the impact of music on their moods and emotions, others appeared less aware of the thinking patterns that were being activated by music or of the fact that more positive outcomes could be achieved by listening to different music. However, for several listeners, involvement in the experiment as a whole was an eye-opening experience, helping them to become more aware of the effects of their usual listening habits, and allowing them an opportunity to experience unexpected mood effects. In several cases this led to changing attitudes towards music selections, heightened awareness of affective impacts, and increased deliberateness of music selection.

These findings thus shed important light on the dilemma posed at the outset of this chapter: the fact that people prefer to listen to self-selected music, but particularly in the case of people with the impaired mood regulation capacities associated with depression, may lack the requisite awareness to select music effectively. Participants respond more to music that is personally relevant, both in terms of the lyrical content and genre preferences.

This highlights the fact that while prescribed music can create some useful affective changes in the short term, interventions that target awareness are likely to be more efficacious in achieving long-term mood effects from music listening. In particular, people with tendencies to rumination can be helped to learn the kind of music that is likely to trigger negative thinking patterns and alternative music that may instead promote more positive messages about the individual and the world in general. In fact, interventions that address music use could potentially be accessible through online or other self-help mediums, and could provide a useful method for educating individuals about general behaviors that can exacerbate depressive symptoms—an approach to the topic that may be more attractive to individuals who are resistant to professional help than traditional therapeutic programs.

A further issue that appears to have an influence on how music affects the mood of the listener is the social situation in which it is heard. The effect of contextual factors will be discussed in the following chapter.

References

Anderson, C. A., Carnagey, N. L., & Eubanks, J. (2003a). Exposure to violent media: The effects of songs with violent lyrics on aggressive thoughts and feelings. *Journal of Personality and Social Psychology, 84*(5), 960–971.

Anderson, M. J., Marwit, S. J., Vandenberg, B., & Chibnall, J. T. (2005). Psychological and religious coping strategies of mothers bereaved by the sudden death of a child. *Death Studies, 29*, 811–826.

Block, M., Stern, D. B., Raman, K., Lee, S., Carey, J., Humphreys, A. A., … Breiter, H. C. (2014). The relationship between self-report of depression and media usage. *Frontiers in Human Neuroscience, 12*(8), 712.

Browning, C. A. (2000). Using music during childbirth. *Birth, 27*(4), 272–276.

Carver, C. S., Scheier, M. F., & Weintraub, J. K. (1989). Assessing coping strategies: A theoretically based approach. *Journal of Personality and Social Psychology, 56*, 267–283.

Cooke, M., Chaboyer, W., Schluter, P., & Hiratos, M. (2005). The effect of music on preoperative anxiety in day surgery. *Journal of Advanced Nursing, 52*(1), 47–55.

Cooke, M., Moyle, W., Shum, D., Harrison, S. D., & Murfield, J. E. (2010). A randomized controlled trial exploring the effect of music on quality of life and depression in older people with dementia. *Journal of Health Psychology, 15*(5), 765–776.

Curran, S. L., Andrykowski, M. A., & Studts, J. L. (1995). Short form of the profile of mood states (POMS-SF): Psychometric information. *Psychological Assessment, 7*(1), 80–83.

Erkkila, J., Punkanen, M., Fachner, J., Ala-Ruona, E., Pontio, I., Tervaniemi, M., … Gold, C. (2011). Individual music therapy for depression: Randomised controlled trial. *The British Journal of Psychiatry, 199*, 132–139.

Forer, B. R. (1949). The fallacy of personal validation: A classroom demonstration of gullibility. *Journal of Abnormal and Social Psychology, 44*(1), 118–123.

Gallagher, L. M., Lagman, R., Walsh, D., Davis, M. P., & LeGrand, S. B. (2006). The clinical effects of music therapy in palliative medicine. *Support Care in Cancer, 14*, 859–866.

Garrido, S., & Schubert, E. (2013). Adaptive and maladaptive attraction to negative emotion in music. *Musicae Scientiae, 17*(2), 145–164. doi:10.1177/1029864913478305.

Garrido, S., Schubert, E., & Bangert, D. (2016). Musical prescriptions for mood improvement: An experimental study. *The Arts in Psychotherapy, 51*, 46–53. doi:10.1016/j.aip.2016.09.002.

Jorm, A., Medway, J., & Christensen, H. (2000). Public beliefs about the helpfulness of interventions for depression: Effects of actions taken when experiencing anxiety and depression symptoms. *Australian and New Zealand Journal of Psychiatry, 34*, 619–626.

Lai, H.-L., Li, Y.-M., & Lee, L.-H. (2012). Effects of music intervention with nursing presence and recorded music on psycho-physiological indices of cancer patient caregivers. *Journal of Clinical Nursing, 21*, 745–756.

McWilliams, L. A., Cox, B. J., & Enns, M. W. (2003). Use of the coping inventory for stressful situations in a clinically depressed sample: Factor structure, personality correlates and prediction of distress. *Journal of Clinical Psychology, 59*(12), 1371–1385.

Nair, B. R., Browne, W., Marley, J., & Heim, C. (2013). Music and dementia. *Degenerative Neurological and Neuromuscular Disease, 3*, 47–51.

Nair, B. R., Heim, C., Krishnan, C., D'Este, C., Marley, J., & Attia, J. (2011). The effect of Baroque music on behavioural disturbances in patients with dementia. *Australasian Journal of Ageing, 31*(1), 11–15.

Newman, M. L., Pennebaker, J. W., Berry, D. S., & Richards, J. M. (2003). Lying words: Predicting deception from linguistic styles. *Personality and Social Psychology Bulletin, 29*(5), 665–675.

Pennebaker, J. W. (1993). Putting stress into words: Health, linguistic, and therapeutic implications. *Behaviour Research and Therapy, 31*(6), 539–548.

Pennebaker, J. W., & Graybeal, A. (2001). Patterns of natural language use: Disclosure, personality, and social integration. *Current Directions in Psychological Science, 10*(3), 90–93.

Pennebaker, J. W., Mayne, T. J., & Francis, M. E. (1997). Linguistic predictors of adaptive bereavement. *Journal of Personality and Social Psychology, 72*(4), 863–871.

Rice, S. M., Goodall, J., Hetrick, S. E., Parker, A. G., Gilbertson, T., Amminger, G. P., … Alvarez-Jimenez, M. (2014). Online and social networkgin interventions for the treatment of depression in young people: A systematic review. *Journal of Medical Internet Research, 16*(9), e206–e246.

Rickwood, D. J., Deane, F. P., & Wilson, C. J. (2007). When and how do young people seek professional help for mental health problems? *Medical Journal of Australia, 187*(7), S35–S40.

Sawyer, M. G., Arney, F. M., Baghurst, P. A., Clark, J. J., Graetz, B. W., Kosky, R. J., … Zubrick, S. R. (2000). The mental health of young people in Australia: Key findings from the child and adolescent component of the national survey of mental health and well-being. *Australian and New Zealand Journal of Psychiatry, 35*(6), 806–814.

Schubert, E. (2010). Affective, evaluative, and collative responses to hated and loved music. *Psychology of Aesthetics, Creativity and the Arts, 4*(1), 36–46.

Srnka, K. J., & Koeszegi, S. T. (2007). From words to numbers: How to transform qualitative data into meaningful quantitative results. *Schmalenbach Business Review, 59*, 29–57.

Tausczik, Y. R., & Pennebaker, J. W. (2010). The psychological meaning of words: LIWC and computerized text analysis methods. *Journal of Language and Social Psychology, 29*(1), 24–54.

Trapnell, P. D., & Campbell, J. D. (1999). Private self-consciousness and the five-factor model of personality: Distinguishing rumination from reflection. *Journal of Personality and Social Psychology, 76*(2), 284–304.

Van den Tol, A. J. M., & Edwards, J. (2013). Exploring a rationale for choosing to listen to sad music when feeling sad. *Psychology of Music, 41*(4), 440–465.

10

Listening Context: Group Rumination and Emotional Contagion

Music as a Social Activity

One of the primary functions that music plays in human society is to promote group cohesion and social bonding. Some researchers suggest that music evolved either in parallel with language or as a pre-linguistic form of communication that helped individual primates to form groups and to coordinate joint activities (Cross, 2001; Freeman, 2000). Ellen Dissanayake (2006), in a survey of studies of music in rituals from over thirty traditional societies, proposed six social functions that music plays, including the display of resources, the control and channelling of aggression, the facilitation of courtship, and the establishment and maintenance of social identity.

Emotions in general are believed to promote social survival by helping individuals to form and maintain social relationships, and to establish or maintain a social position in relation to others (Fischer & Manstead, 2008). While positive emotions can serve as 'social glue', displays of negative emotions such as crying are a demonstration of powerlessness and signal the need for social support. Thus, in a wider social context, such displays of vulnerability can actually diminish

S. Garrido, *Why Are We Attracted to Sad Music?*,
DOI 10.1007/978-3-319-39666-8_10

one's perceived social status within a group. However, close social connections are more likely to provide support in response to displays of negative emotions. Studies have shown, therefore, that people cry more often in the presence of their partner or other intimates than in public situations (Vingerhoets & Becht, 1997). Furthermore, the social context in which crying occurs likely influences the psychological effect experienced. Since crying is meant to motivate bystanders to provide solace and comfort, reported mood improvement after crying tend to be higher where such support is received (Bylsma, Croon, Vingerhoets, & Rottenberg, 2011).

From infancy, music serves the function of strengthening intimate relationships. From the early stages of life, families across cultures tend to create rituals that involve music and singing. Musical rituals in early infancy serve the purpose of both regulating arousal and of consolidating parental–infant bonds (Trehub & Trainor, 1998). While such family rituals continue to be important for wellbeing and social cohesion in collectivist and traditional cultures as children get older, in individualistic societies, peer group influences eventually become paramount (Boer & Abubakar, 2014). However, music still continues to play an important role in social relationships.

Throughout life music acts as a social cohesive in various ways. For example, Diana Boer and colleagues (2011) demonstrated in a series of experiments that music creates and strengthens interpersonal relations between young people because of the cues that music preferences give about values. In one of their experiments participants were asked to imagine meeting a stranger. They were then told about the stranger's musical preferences and were asked to indicate the likely values as well as the social attractiveness of the individual. The researchers found that similarity in both music taste and values predicted whether or not the participants rated the hypothetical stranger as socially attractive. This suggests that music choices are a way of communicating values and of making judgments about the values of others and the potential of others to form part of our social group. Even the online sharing of music preferences, such as occurs on sites like Last.Fm and which doesn't involve any face-to-face contact, can foster the development of social ties, albeit relatively weak ones (Baym & Ledbetter, 2009).

Furthermore, research demonstrates that feeling that one's tastes align with the people around you is beneficial for mental health. In general, being part of a group in which people have a sense of shared social identity tends to relieve stress (Häusser, Kattenstroth, van Dick, & Mojzisch, 2012). Thus, Dave Miranda and Patrick Gaudrea (2011) found that congruence of musical taste with both parents and peers reduces negative affect. Multiple studies have shown that particularly amongst adolescents, music can be used as a 'badge' to identify the 'in group' and the 'out group' (North & Hargreaves, 1999; Tarrant, North, & Hargreaves, 2001), and is used in processes of friendship formation (Rentfrow & Gosling, 2006; Selfhout, Branje, ter Bogt, & Meeus, 2009). Since musical identity can suggest acceptance into certain social groups, the sharing of musical taste with others evidently increases the feeling of belonging and of having social support, important factors in mental health.

In addition to the role that music preferences play in the establishment of social groups and personal identity, the act of engaging with music in combination with other individuals also has a number of social effects. One of the primary ways in which people consolidate affiliations with other individuals is through experiencing emotions with them. Romantically involved couples and college roommates, for example, actually become more emotionally similar the longer they are associated with each other (Anderson, Keltner, & John, 2003). Furthermore, the degree of emotional convergence achieved in these relationships is predictive of the likelihood that the partnership will survive, suggesting the importance of sharing emotions in strengthening intimate relationships.

Empathy, as discussed in Chap. 7, is believed to occur through a process of unconscious motor mimicry, which causes an individual to experience parallel emotions to those that they perceive as being expressed by the other person (Vreeke & Van der Mark, 2003). Studies using electromyography (EMG) to record the electrical activity of facial muscles have demonstrated that when people are observing the emotional expressions of others, their own facial expressions are reflecting the observed emotions in minute, subtle changes in the muscles, even when there is no noticeable change in facial expression (Lundqvist, 1995; Wild, Erb, Eyb, Bartels, & Grodd, 2003). Robert Levenson, Paul Ekman and Wallace Friesen (1983) have shown that mimicking the facial expressions of primary emotions results in patterns of activity in the autonomic nervous system that suggest the real experience of the emotions being mimicked, thereby enabling emotions to be shared. Thus Elaine Hatfield and colleagues (Hatfield, Rapson, & Le, 2011) argue that mimicry of observed expressions of emotion synchronize and coordinate social interactions, facilitating emotional closeness.

Emotions shared when listening to music have a similar effect. As discussed in Chap. 7, emotional contagion and entrainment are believed to be among the key mechanisms by which emotional responses to music are evoked (Juslin & Vastfjall, 2008). There is extensive evidence that group synchronization to a beat influences behaviour towards the group and those perceived as being outside that group. Sebastian Kirschner and Michael Tomasello (2010), for example, have found that joint music-making in a group of four-year olds significantly increased cooperative and helpful behaviours compared to a control group that had no musical activities. The authors argued that the act of synchronizing voices and movements helps to increase commitment to the group and allows it to focus on collective goals. Other studies have shown similar increases in prosocial behaviours after moving together to a shared musical beat (Cirelli, Einarson, & Trainor, 2014). Conversely, Scott Wiltermuth (2012) has shown that adults who move synchronously to music with others in a group are more likely to subsequently comply with requests by someone from the group to do something unpleasant or aggressive toward another group of individuals. This goes some way toward explaining the phenomenon of mob behaviour and the frequency with which rallies may precede violent and illegal activities that individuals would often not engage in alone.

There is also evidence that emotional experiences are amplified in group settings. Social facilitation theory predicts that where others are present, arousal, and hence often performance, increases (Zajonc & Sales, 1966). One of the earliest experiments in this field was by Norman Triplett (1898), who found that children asked to wind fishing line around a reel worked faster when in the presence of another person doing the same task. With regard to music, Alexandra Lamont (2009) has found that the strongest emotional experiences with music tend to occur at live events such as concerts or festivals. In a survey of a concert audience in Durham,

UK (described in Chap. 2), my colleagues and I also found that emotional contagion between members of the audience contributed to their emotional response. It is therefore likely that emotional experiences are amplified by the emotional contagion that occurs in the midst of a large group of listeners who are all responding to the same music. This is a phenomenon that is also frequently observed in movie theatres (Coplan, 2006).

However, the increased intensity of emotional experiences that can occur in group musical engagement only seems to occur where the listener is aware of the emotional response of other listeners. Patrik Juslin and colleagues (Juslin, Liljeström, Laukka, Västfjäll, & Lundqvist, 2011) found that more intense musical emotions occurred when people listened to music with a close friend than when they listened alone (see also Liljeström, Juslin, & Västfjäll, 2013). Conversely, in another study (Egermann et al., 2011), listening alone was found to be more arousing than listening in a group. However, in the latter study listeners were not aware of how the other listeners in the group were responding to the music. Thus, it has been suggested that emotional amplification occurs through a process of social feedback (Egermann, Kopiez, & Altenmüller, 2013).

In fact, as discussed in Chap. 4, our emotions in general are influenced by our appraisal of a situation. Where social feedback is taking place, this likely has an influence on the appraisal that a listener would make of the emotions being experienced (Manstead & Fischer, 2001). Furthermore, strong motivations exist for conforming to perceived group norms. The evidence suggests that music listeners make aesthetic choices on the basis of social feedback (Salganik, Dodds, & Watts, 2006). Neurological research confirms that where there is a mismatch between one's own preferences and that of the majority, this creates a sense of anxiety, in adolescents at least, motivating them to conform to what appears to be most popular (Berns, Capra, Moore, & Noussair, 2010). Thus, it appears that where social feedback is available in a music listening situation, whether it be through voiced opinions, online popularity ratings, or the expressions of emotional response, this can influence both liking of music, emotional appraisal, and the intensity of emotional response through a process of emotional contagion.

That the social circumstances of music listening has an influence on emotional response was also confirmed by the study I conducted with Daniel Bangert and Emery Schubert which is described in the previous chapter of this volume (Garrido et al., 2016). In that study, participants listened to a researcher-selected playlist regularly over a four-week period and they completed diaries to describe the circumstances in which they listened to the music and also its affective impact. Since participants listened to the same music in various situations, participant diaries illuminated some interesting things about how social settings influenced their emotional response to the music.

We found that where participants reported disliking particular songs on their assigned playlist when listening alone, they frequently reported enjoying listening to it in the company of friends. Sometimes the affective impact changed simply through observing the response of other people to the music and at times it occurred because the music appeared more suited to group activities than solitary ones. Conversely, more reflective songs appeared to have a greater affective impact when heard in a private, solitary situation in which participants could concentrate and become fully absorbed in the music. These findings are unsurprising given that people are probably more likely to restrain themselves from crying in the presence of others and are therefore less likely to become emotionally engaged in sad music to the extent that they might otherwise when in the presence of others.

Music and Group Rumination

Given that group settings and social feedback can at times amplify the intensity of emotions experienced in response to music, and that, as we have established in previous chapters, sad music can actually intensify depression in some listeners, is there the potential for group listening to sad music to have a doubly dangerous effect on people with tendencies to depression? Amanda Rose (2002) used the term "co-rumination" to refer to the "extensive discussion and revisiting" of problems and focusing on negative feelings that was associated with both close relationships and also emotional difficulties (p. 1803). Dave Miranda and colleagues

(Miranda, Gaudrea, Debrosse, Morizot, & Kirmayer, 2012) applied this term to some social groups which form around music, in which people may engage in excessive group discussions about music that focuses on the exploration of dark themes and their own personal problems. In a former study, Miranda and Claes (2009) had found that music preferences and depression levels in their adolescent participants were closely associated with those of their peers. Thus, it seems possible that some kind of group rumination may occur amongst peers with preferences for sad music.

Indeed, entire musical subcultures such as "goth" or "emo" (an abbreviation of 'emotional') have sprung up around the exploration of sadness and depression through music. The music popular with such groups has been blamed for occurrences of teen suicides, such as the double suicide of two teenage girls in 2007 in Australia. The two girls apparently hanged themselves from the same tree in a park near Melbourne after months of posts on a social media site that documented their obsession with "emo" music and a downward spiral of depressive thinking.

Public outrage over such events apparently involving music has led, in many parts of the world, to cries for the banning of music with suicidal themes. In Russia, a special governmental committee was formed to deal with issues relating to the emo subculture, resulting in a bill proposing to regulate emo websites and ban affiliates from wearing their characteristic all-black garb in schools and government buildings. It was claimed that the subculture posed a "social danger and a threat to national stability" (Michaels, 2008).

Media attention has often augmented concerns that such musical subcultures foster subversive and suicidal tendencies in their affiliates, not only in relation to the emo subculture but also with regard to other music. For example, lawsuits were brought against the rock musician Ozzy Osbourne and the band Judas Priest, claiming that they bore some responsibility for the suicides of their teenage fans. Publicity fanned the flames of public outrage, although the cases were eventually dismissed. Some question still remains over the extent to which music (and the artists behind it) can be blamed for such events.

Several lines of argument are often used in relation to the effect of so-called 'problem music' on behaviour. Social Learning Theory advocates the idea that displays of certain behaviour within the media encourages the perception of such behaviour as both normal and acceptable. For example, in one experiment, children that watched a model engaging in aggressive behaviour with an inflatable doll became more aggressive in their own behaviour (Bandura, Ross, & Ross, 1961). Similar effects seem to exist in relation to aggressive films and computer games (Bushman & Huesmann, 2006).

Some studies seem to support this idea in relation to music listening, with correlations having been found between heavy metal music and personality traits such as aggressiveness, moodiness and pessimism (Wells & Hakanen, 1991), and between rock/metal, depression and suicidal vulnerability (Martin, Clarke, & Colby, 1993). Associations have also been found between clinical depression and mood disorders and a preference for rap, heavy metal and techno music (Doak, 2003). Of course, correlational studies do not demonstrate causality, and therefore do not establish whether aggressive and depressed people are attracted to this music because of their moods or whether their moods are somehow exacerbated by the music.

Nevertheless, there is experimental evidence that aggressive music with violent lyrics increases feelings of aggression in people more than the same music without the lyrics (Anderson, et al., 2003). Other studies have shown that music with suicidal lyrics can prime suicidal thoughts in the listener (Rustad, Small, Jobes, Safer, & Peterson, 2003). While this suggests strongly that lyrics may have the power to encourage certain beliefs and behaviours, experimental evidence in relation to music without lyrics is lacking.

However, other studies suggest an alternative viewpoint, indicating that people are attracted to particular genres in order to give them an outlet for their negative emotions (Baker & Homan, 2007; Lacourse, Claes, & Villeneuve, 2001). Drive Reduction Theory argues that when bodily tension is created by feelings of aggression or grief, for example, an individual will seek an outlet for these emotions in order to achieve a state of emotional equilibrium. Thus, it is argued that genres such as rap, metal or the music popular with the emo subculture, allow negative emotions to be released in a harmless way, reducing the likelihood that the person will express these emotions in less appropriate ways (Anastasi, 2005; Berkowitz, 1962).

As previous chapters of this book have emphasized, listening to sad music can fulfil positive psychological functions. It seems unlikely, therefore, that genre is of itself a risk factor for psychopathology or deviant behaviour (Miranda & Claes, 2004). In fact, some studies have shown that while distressed youths often demonstrate a preference for genres such as metal, they do not report a more negative effect of the music on their mood than people who listen to other genres (McFerran, Garrido, O'Grady, Grocke, & Sawyer, 2014).

However, people with vulnerabilities such as anger or depression may be more susceptible to the influence of music that could aggravate their particular emotional sensitivities (Bushong, 2002). Rebecca Peterson, Martin Safer and David Jobes (2008), for example, found that people with high levels of neuroticism, low self-esteem and low scores in openness to experience were more likely to write stories containing suicide-related content after listening to sad music, suggesting their greater vulnerability to suicidal priming.

Just as individual differences influences the effect of music with suicidal lyrics, or music that focuses on negative themes, similar individual differences likely exist in how people are affected by group rumination with music. Groups of individuals repetitively listening to depressing music while talking about personal problems and negative emotions could potentially have healthy effects on mood and mental health if it increases perceived social support for members of the group or if it results in a resolution of negative emotions. However, it seems possible that group rumination could serve as a particularly compelling force on the more vulnerable members in such a group, with negative outcomes for their wellbeing. On the other hand, merely listening to music could have an isolating effect on an individual, promoting social withdrawal and increasing tendencies to private rumination.

How Do the Social Circumstances of Listening Influence the Impact of Sad Music?

Thus, the question of how the social circumstances of music listening influence the affective outcomes of listening to sad music is an important one to consider in exploring the effect of sad music on mental health and wellbeing. I explored this further in an online survey of 700 participants, ranging in age from 16 to 74 years of age (mean age of 24.9 years). Around 40 percent of these participants were currently suffering moderate to severe levels of depression as measured by a short form of the Depression-Anxiety-Stress-Scale (Henry & Crawford, 2005). Within the survey, participants answered a number of questions relating to their ways of using music, as well as nominating a song that made them feel sad and rating that song according to valence and arousal levels. During the analysis phase lyrics to the nominated songs were obtained and analysed using Linguistic Inquiry and Word Count (LIWC) (Tausczik & Pennebaker, 2010) in order to explore the thematic content.

A factor analysis of survey items was conducted to establish patterns of music use. Six distinct patterns of behaviour around music listening were identified. A Group Rumination factor reflected a tendency to listen to sad music with others while talking about sad things or personal problems, while a Social Connection factor suggested a preference for listening to music or talking about it with others more generally, whether the music was happy or sad. On the other hand, a Solitary Reflection factor indicated a propensity to listen to music while alone for the purpose of reflection or coping. Other listeners evinced a preference for music that expressed a message that they could individually relate to, a factor I labelled Personal Meaning. For other listeners, music listening was Artist Centred, with a strong focus on the musicians themselves, or for purposes of Aesthetic Appreciation.

People with moderate to high levels of depression in this sample tended to nominate music that had more negative valence, lower arousal levels and more feeling words in the lyrics than less depressed participants. They also had higher rumination scores and reported less positive mood effects from listening to sad music when sad. It was further revealed that people with moderate to high levels of depression were more likely to listen to music for Social Connection purposes and to engage in Group Rumination, and less likely to listen to music for Solitary Reflection than people with either mild or no depression. Furthermore, their listening choices tended to be more Artist Centred and less for the purposes of Aesthetic Appreciation. On the other hand, people with either no or only mild depression tended to nominate 'sad music' that had comparatively more positive valence and higher arousal than the selections of their more depressed counterparts, and generally reported more positive mood effects from listening to it.

These results suggest that people with high levels of depression do like to connect with other people for the purpose of sharing music and to talk about its relevance to their own feelings. Surprisingly, given the social connections involved, it seems that such a pattern of music use has less positive mood outcomes than a pattern of using music for purposes of Solitary Reflection. This tends to confirm the results of the studies reported in previous chapters which indicates that reflectiveness is a healthy coping mechanism distinct from rumination (Garrido & Schubert, 2013; Trapnell & Campbell, 1999) that can actually help people to reach emotional resolution when experiencing negative emotions resulting from adverse life events.

Other studies also corroborate the relationship between co-rumination and negative mental health outcomes. Rose and colleagues (2007), for example, conducted a longitudinal study in which it was found that co-rumination was predictive of increased depression and anxiety in adolescent girls over a six-month period. However, since co-rumination also resulted in stronger social bonds, the authors concluded that this might mean that at-risk populations go undetected because of the seeming strength of their supportive networks. Thus, it seems that co-rumination may provide another example of how adaptive patterns of coping malfunction in cases of depression. Strong social connections—generally a protective factor against depression—can, where rumination is involved, lead to excessive dwelling on negative emotions resulting in increased depressive symptoms in vulnerable individuals. Music can form a strong basis for the sharing of negative emotions, working along with the social setting to intensify the emotions experienced.

Another interesting finding from the online survey was the fact that higher levels of depression were also associated with an Artist Centred-listening style. Readers might remember the case of Sarah from Chap. 8, who indicated a strong affinity with the artists whose music she listened to. She spent large amounts of time reading about their personal lives online, and reflected on their lives and the similarity to her own life when listening to their music. The fact that this kind of listening pattern is associated with negative mental health outcomes is supported by studies that suggest that a high interest in, and over-identification with music celebrities are correlated with social alienation and low self-esteem, and are particular risk factors in people with a history of depression and suicide (Kistler, Rodgers, Power, Austin, & Hill, 2010; Lacourse et al., 2001; Levesque, 2010).

The use of sad songs with a high content of feeling words in people with high levels of depression is also perhaps reflective of music that is serving maladaptive coping strategies. James Pennebaker and colleagues (1997) found that the use of words related to cognitive mechanisms and insight in text indicates that processes of reflection and reappraisal are occurring, which can lead to greater health improvements. The use of more emotive words, on the other hand, could be suggestive of an emotion-oriented coping style, which is generally believed to be a less useful coping strategy (Carver et al., 1989).

It is evident from this discussion that music plays an important role in the formation and maintenance of social relationships. The sharing of emotions through music strengthens social bonds from the earliest days of life and throughout the lifespan. Sharing of negative emotion, in particular, is more likely to happen in close or intimate relationships. People tend to restrain themselves from crying in public, and to experience less intense sadness in response to music when in the company of people they are not emotionally close to.

However, in close relationships, sharing sadness has a cementing effect on the relationship and it can serve the adaptive function of signalling a need for social support. Where this sharing brings about the needed help or support, the outcome may be positive. Where other individuals in the group do not share the same need for support they may be able to provide a useful distraction from the intensity of negative emotions that are being experienced.

However, in close relationships processes of emotional contagion can cause sadness to spread from one individual to another. The sharing of sad music can also result in an amplification of the emotions experienced through mechanisms of social feedback. Thus, among distressed friends, group rumination by listening to depressing music can feed and even magnify patterns of ruminative thinking, resulting in deleterious effects on mood and mental health. Nevertheless, the need for social support is real, and this is likely why people with tendencies to depression seek out connections with people experiencing similar feelings, despite the potential for their mood states to be worsened. It is possible that an artist-centred style of musical engagement provides a stand-in or substitute for real emotional connections with other like-minded social intimates.

Thus, group musical engagement can both diffuse the negative emotions evoked by sad music and also create a synergistic heightening of emotional effects, depending on the dominant affective responses of the individuals in the group. Where the effect is an increase in emotional intensity, whether the mental health outcomes are positive or negative for the members of the group again likely depends on the thought patterns triggered, as it does for sad music listening in solitary situations. Vulnerable individuals with predispositions toward rumination may suffer the worst outcomes from group rumination, with negative thoughts and feelings becoming more deeply entrenched by social feedback from the group. Outcomes are likely more positive where the group interactions are able to provide an opportunity to obtain practical assistance or to engage in processes of cognitive reframing of events.

This book has thus far established that the reasons for listening to sad music are varied, and that the effect it has on the individual is influenced by a complex interaction of personal and group variables. While a number of positive psychological functions can be served by listening to sad music, perhaps by the majority of listeners, for a minority the effect may be to exacerbate tendencies to depression. The following chapters will explore specific situations in which sad music seems to be particularly attractive to listeners, and the evidence relating to the adaptive and maladaptive purposes sad music can play in such situations.

References

Anastasi, A. P. (2005). Adolescent boys' use of Emo music as their healing lament. *Journal of Religion and Health, 44*(3), 303–319.

Anderson, C. A., Carnagey, N. L., & Eubanks, J. (2003). Exposure to violent media: The effects of songs with violent lyrics on aggressive thoughts and feelings. *Journal of Personality and Social Psychology, 84*(5), 960–971.

Baker, S., & Homan, S. (2007). Rap, recidivism and the creative self: A popular music programme for young offenders in detention. *Journal of Youth Studies, 10*(4), 459–476.

Bandura, A., Ross, D., & Ross, S. A. (1961). Transmission of aggression through imitation of aggressive models. *Journal of Abnormal and Social Psychology, 63*, 575–582.

Baym, N. K., & Ledbetter, A. (2009). Tunes that bind? Predicting friendship strength in a music-based social network. *Information, Communication and Society, 12*(3), 408–427.

Berkowitz, L. (1962). *Aggression: A social psychological analysis*. New York: McGraw-Hill Book Company.

Berns, G. S., Capra, C. M., Moore, S., & Noussair, C. (2010). Neural mechanisms of the influence of popularity on adolescent ratings of music. *Neuroimage, 49*(3), 2687–2696.

Boer, D., & Abubakar, A. (2014). Music listening in families and peer groups: Benefits for young people's social cohesion and emotional well-being across four cultures. *Frontiers in Psychology, 5*, 392.

Boer, D., Fischer, R., Strack, M., Bond, M. H., Lo, E., & Lam, J. (2011). How shared preferences in music create bonds between people: Values as the missing link. *Personality and Social Psychology Bulletin, 20*(10), 1–13. doi:10.1177/0146167211407521.

Bushman, B. J., & Huesmann, R. (2006). Short-term and long-term effects of violent media on aggression in children and adults. *Archives of Pediatric Adolescent Medicine, 160*(4), 348–352.

Bushong, D. J. (2002). Good music/bad music: Extant literature on popular music media and antisocial behavior. *Music Therapy Perspectives, 20*(2), 69–79.

Bylsma, L. M., Croon, M. A., Vingerhoets, A. J. J. M., & Rottenberg, J. (2011). When and for whom does crying improve mood? A daily diary study of 1004 crying episodes. *Journal of Research in Personality, 45*(4), 385–392.

Carver, C. S., Scheier, M. F., & Weintraub, J. K. (1989). Assessing coping strategies: A theoretically based approach. *Journal of Personality and Social Psychology, 56*, 267–283.

Cirelli, L. K., Einarson, K. M., & Trainor, L. (2014). *Interpersonal synchrony increases prosocial behavior in infants*. Paper presented at the 12th International Conferece on Music Perception and Cognition and 8th Triennial Conference of the European Society for the Cognitive Science of Music, Thessaloniki, Greece.

Coplan, A. (2006). Catching characters' emotions: Emotional contagion responses to narrative fiction film. *Film Studies, 8*, 26–38.
Cross, I. (2001). Music; cognition; culture; evolution. *Annals of the New York Academy of Science, 930*, 28–42.
Dissanayake, E. (2006). Ritual and ritualization: Musical means of conveying and shaping emotion in humans and other animals. In S. Brown & U. Voglstein (Eds.), *Music and manipulation: On the social uses and social control of music* (pp. 31–56). Oxford & New York: Berghahn Books.
Doak, B. A. (2003). Relationships between adolescent psychiatric diagnoses, music preferences and drug preferences. *Music Therapy Perspectives, 21*(2), 69–76.
Egermann, H., Kopiez, R., & Altenmüller, E. (2013). The influence of social normative and informational feedback on musically induced emotions in an online music listening setting. *Psychomusicology, 23*(1), 21–32.
Egermann, H., Sutherland, M. E., Grewe, O., Nagel, F., Kopiez, R., & Altenmueller, E. (2011). Does music listening in a social context alter experience? A physiological and psychological perspective on emotion. *Musicae Scientiae, 15*(3), 307–323. doi:10.1177/1029864911399497.
Ekman, P., Levenson, R. W., & Friesen, W. V. (1983). Autonomic nervous sytem activity distinguishes among emotions. *Science, 221*(4616), 1208–1210.
Fischer, A. H., & Manstead, A. S. R. (2008). Social functions of emotion. In M. Lewis, J. M. Haviland-Jones, & L. F. Barrett (Eds.), *Handbook of emotions* (3rd ed., pp. 456–469). New York: The Guildford Press.
Freeman, W. J. A. (2000). *Neurobiological role of music in social bonding*. Florence, Italy.
Garrido, S., & Schubert, E. (2013). Adaptive and maladaptive attraction to negative emotion in music. *Musicae Scientiae, 17*(2), 145–164. doi:10.1177/1029864913478305.
Garrido, S., Schubert, E., & Bangert, D. (2016). Musical prescriptions for mood improvement: An experimental study. *The Arts in Psychotherapy, 51*, 46–53. doi:10.1016/j.aip.2016.09.002.
Hatfield, E., Rapson, R. L., & Le, Y.-C. L. (2011). Emotional contagion and empathy. In J. Decety & W. Ickes (Eds.), *The social neuroscience of empathy* (pp. 19–30). Boston, MA: MIT Press.
Häusser, J. A., Kattenstroth, M., van Dick, R., & Mojzisch, A. (2012). "We" are not stressed: Social identity in groups bufferes neuroendocrine stress reactions. *Journal of Experimental Social Psychology, 48*(4), 973–977.

Henry, J. D., & Crawford, J. R. (2005). The short-form version of the Depression Anxiety Stress Scales (DASS-21): Construct validity and normative data in a large non-clinical sample. *British Journal of Clinical Psychology, 44*(2), 227–239.

Juslin, P. N., Liljeström, S., Laukka, P., Västfjäll, D., & Lundqvist, L.-O. (2011). Emotional reactions to music in a nationally representative sample of Swedish adults: Prevalence and causal influences. *Musicae Scientiae, 15*(2), 174–207.

Juslin, P. N., & Vastfjall, D. (2008). Emotional response to music: The need to consider underlying mechanisms. *Behavioral and Brain Sciences, 31*, 559–621.

Kirschner, S., & Tomasello, M. (2010). Joint music making promotes social behavior in 4-year old children. *Evolution and Human Behavior, 31*, 354–364.

Kistler, M., Rodgers, K. B., Power, T., Austin, E. W., & Hill, L. G. (2010). Adolescents and music media: Toward an involvement-mediational model of consumption and self-concept. *Journal of Research on Adolescence, 20*(3), 616–630.

Lacourse, E., Claes, M., & Villeneuve, M. (2001). Heavy metal music and adolescent suicidal risk. *Journal of Youth and Adolescence, 30*(3), 321–332.

Lamont, A. (2009). Strong experiences of music in university students. Paper presented at the *Proceedings of the 7th Triennial Conference of the European Society for the Cognitive Sciences of Music*, Jyväskylä, Finland.

Levesque, R. J. R. (2010). Idols and idolization. In R. J. R. Levesque (Ed.), *Encyclopedia of adolescence* (pp. 1377–1379). New York: Springer.

Liljeström, S., Juslin, P. N., & Västfjäll, D. (2013). Experimental evidence of the roles of music choice, social context, and listener personality in emotional reactions to music. *Psychology of Music, 41*(5), 579–599.

Lundqvist, L.-O. (1995). Facial EMG reactions to facial expressions: A case of facial emotional contagion? *Scandinavian Journal of Psychology, 36*, 130–141.

Manstead, A. S. R., & Fischer, A. H. (2001). Social appraisal: The social world as object of and influence on appraisal processes. In K. R. Scherer, A. Schorr, & T. Johnstone (Eds.), *Appraisal processes in emotion: Theory, research, application*. New York: Oxford University Press.

Martin, G., Clarke, M., & Colby, P. (1993). Adolescent suicide: Music preference as an indicator of vulnerability. *Journal of the American Academy of Child & Adolescent Psychiatry, 32*(3), 530–535.

McFerran, K., Garrido, S., O'Grady, L., Grocke, D., & Sawyer, S. M. (2014). Examining the relationship between self-reported mood management and music preferences in Australian teenagers. *Nordic Journal of Music Therapy*. doi:10.1080/08098131.2014.908942.

Michaels, S. (2008, July 22). Russia wages war on emo kids. *Guardian*. Retrieved from http://www.guardian.co.uk/music/2008/jul/22/russian.emo
Miranda, D., & Claes, M. (2004). Rap music genres and deviant behaviors in French-Canadian adolescents. *Journal of Youth and Adolescence., 33*(2), 113–122.
Miranda, D., & Claes, M. (2009). Music listening, coping, peer affiliation and depression in adolescence. *Psychology of Music, 37*(2), 215–233.
Miranda, D., & Gaudrea, P. (2011). Music listening and emotional well-being in adolescence: A person- and variable-oriented study. *Revue Europeenne de Psycho, 61*, 1–11.
Miranda, D., Gaudrea, P., Debrosse, R., Morizot, J., & Kirmayer, L. (2012). Music listening and mental health: Variations on internalizing psychopathology. In A. R. M. Raymond, G. Kreutz, & L. Mitchell (Eds.), *Music, health and wellbeing* (pp. 513–530). New York: Oxford University Press.
North, A. C., & Hargreaves, D. J. (1999). Music and adolescent identity. *Music Education Research, 1*(1), 75–92.
Pennebaker, J. W., Mayne, T. J., & Francis, M. E. (1997). Linguistic predictors of adaptive bereavement. *Journal of Personality and Social Psychology, 72*(4), 863–871.
Peterson, R. J., Safer, M. A., & Jobes, D. A. (2008). The impact of suicidal rock music lyrics on youth: An investigation of individual differences. *Archives of Suicide Research, 12*(2), 161–169.
Rentfrow, P. J., & Gosling, S. D. (2006). Message in a ballad: The role of music preferences in interpersonal perception. *Psychological Science, 17*(3), 236–242.
Rose, A. J. (2002). Co-rumination in the friendships of girls and boys. *Child Development, 73*(6), 1830–1843.
Rose, A. J., Carlson, W., & Waller, E. M. (2007). Prospective associations of co-rumination with friendship and emotional adjustment: Considering the socioemotional trade-offs of co-rumination. *Developmental Psychology, 43*(4), 1019–1031.
Rustad, R. A., Small, J. E., Jobes, D. A., Safer, M. A., & Peterson, R. J. (2003). The impact of rock videos and music with suicidal content on thoughts and attitudes about suicide. *Suicide and Life-Threatening Behavior, 33*(2), 120–131.
Salganik, M. J., Dodds, P. S., & Watts, D. J. (2006). Experimental study of inequality and unpredictability in an artificial cultural market. *Science, 311*, 854–856.
Selfhout, M. H., Branje, S. J., ter Bogt, T. F., & Meeus, W. H. (2009). The role of music preferences in early adolescents' friendship formation and stability. *Journal of Adolescence, 32*(1), 95–107.

Tarrant, M., North, A. C., & Hargreaves, D. J. (2001). Social categorization, self-esteem, and the estimated musical preferences of male adolescents. *The Journal of Social Psychology, 141*(5), 565–581.

Tausczik, Y. R., & Pennebaker, J. W. (2010). The psychological meaning of words: LIWC and computerized text analysis methods. *Journal of Language and Social Psychology, 29*(1), 24–54.

Trapnell, P. D., & Campbell, J. D. (1999). Private self-consciousness and the five-factor model of personality: Distinguishing rumination from reflection. *Journal of Personality and Social Psychology, 76*(2), 284–304.

Trehub, S., & Trainor, L. (1998). Singing to infants: Lullabies and play songs. In L. P. Lipsitt, C. K. Tovee-Collier, & H. Hayne (Eds.), *Advances in infancy research* (Vol. 12, pp. 43–78). Santa Barbara, CA: Greenwood Publishing Group.

Triplett, N. (1898). The dynamogenic factors in pacemaking and competition. *The American Journal of Psychology, 9*(4), 507–533.

Vingerhoets, A. J. J. M., & Becht, M. C. (1997). The ISAC study: Some preliminary findings. Paper presented at the *Annual meeting of the American Psychosomatic Society,* Santa Fe, NM.

Vreeke, G. J., & Van der Mark, I. L. (2003). Empathy, an integrative model. *New Ideas in Psychology, 21*(3), 177–207.

Wells, A., & Hakanen, E. A. (1991). The emotional use of popular music by adolescents. *Journalism & Mass Communication Quarterly, 68*(3), 445–454.

Wild, B., Erb, M., Eyb, B., Bartels, M., & Grodd, W. (2003). Why are smiles contagious? An fMRI study of the interaction between perception of facial affect and facial movements. *Psychiatry Research: Neuroimaging, 123*, 17–36.

Wiltermuth, S. S. (2012). Synchronous activity boosts compliance with requests to aggress. *Journal of Experimental Social Psychology, 48*(1), 453–456.

Zajonc, R. B., & Sales, S. M. (1966). Social facilitation of dominant and subordinate responses. *Journal of Experimental Social Psychology, 2*(2), 160–168.

11

Nostalgia and Mixed Emotions in Response to Music

What are Mixed Emotions?

Many important milestone events in our lives seem to be accompanied by both positive and negative emotions. For example, the achievement of a major life goal may leave an individual feeling pleased that they have reached their objective while sad to be leaving behind an enjoyable phase of their life (Aaker, Drolet, & Griffin, 2008). As discussed in Chap. 2, people sometimes report emotions in response to music that appear to reflect both positive and negative affect as well. The evidence discussed in the subsequent chapters has supported the idea that people can experience sadness as pleasurable. However, it remains unclear whether listeners who enjoy listening to sad music are experiencing a distinct form of sadness, an experience of 'everyday' sadness in which displeasure is dissociated, oscillations between positive and negative affect, or the simultaneous experience of both pleasant and unpleasant emotions. Thus, no discussion of the phenomenon of our attraction to sad music would be complete without some discussion of mixed emotions, or the experience of two opposing emotions such as happiness or sadness in synchrony.

S. Garrido, *Why Are We Attracted to Sad Music?*,
DOI 10.1007/978-3-319-39666-8_11

In fact, whether or not it is actually possible to experience mixed emotions has been the subject of much debate in the psychological literature. The eminent Victorian philosopher Alexander Bain (1818–1903) argued that some emotions were so incompatible that they could not occur simultaneously. He asserted, for example, that "confidence and doubt cannot co-exist any more than hot and cold, fire and water, or acid and alkali" (1865, p. 546). Socrates, on the other hand, is reported by Plato (in *Philetus*) to have spoken at length about "mixed pleasures", or pleasures that can include some degree of pain.

However, as described in Chap. 2, commonly accepted models of emotion such as the circumplex model (Russell, 1979) tend to conceptualize emotions as consisting of two dimensions—arousal and valence—on which all emotions can be mapped. According to such models, valence is a single dimension on which positive or pleasurable emotions exist at one end of the continuum, while negative or unpleasant emotions exist at the opposite end. The two are thus mutually exclusive. The argument that positive and negative emotions lie at opposite ends of a continuum, however, is inherently problematic since logically it suggests that anything but the most intense form of happiness is accompanied by some level of sadness, and excludes the possibility of neutral affective states altogether (Larsen & McGraw, 2011).

In recent decades a number of empirical studies have investigated the possibility of mixed emotions occurring simultaneously. Eshkol Rafaeli and colleagues (2007) found that individuals demonstrated differing capacities for affective synchrony (overlapping experiences of positive and negative affective states), for a-synchrony (independently fluctuating levels of positive and negative emotions) and for de-synchrony (positive and negative affect operating as bipolar opposites). According to the authors, these capacities were stable dispositional traits that were associated with particular cognitive representations of self and emotions.

Mixed emotions have also been documented in response to music and in other aesthetic contexts. In one study, for example, the film *Life is Beautiful* was found to evoke mixed emotional experiences in viewers (Larsen, McGraw, & Cacioppo, 2001). Across two studies, Patrick Hunter and colleagues (2008, 2010) found that even where not directly asked to think about mixed emotions, participants who listen to music with mixed affective cues (e.g., a slow tempo but a major key or a fast tempo but a minor key) are more likely to report simultaneous experiences of positive and negative emotions than they are when listening to music with matched affective cues (e.g., major key and fast tempo).

Contemporary research in neuropsychology tends to support the notion that positive and negative emotions are not bivariate, but are instead separable dimensions that rely on parallel systems of approach and avoidance (Cacciopo, Gardner, & Berntson, 1999). Facial expressions also provide evidence of mixed emotions. For example, one study found that scores on a self-report measure of ambivalent attitudes toward smoking were positively correlated with the display of facial expressions that demonstrated mixed emotions when watching a burning cigarette (Griffin & Sayette, 2008). Thus, it seems that while positive and negative emotions are most often experienced as dichotomous, it is possible to experience them simultaneously (Rafaeli et al., 2007).

Individual differences exist in the propensity to experience mixed emotions as well as in the level of comfort one feels when having such an experience. Chin Ming Hui and colleagues (2009), for example, have found that dialectical thinkers—people who have a greater ability to accept and embrace contradictory emotions—were more likely to experience mixed emotions than non-dialectical thinkers. Dialectical thinking tends to be higher in both Asian cultures and in older individuals (Williams & Aaker, 2002). Studies in consumer behavior have also shown that people with high levels of abstract thinking respond better to advertisements that make mixed emotional appeals (Hong & Lee, 2010). Similarly, impulsivity appears to influence the experience of mixed emotions in response to indulgent consumption (Ramanathan & Williams, 2007). Thus, personality plays a role in an individual's proclivity for experiencing mixed emotions.

Whether one experiences mixed emotions or a single emotion may also change depending on the stressfulness of an individual's situation. Alex Zautra and colleagues (2000) found that affective experiences became more polarized in situations of high stress. They argue that the processing of multiple emotions at the same time utilizes more of the available resources than bipolar processing, and thus in stressful situations, when resources need to be conserved, individuals tend to differentiate a single emotion. However, Karin Coifman and colleagues (2007) have found that resilient individuals tended to be more capable of processing complex affective experiences and experienced less polarity of affect, a fact which contributed to their ability to cope with adverse life events. Rafaeli and colleagues (2007) similarly argue that holding an "evaluatively integrated view" of the world (p. 931) can lead to an individual being able to moderate their affective responses more effectively.

It may, in fact, be that such individuals actually experience less stress because of their ability to accept ambiguity. Zautra's study, for example, did not report how comfortable their participants were with the experience of mixed emotions. Studies reveal that people often respond to experiences of mixed emotions with discomfort and tend to try to find ways to resolve their feelings of conflict (Williams & Aaker, 2002). This conflict tends to drive people to reappraise events according to a single dominant emotion, meaning that, over time, experiences of mixed emotions become remembered as more unipolar (Aaker et al., 2008). Cultural perceptions of the undesirability of cognitive or emotional dissonance might prompt a desire to rationalize the experience (Williams & Aaker, 2002).

It is possible, therefore, that the participants in Zautra's study reported higher levels of stress because of their relatively high level of discomfort with ambivalence while tending to distort reports of their affective experiences. Participants who were more comfortable with ambivalence, on the other hand, may have been more successful both at moderating their experience of stress and in accurately reporting their experience of mixed emotions. It may be that while situations that are only mildly urgent benefit from the ability to evaluate multiple perspectives, situations of high stress more often require rapid reactions and thus clear and singular emotional experiences are more adaptive in such circumstances. However, appraisals of a situation as highly stressful may in turn be fed by one's individual level of discomfort with ambiguous affective responses.

Thus, while most people tend to primarily report the experience of single emotions, there is considerable evidence that the experience of mixed emotions is both biologically possible and reported as occurring in response to many events and stimuli, including music. Whether one tends to report experiencing mixed emotions is influenced by both cultural perceptions of the normalcy of ambiguity, and one's personality.

Arguments suggest that the experience of mixed emotions is adaptive and displays an ability to integrate multiple perspectives in evaluating a situation. Alternative arguments suggest that in situations of high stress the processing of single emotions is more adaptive. However, the level of comfort that one feels with ambiguous affective reactions may influence both how individuals report their emotional experiences and also the cognitive efforts made to resolve affective conflicts.

What is Nostalgia?

One specific example of a mixed emotion that is prominently reported in studies about music listening is that of nostalgia, which is often described as being a 'bittersweet' experience. It is frequently experienced by both young and old across cultures (Wildschut, Sedikides, Arndt, & Routledge, 2006), and is one of the most frequent experiences described when listening to sad music. Annemieke Van den Tol and Jane Edwards (2013) reported that when feeling sad, study participants selected sad music to listen to, in part because of its power to facilitate the retrieval of episodic memories. Music is, in fact, one of the most powerful triggers of nostalgic memories (Barrett et al., 2010).

Nostalgia was originally regarded as a serious pathological disorder (Dickinson & Erben, 2006). It was first documented by the Swiss physician Johannes Hofer (1934, originally 1678), who observed it in the case of soldiers who developed symptoms of melancholy and extreme homesickness when fighting far from their homeland. Instances of nostalgia were also recorded in the nineteenth century in cases of children taken from their mothers to live with their wet-nurses, who were subsequently returned to their mothers and separated from the wet-nurse to whom they had become accustomed (Roth, 1991). Early in the twentieth century, psychoanalytic approaches began to see all cases of nostalgia as being associated with the loss of the mother's breast or regarded as an expression of the oedipal complex (Kaplan, 1987).

The understanding of nostalgia as a pathological condition persisted until later in the twentieth century, when the term took on its current meaning (Loveland, Smeesters, & Mandel, 2010). Hence a more modern understanding, as defined by *The New Oxford Dictionary of English* ("Nostalgia," 1998), is of nostalgia as "a sentimental longing or wistful affection for the past". Rather than being considered a disorder or ailment, nostalgia is now regarded as a normal and common experience, with over 80 percent of British undergraduate students reporting incidents of nostalgia at least once a week (Wildschut et al., 2006).

Nostalgia is often triggered by feelings of loneliness and depression. Tim Wildschut and colleagues (2006), for example, found that participants were more prone to nostalgia when in a negative mood than when they were experiencing a positive or neutral mood. Nostalgia-proneness has also been found to be associated with the Sadness dimension of the Affective Neuroscience Personality Scale and with Neuroticism from the Big Five Personality Index (Barrett et al., 2010).

It has been argued that when people feel either sad or socially isolated, nostalgia can serve a number of positive psychological functions. For example, it has been argued that nostalgic remembering helps an individual to reinterpret and recover the past (Cassia, 2000), to evoke positive affect and to counteract a negative mood (Wildschut et al., 2006), to increase self-esteem and foster stronger social connections (Wildschut, Sedikides, Routledge, Arndt, & Cordaro, 2010), to cope with existential threat (Sedikides, Wildschut, Arndt, & Routledge, 2008), to find meaning (Routledge et al., 2011), to construct identity (Khorsandi & Saarikallio, 2013), to satisfy a need to belong by reconnecting with people from the past (Loveland et al., 2010), and to cope with discontinuity in life (Sedikides, Wildschut, Gaertner, Routledge, & Arndt, 2008). Thus, nostalgia appears to be a resource that is accessed as a psychological buffer in times of distress, and is associated with a number of adaptive coping strategies (Batcho, 2013; Garrido, 2016).

Despite these positive psychological functions, nostalgia is understood to be a complex emotion (in comparison with primary emotions such as anger or fear), which can involve both positive and negative affect. Nostalgia entails both the enjoyment of remembering the past and the painful knowledge that the past is irretrievable. The yearning for the past can be both for past stages and events in one's own life (personal nostalgia) and for past historical periods through which one has not necessarily lived (historical nostalgia) (Holbrook, 1993; Marchegiani & Phau,

2013). Discontentment with modern society may lead some to find comfort in dwelling in past periods of history when life was somewhat simpler (Lowenthal, 1981). The allure of both historical and personal nostalgia can be seen in the popularity of vintage fashion, period dramas and movies, and the revival of interest in pop culture personalities and items commemorating them amongst youths who were not alive when their idol was first popular (Galt, 2006).

There is also additional evidence that nostalgia does not always have psychologically healthy effects. For example, in complicated grief, obsession with loss of the idealized past can worsen depression (Nolen-Hoeksema, Parker, & Larson, 1994). An over-obsession with the past may also result in negative outcomes for migrants, leading to a failure to adjust to new surroundings and increased feelings of isolation (Lijtmaer, 2001; Zinchenko, 2011). Some forms of schizophrenia also involve a delusional system of idealized memories of the past, in which the sufferer can become completely absorbed (Moritz, Woodward, Cuttler, & Whitman, 2004).

Other studies similarly report differing outcomes for nostalgic remembering. Constantine Sedikides et al. (2010), for example, found that nostalgia enabled a sense of self-continuity for happy but not unhappy persons. They thus argue that "when happiness is low, engaging in nostalgic reverie about the past may make the present seem particularly bleak by comparison" (p. 234). Bas Verplanken (2012) similarly observed that even though nostalgia initially resulted in an increase in positive affect in his sample, it ultimately increased anxiety and depression in people who were habitual worriers. Interestingly, Philip Zimbardo and John Boyd (1999) found that one's perspective on the past can influence the effect of nostalgic remembering on an individual. They argue that people who tend to think a great deal about the past can view the past in either positive or negative terms. In their study, it was having a negative perspective of the past that was correlated with depression. Other studies have also shown that individual differences exist both in the content of nostalgic memories, the functions it serves and whether the consequences of nostalgia are positive or negative (Hart et al., 2011; Iyer & Jetten, 2011).

These studies suggest that despite the potential psychological functions nostalgia can fill, it does not have a wholesale positive effect. Frederick

Barrett et al. (2010) thus proposed two distinctive nostalgia-prone personality profiles: the brooding, neurotic ruminator, and the individual whose thoughts about the past are motivated by curiosity and wonder. Readers who have been following the narrative of this volume from the beginning will likely immediately recognize the similarity between these archetypes and the two types of private self-attention described by Paul Trapnell and Jennifer Campbell (1999): rumination and reflectiveness (see Chap. 5 for more information). According to Trapnell and Campbell, rumination is a maladaptive focus on negative and pessimistic thoughts that is strongly predictive of depression, while reflectiveness is a form of self-analysis that is highly adaptive and psychologically healthy. This distinction may prove to be an effective way of further understanding the 'bittersweet' effects of nostalgia and the mixed outcomes of nostalgic remembering indicated in the literature.

Nostalgia and Sad Music

Nostalgia is one of the most prominent emotions evoked by music (Zentner et al., 2008). It can be a strong catalyst for the memory of particular events, people, places or emotions. This effect is often known as the 'Darling, they're playing our song' phenomenon—a reference to the fact that songs so often become associated with particular relationships or periods of time in our lives. In fact, it has been found that nostalgia is triggered more often in the context of music than in non-musical contexts. Patrick Juslin et al. (2008), for instance, conducted a study of 32 college students using experience sampling methods and found that students reported feeling nostalgia and longing more often when listening to music than when engaging in other activities, particularly during solitary listening.

Two factors appear to influence whether or not a particular piece of music will trigger an episode of nostalgia in the listener: the autobiographical relevance of the music to the individual, and how 'nostalgia-prone' they are (Barrett et al., 2010). My own studies tend to confirm this. In a series of five case studies that examined why people listen to sad music (Garrido & Schubert, 2011), four of the five participants that we interviewed reported that sad music often evoked nostalgic memories. The sadness experienced with nostalgia-evoking music was often more intense than songs that were sad in a more general way, leading some of the participants to avoid listening to such songs except in particular circumstances such as where they wanted to process their feelings about the events they were remembering.

Our participants reported that memories could be triggered by music via several kinds of autobiographical links: songs that had been heard on a specific occasion; songs with themes relating to a certain situation or event of which the individual has personal memories; songs that were liked by a particular other person of whom memories were evoked; and songs with a general emotional tone that tended to provoke memories of a time in which similar emotions were experienced. For example, one participant whose father had died had specific songs that brought back potent memories of times spent playing music with him. However, for other participants, music about parties or holidays that were less specifically related to actual events could trigger memories of time passed with friends or family road trips, for example. Thus, even where the music was not related specifically to a particular episodic memory, it could still evoke nostalgic connections.

How likely an individual is to feel nostalgic can be quantified by various psychometric measures of nostalgia-proneness. The Southampton Nostalgia Scale (SNS; Routledge, Arndt, Sedikides, & Wildschut, 2008), for example, asks participants to answer five questions relating to the frequency with which they experience episodes of nostalgic remembering. Measured in this way, nostalgia-proneness is believed to reflect a stable, trait-level disposition toward nostalgia. Batcho's Nostalgia Inventory (BNI; Batcho, 1995), on the other hand, asks respondents to rate a number of items from when they were younger, such as family, friends, music, or the way society was, according to how much they miss those things. Thus this scale captures the degree of longing that an individual experiences in relation to things from their past.

The SNS was used in a study I conducted with Emery Schubert (2013), in which we explored the connection between nostalgia-proneness and a liking for sad music. Interestingly, we found significant positive correlations between absorption and nostalgia-proneness, suggesting that a person with strong tendencies toward absorption is likely to experience more frequent episodes of nostalgic remembering than people with low scores. We also found correlations between nostalgia-proneness and both rumination and reflectiveness. In addition, nostalgia-proneness was significantly correlated with a liking for sad music, as measured by the LSMS,[1] although it was a lesser influence on LSMS scores than absorption or reflectiveness. These results tend to support the idea discussed above regarding the two archetypal forms of nostalgic remembering, as well as suggesting that listening to sad music can trigger such remembering.

In a subsequent study (Garrido & Schubert, 2015a) participants listened to a self-selected piece of sad music and answered questions relating to how the music had made them feel as well as completing other mood measures including a short form of the POMS (Curran et al., 1995). In relation to how the music made them feel, one question asked participants to rate the statement: "The music reminded me of past events. It was a bittersweet nostalgic experience." Regression analyses on this item demonstrated that both rumination and reflectiveness scores were significant predictors of feeling nostalgic in response to the self-selected sad song. Interestingly, baseline scores on the Confusion subscale of the POMS were also a significant predictor, suggesting that nostalgic remembering in response to sad music is less likely to have positive outcomes where it is associated with some cognitive and emotional disturbances or ambiguity. Thus, it appears that, as suggested by Barrett et al. (2010), nostalgia can be associated with both healthy and unhealthy coping styles and reflects some emotional conflict and confusion.

My colleague Jane Davidson and I (2014) set out to further explore the connection between nostalgia and music use in a study of 213 undergraduate students. Our participants completed a survey which included both the SNS and the BNI, as well as answering questions about their music preferences and questions about the degree to which they enjoyed experiences of nostalgia. We examined these measures in relation to genre preferences. While there were no significant differences between groups on the frequency of their nostalgic experiences as measured by the SNS or the degree to which they missed the past as measured by the BNI,

[1] See Chap. 6 for more information.

participants who reported a preference for New Age music were the least likely to enjoy nostalgic listening of the sample, while those who preferred Heavy Metal music reported enjoying remembering the past.

This interesting difference in music choices could be understood as reflecting the different coping styles of the participants. Heavy metal music typically involves themes of death, personal trauma and other "dark and depressing topics" (Weinstein, 1991) and has been described as a "subculture of alienation" (Arnett, 1993). A liking for metal music has also been found to be associated with depression (Doak, 2003; Lacourse et al., 2001). Listening to New Age music, on the other hand, has been found to produce increased feelings of ease, restedness, thankfulness and love and to decrease feelings of hostility and tension (McCraty, Barrios-Choplin, Atkinson, & Tomasino, 1998). These associations between genre preferences and nostalgia ratings confirm the ideas presented in previous studies that people who have a struggle with their mental health are attracted both to remembering the past and to the exploration of dark themes in their music, while those with low nostalgia-proneness prefer to use more centering and calming forms of music to cope with stress. However, a correlational study of this nature cannot confirm the direction of the relationship, i.e., whether the attraction to nostalgia contributes to affective disturbances or whether it is sought in time of disturbance as a resource for counteracting it. This was an issue that required further examination.

Nostalgia and Rumination

That nostalgia can form part of both healthy and unhealthy coping mechanisms was further supported by a series of two studies that I conducted (Garrido, 2016). In the first of these, 85 males and 128 female undergraduate students with a mean age of 21.5 years completed an online survey that included the BNI, the SNS, and Trapnell and Campbell's Rumination–Reflection Questionnaire (RRQ; 1999). They also completed the Beck Depression Inventory (BDI; Beck, Ward, Mendelson, Mock, & Erbaugh, 1961), a scale that has been widely used as a measure of depression in both clinical and normative populations.

As expected, rumination was correlated with both measures of nostalgia-proneness and with depression. Interestingly, depression as measured by the BDI was correlated only with the BNI and not with the SNS. The reader may recall that the BNI measures the degree to which a person longs for the past, while the SNS measures the frequency that an individual experiences nostalgic remembering. This indicates that the frequency with which one experiences nostalgia is not related to depression levels. Rather, it is the strength of one's longing for the past that is more closely associated with depression. It was further found that the direct effect of nostalgia on depression levels dropped when controlling for rumination, suggesting that the relationship between nostalgia-proneness and depression is at least partially mediated by a ruminative thinking style. Thus, it seems that where nostalgia and rumination occurs together, the outcome may be one of increased depression.

These results illuminate the possibility that people with ruminative tendencies may tend to focus more on negative memories, view the past in a more negative light, or compare the past more unfavourably with the present—thinking patterns that could conceivably exacerbate a depressed mood. Such a conclusion is supported by studies that have found that rumination is associated with negatively biased memory recall (Lyubomirsky et al., 1998) and a general tendency to interpret stimuli as negative (Raes et al., 2006).

Given the evident relationship between rumination and nostalgia, it is also possible that other coping styles could be involved in how people use music to facilitate remembering the past in times of psychological distress. In addition to rumination, other maladaptive coping styles can include avoidance, escape and denial, while adaptive coping can take the form of problem-solving behaviours, seeking social support or using humour, among other things (Carver et al., 1989; Thompson et al., 2010).

However, one difficulty with investigating the effect of nostalgia on ruminators is the low level of awareness that many people have of the actual effects of their behavior on mood. Studies suggest a tendency on the part of ruminators to rationalize ruminative behavior and to claim benefits from engaging in rumination despite the fact that it prolongs their depression. For example, Barnhofer et al. (2006) reported that participants in their study believed that ruminating on past mistakes would help them to better understand their emotions and avoid making similar mistakes in the future. Similarly, participants in Watkins and Baracaia's study (2001) believed that they would benefit from the increase in the self-awareness of rumination. However, the fact that rumination worsens or perpetuates a depressed mood is well established in the literature (Nolen-Hoeksema & Morrow, 1993). Several studies have reported a mismatch between actual mood outcomes of particular behavior and the self-perceived effects in the case of people with impaired mood regulatory capacities (Garrido & Schubert, 2015b; McFerran et al., 2013).

One way to overcome this difficulty could be to use implicit measures of affective state. Implicit measures attempt to assess affective state indirectly, based on the assumption that participants unconsciously display information about their own affective state when engaging in other tasks such as rating the affective content of words (Quirin, Kazen, & Kuhl, 2009), word-stem completion and word categorization (DeWall & Baumeister, 2007), or an examination of overall processing style (Ruys & Stapel, 2008). Such measures enable mood to be assessed without participant awareness so that results are not distorted either intentionally or by a lack of awareness of one's own affective state (Jostman, Koole, van der Wulp, & Fockenberg, 2006).

These issues were addressed in a second study that I conducted (Garrido, 2016), which aimed to test the affective outcomes of listening to nostalgic music using both direct and implicit measures, and to explore interactions between coping style and nostalgia. Participants in this study were recruited via a website hosted by the Australian Broadcasting Company (ABC) and promoted by various ABC radio stations and print media. A sample of 715 participants with a mean age of 39.5 years responded and completed an online survey. Embedded in the survey was a quasi-experimental question designed to induce feelings of nostalgia in participants while doing the survey by asking them to listen to a self-selected piece of music that makes them feel nostalgic. A time stamp feature in the survey software acted as a compliance check so that I could assess whether or not people had spent a reasonable enough time on the task to have completed it as requested.

Prior to retrieving their self-selected music participants were asked whether they thought the music they were about to listen to would lift or lower their mood. They were also asked to indicate their current mood by selecting from a list of seven adjectives. After listening to their self-selected nostalgic music, participants were then questioned about its affective impact on them, which also acted as a check of the degree to which nostalgia had effectively been induced. In addition to the BNI and the RRQ, the Coping Orientations to Problems Experienced Scale (COPE; Carver et al., 1989) was used, which contains subscales to assess both positive and negative coping styles. An implicit mood measure was also included after the nostalgic mood induction. The Implicit Positive and Negative Affect Test (IPANAT; Quirin et al., 2009) is designed to indirectly assess positive and negative affect by asking participants to rate the extent to which words from an artificial language convey certain emotions. Scores are then aggregated to form positive and negative affect subscales.

Results indicated that there were associations between nostalgia-proneness as measured by the BNI and both positive and negative coping styles on the COPE. The BNI was also correlated with rumination and with a negative affective outcome from listening to the self-selected nostalgic music. A negative affective outcome was furthermore, positively correlated with Rumination, Denial and Behavioural Disengagement, and negatively correlated with the adaptive coping style of Active coping. These correlations give a preliminary indication that nostalgia is associated with both positive and negative coping styles, but that a negative outcome might be more likely in the case of people with maladaptive coping styles such as rumination or denial.

The majority of participants reported being in a positive mood prior to listening to their nostalgic music selection. Only 84 of the participants reported a predominantly negative affective impact from the music. However, the implicit mood measures indicated the presence of a higher level of negative moods after music listening than the questions that asked directly about the effect of the music. This tends to suggest some disconnect between the self-perceived and actual affective outcomes as suggested in previous studies (Garrido & Schubert, 2015a, 2015b). A regression model confirmed that rumination was predictive of a negative affective outcome from listening to the nostalgic music, and an inverse relationship between negative affective outcome and an active coping style was found.

The study confirmed associations found in the studies described above between nostalgia-proneness and both adaptive and maladaptive coping styles, particularly rumination. These results suggest that while nostalgia may provide many positive psychological benefits resulting in an improved mood for the majority of people, where individuals tend towards maladaptive coping styles, the outcome of nostalgic episodes may be less positive. These results are in harmony with other studies cited above which confirm the idea that nostalgia does not have positive effects on all people.

Previous studies have established that people in a depressed mood are strongly attracted to nostalgic remembering and that engaging in it increases positive affect. This study confirmed these findings, with the majority of participants demonstrating positive affective outcomes in both self-perceived effects of listening to nostalgic music and in implicit mood measures. However, the results also demonstrate that this is not true of all people. It was also evident from this study that, as in other studies relating to maladaptive behavior, participants were either not aware of actual mood effects or tend to rationalize and justify their maladaptive behavior (Barnhofer et al., 2006). Thus, when directly questioned about the effect of the nostalgic music on their mood, some people reported a positive effect while implicit mood measures captured indications of a negative affective state.

The finding that the relationship between nostalgia-proneness and depression is at least partially mediated by nostalgia suggests that where there are tendencies to depression, nostalgic remembering may tend to exacerbate patterns of negative thinking, resulting in less positive affective outcomes. Nostalgia may also form part of other maladaptive coping strategies by, for example, providing further escape from present reality by people with high scores in denial. These results indicate that individuals prone to unhealthy thought patterns may not experience the same benefits from remembering the past that other people do, despite what they report. It may be that although the immediate effect of remembering happy episodes in the past is enjoyable, the dichotomy between the perceived ideal of the past and the reality of the present may ultimately result in increased depression or anxiety (Verplanken, 2012). Whether the nostalgic episode results in an experience of positive or negative outcomes may greatly depend on the individual's habitual way of viewing the past, rather than the frequency with which they indulge in nostalgia.

The role of habitual coping styles and thinking patterns was further highlighted by a study in which myself and my colleagues, Emery Schubert and Daniel Bangert (Garrido et al., 2016), collected music listening diaries from 176 participants who had been assigned a playlist (either happy or sad) to listen to over a four-week period.[2] In that study, both songs with lyrics and instrumental music were able to trigger potent memories in participants, and feelings of nostalgia, although song lyrics did appear to have a more powerful effect. Content analysis of the diary entries revealed a higher frequency of discussion about memories in the sad music listening group, suggesting that sad music tended to be more evocative of nostalgic feelings than happy music. Much of the time participants described this as a positive experience:

> I would say this song had the most positive effect on my mood. I believe this is because it creates a sense of nostalgia and reminds me of spending time at home with my Dad as this is the kind of music he enjoys (Female, aged 20).

For other participants the effect of nostalgia was to increase feelings of sadness or discontent. For example, some participants found that the music increased feelings of homesickness, or strong feelings of missing people from whom they were separated. For others, the knowledge that the past is gone forever intensified this negative effect: "I experienced a profound melancholy not because I'm yearning for that moment to return, but because of the sheer finality and irrevocability of these moments" (Male, aged 21). Another participant described the bittersweet effect of memories, which ultimately resulted in a dampening of his mood: "'Tiny Dancer' reminded me of my deceased Uncle and that gave me happy and sad memories … I was incredibly burdened by these memories, in fact I was a little number by the end of the day" (Male, aged 22).

As is evident from the words of the above participant, music that prompted nostalgic memories tended to have a stronger affective impact

[2] This study is further described in Chap. 9.

than music that stimulated other thoughts. Where the memories were positive, the affective outcomes also tended to be positive, while where negative memories were triggered the affective outcome of music listening tended to be long-lasting and negative. The contrast can be illustrated by the following two examples:

> It reminded me of a friend that I haven't seen in a while. He used to sing this kind of music. So this song made me reminisce a little and it felt good. (Female, aged 24)
>
> The first emotion to come to mind when listening was nostalgia because this song was introduced to me by a friend, and as a result that friend came to mind. It then blended into some sadness upon the realization that we grew apart over the years due to life being life. (Male, aged 23)

Further qualitative analysis revealed that where sad memories, dissatisfaction with the present, or ruminative thinking were triggered by the music, the affective outcome tended to be negative. On the other hand, where positively perceived memories, and optimistic thoughts about the present or oneself were triggered, the affective outcome tended to be positive.

These examples illustrate that a variety of affective conditions seem to have been experienced in connection with nostalgic memories, including experiences of single emotions, and both sequential and simultaneous experiences of opposite emotions. Whether the emotions experienced were predominantly positive or negative depended largely on the perspective the individual took of the past. This is, in turn, likely largely related to the habitual thinking patterns that each individual has developed for coping with adverse events. While this research reveals that the frequency of nostalgic listening is associated with both rumination and reflectiveness, and therefore both adaptive and maladaptive coping styles, only the degree to which one longs for the past—which suggests a level of discontent with the present—was predictive of depression.

Thus, it seems that just as the healthy tendency toward self-reflection becomes distorted in people with depression resulting in excessive thinking about negative feelings, so the psychologically useful process of reconnecting with one's past by indulging in nostalgic remembering can also become disrupted where there are tendencies to depression. Whereas a person who is experiencing distress or loneliness in the present may use memories as a way of feeling more connected with people or of reliving positive experiences, in people with tendencies to depression thoughts about the past become a source of discontent and can result in mood deterioration where the focus is on negative aspects of the past, or the irretrievable loss of things from the past. Furthermore, nostalgia can reflect some level of emotional conflict and confusion, and individuals may have varying abilities to tolerate this ambiguity.

Sad music appears to be one of the most potent triggers of nostalgic memories, and is one of the most frequent reasons that people report for listening to sad music when experiencing some distress. However, the effect of such remembering is not universally positive, and appears to be closely linked to individual differences such as rumination, which has also proven to be an important variable in the studies discussed in previous chapters of this volume.

Falling in love is also one of the most potent emotional experiences that a human being will ever have. However, it too is accompanied from time to time by mixed emotions and feelings of ambiguity. The following chapter will explore the use of sad music to cope with situations of heartbreak or unhappy love.

References

Aaker, J., Drolet, A., & Griffin, D. (2008). Recalling mixed emotions. *Journal of Consumer Research, 35*, 268–279.

Arnett, J. (1993). Three profiles of heavy metal fans: A taste for sensation and a subculture of alienation. *Qualitative Sociology, 16*(4), 423–443.

Bain, A. (1865). *The emotions and the will.* London: Longmans, Green.

Barnhofer, T., Kuehn, E.-M., de Jong-Meyer, R., & Williams, J. M. G. (2006). Beliefs about the benefits of rumination in depressed men and women with and without a history of assault. *Behavioral and Cognitive Psychotherapy, 35*, 317–324.

Barrett, F. S., Grimm, K. J., Robins, R. W., Wildschut, T., Sedikides, C., & Janata, P. (2010). Music-evoked nostalgia: Affect, memory, and personality. *Emotion, 10*(3), 390–403.

Batcho, K. I. (1995). Nostalgia: A psychological perspective. *Perceptual and Motor Skills, 80*, 131–143.
Batcho, K. I. (2013). Nostalgia: Retreat or support in difficult times? *The American Journal of Psychology, 126*(3), 355–367.
Beck, A. T., Ward, C. H., Mendelson, M., Mock, J., & Erbaugh, J. (1961). An inventory for measuring depresion. *Archives of General Psychiatry, 4*, 561–571.
Cacciopo, J. T., Gardner, W. L., & Berntson, G. G. (1999). The affect system has parallel and integrative processing components: Form follows function. *Journal of Personality and Social Psychology, 76*(5), 839–855.
Carver, C. S., Scheier, M. F., & Weintraub, J. K. (1989). Assessing coping strategies: A theoretically based approach. *Journal of Personality and Social Psychology, 56*, 267–283.
Cassia, P. S. (2000). Exoticizing discoveries and extraordinary experiences: "Traditional" music, modernity, and nostalgia in Malta and other Mediterranean societies. *Ethnomusicology, 44*(2), 281–301.
Coifman, K. G., Bonanno, G. A., & Rafaeli, E. (2007). Affect dynamics, bereavement and resilience to loss. *Journal of Happines Studies, 8*, 371–392.
Curran, S. L., Andrykowski, M. A., & Studts, J. L. (1995). Short form of the profile of mood states (POMS-SF): Psychometric information. *Psychological Assessment, 7*(1), 80–83.
Davidson, J., & Garrido, S. (2014). *My life as a playlist*. Perth: University of Western Australia Publishing.
DeWall, C. N., & Baumeister, R. F. (2007). From terror to joy: Automatic tuning to positive affective information following mortality salience. *Psychological Science, 18*, 984–990.
Dickinson, H., & Erben, M. (2006). Nostalgia and autobiography: The past in the present. *Auto-Biography, 14*, 223–244.
Doak, B. A. (2003). Relationships between adolescent psychiatric diagnoses, music preferences and drug preferences. *Music Therapy Perspectives, 21*(2), 69–76.
Galt, R. (2006). *The new European cinema: Redrawing the map*. New York: Columbia University Press.
Garrido, S. (2016). The painful past: Is nostalgia a healthy coping mechanism or rumination? *Journal of Personality & Social Psychology*. Retrieved from http://dx.doi.org/10.1016/j.paid.2016.07.021.
Garrido, S., & Schubert, E. (2011). Negative emotion in music: What is the attraction? A qualitative study. *Empirical Musicology Review, 6*(4), 214–230.

Garrido, S., & Schubert, E. (2015a). Moody melodies: Do they cheer us up? A study of the effect of sad music on mood. *Psychology of Music, 43*(2), 244–261. doi:10.1177/0305735613501938.

Garrido, S., & Schubert, E. (2015b). Music and people with tendencies to depression. *Music Perception, 32*(4), 313–321. doi:10.1525/MP.2015.32.4.313.

Garrido, S., Schubert, E., & Bangert, D. (2016). Musical prescriptions for mood improvement: An experimental study. *The Arts in Psychotherapy, 51*, 46–53. doi:10.1016/j.aip.2016.09.002.

Griffin, K., & Sayette, M. (2008). Facial reactions to smoking cues relate to ambivalence about smoking. *Psychology of Addictive Behaviour, 22*(4), 551–556.

Hart, C. M., Sedikides, C., Wildschut, T., Arndt, J., Routledge, C., & Vingerhoets, J. J. M. (2011). Nostalgic recollections of high and low narcissists. *Journal of Research in Personality, 45*(2), 238–242.

Hofer, J. (1934 [1678]). Medical dissertation of nostalgia. *Bulletin of Historical Medicine*, 2, 376-391.

Holbrook, M. B. (1993). Nostalgia and consumption preferences: Some emerging patterns of consumer tastes. *Journal of Consumer Research, 20*, 245–256.

Hong, J., & Lee, A. Y. (2010). Feeling mixed but not torn: The moderating role of construal level in mixed emotions appeals. *Journal of Consumer Research, 37*, 456–472.

Hui, C. M., Fok, H. K., & Bond, M. H. (2009). Who feels more ambivalence? Linking dialectical thinking to mixed emotions. *Personality and Individual Differences, 46*, 493–498.

Hunter, P. G., Schellenberg, E. G., & Schimmack, U. (2008). Mixed affective responses to music with conflicting cues. *Cognition & Emotion, 22*(2), 327–352.

Hunter, P. G., Schellenberg, E. G., & Schimmack, U. (2010). Feelings and perceptions of happiness and sadness induced by music: Similarities, differences and mixed emotions. *Psychology of Aesthetics, Creativity and the Arts, 4*(1), 47–56.

Iyer, A., & Jetten, J. (2011). What's left behind: Identity continuity moderates the effect of nostalgia on well-being and life choices. *Journal of Personality and Social Psychology, 101*, 94–108.

Jostman, N., Koole, S. L., van der Wulp, N. Y., & Fockenberg, D. A. (2006). Subliminal affect regulation: The moderating role of action vs state orientation. *European Psychologist, 10*, 209–217.

Juslin, P. N., Liliestrom, S., Västfjäll, D., Barradas, G., & Silva, A. (2008). An experience sampling study of emotional reactions to music: Listener, music, and situation. *Emotion, 8*, 668–683.

Kaplan, H. A. (1987). The psychopathology of nostalgia. *Psychoanalytic Review, 74*(4), 465–486.

Khorsandi, A., & Saarikallio, S. (2013). Music-related nostalgic experiences of young migrants. Paper presented at the *3rd International Conference on Music & Emotion (ICME3)*, Jyväskylä, Finland.

Lacourse, E., Claes, M., & Villeneuve, M. (2001). Heavy metal music and adolescent suicidal risk. *Journal of Youth and Adolescence, 30*(3), 321–332.

Larsen, J. T., & McGraw, A. P. (2011). Further evidence for mixed emotions. *Personality Processes and Individual Differences, 100*(6), 1095–1100.

Larsen, J. T., McGraw, A. P., & Cacioppo, J. T. (2001). Can people feel happy and sad at the same time? *Journal of Personality and Social Psychology, 81*(4), 684–696.

Lijtmaer, R. M. (2001). Splitting and nostalgia in recent immigrants: Psychodynamic considerations. *Journal of the American Academy of Psychoanalysis, 29*(3), 427–438.

Loveland, K. E., Smeesters, D., & Mandel, N. (2010). Still preoccupied with 1995: The need to belong and preference for nostalgic products. *Journal of Consumer Research, 37*, 393–408.

Lowenthal, D. (1981). Dilemmas of preservation. In M. Binney & D. Lowenthal (Eds.), *Our past before us: Why do we save it?* London: Temple Smith.

Lyubomirsky, S., Caldwell, N. D., & Nolen-Hoeksema, S. (1998). Effects of ruminative and distractive responses to depressed mood on retrieval of autobiographical memories. *Journal of Personality and Social Psychology, 75*(1), 166–177.

Marchegiani, C., & Phau, I. (2013). Personal and historical nostalgia—A comparion of common emotions. *Journal of Global Marketing, 26*(3), 137–146.

McCraty, R., Barrios-Choplin, B., Atkinson, M., & Tomasino, D. (1998). The effects of different types of music on mood, tension, and mental clarity. *Alternative Therapies in Health and Medicine, 4*(1), 75–84.

McFerran, K., Garrido, S., & Saarikallio, S. (2013). A critical interpretive synthesis of the literature linking music and adolescent mental health. *Youth & Society*. doi:10.1177/0044118X13501343.

Moritz, S., Woodward, T. S., Cuttler, C., & Whitman, J. C. (2004). False memories in schizophrenia. *Neuropsychology, 18*(2), 276–283.

Nolen-Hoeksema, S., & Morrow, J. (1993). Effects of rumination and distraction on naturally occurring depressed mood. *Cognition & Emotion, 7*(6), 561–570.

Nolen-Hoeksema, S., Parker, L. E., & Larson, J. (1994). Ruminative coping with depressed mood following loss. *Journal of Personality and Social Psychology, 67*(1), 92–104.

Nostalgia. (1998). *The New Oxford Dictionary of English*. Oxford, 1226.

Quirin, M., Kazen, M., & Kuhl, J. (2009). Nonsense sounds happy or helpless: The Implicit Positive and Negative Affect Test (IPANAT). *Journal of Personality and Social Psychology, 97*(3), 500–516.

Raes, F., Hermans, D., & Williams, J. M. G. (2006). Negative bias in the perception of others' facial emotional expressions in major depression: The role of depressive rumination. *Journal of Nervous and Mental Disease, 194*(10), 796–799.

Rafaeli, E., Rogers, G. M., & Revelle, W. (2007). Affective synchrony: Individual differences in mixed emotions. *Personality and Social Psychology Bulletin, 33*, 915–933.

Ramanathan, S., & Williams, P. (2007). Immediate and delayed emotional consequences of indulgence: The moderating influence of personality type on mixed emotions. *Journal of Consumer Research, 34*, 212–223.

Roth, M. S. (1991). Dying of the past: Medical studies of nostalgia in nineteenth century France. *History and Memory, 3*(1), 5–29.

Routledge, C., Arndt, J., Sedikides, C., & Wildschut, T. (2008). A blast from the past: The terror management function of nostalgia. *Journal of Experimental Social Psychology, 44*, 132–140.

Routledge, C., Arndt, J., Wildschut, T., Sedikides, C., Juhl, J., Vingerhoets, A. J. J. M., & Schlotz, W. (2011). The past makes the present meaningful: Nostalgia as an existential resource. *Journal of Personality and Social Psychology, 101*(3), 638–652.

Russell, J. A. (1979). Affective space is bipolar. *Journal of Personality and Social Psychology, 37*, 345–356.

Ruys, K. I., & Stapel, D. A. (2008). How to heat up from the cold: Examining the preconditions for (unconscious) mood effects. *Journal of Personality and Social Psychology, 94*, 777–791.

Schubert, E. (2013). Loved music can make a listener feel negative emotions. *Musicae Scientiae, 17*(1), 11–26.

Sedikides, C., Wildschut, T., Arndt, J., & Routledge, C. (2008a). Nostalgia: Past, present and future. *Current Directions in Psychological Science, 17*(5), 304–307.

Sedikides, C., Wildschut, T., Gaertner, L., Routledge, C., & Arndt, J. (2008b). Nostalgia as enabler of self-continuity. In F. Sani (Ed.), *Individual and collective self-continuity: Psychological perspectives*. Marwah, NJ: Lawrence Erlbaum Associates.

Sedikides, C., Wildschut, T., Gaertner, L., Routledge, C., & Arndt, J. (2010). Nostalgia as enabler of self-continuity. In F. Sani (Ed.), *Self continuity: Individual and collective perspectives*. New York: Psychology Press.

Thompson, R. J., Mata, J., Jaeggi, S. M., Buschkuehl, M., Jonides, J., & Gotlib, I. H. (2010). Maladaptive coping, adaptive coping, and depressive symptoms: Variations across age and depressive state. *Behavior Research Therapy, 48*(6), 459–466.

Trapnell, P. D., & Campbell, J. D. (1999). Private self-consciousness and the five-factor model of personality: Distinguishing rumination from reflection. *Journal of Personality and Social Psychology, 76*(2), 284–304.

Van den Tol, A. J. M., & Edwards, J. (2013). Exploring a rationale for choosing to listen to sad music when feeling sad. *Psychology of Music, 41*(4), 440–465.

Verplanken, B. (2012). When bittersweet turns sour: Adverse effects of nostalgia on habitual worriers. *European Journal of Social Psychology, 42*, 285–289.

Watkins, E., & Baracaia, S. (2001). Why do people ruminate in dysphoric moods? *Personality and Individual Differences, 30*, 723–734.

Weinstein, D. (1991). *Heavy metal: A cultural sociology*. New York: Lexington Books.

Wildschut, T., Sedikides, C., Arndt, J., & Routledge, C. (2006). Nostalgia: Content, triggers, functions. *Journal of Personality and Social Psychology, 91*(5), 975–993.

Wildschut, T., Sedikides, C., Routledge, C., Arndt, J., & Cordaro, P. (2010). Nostalgia as a repository of social connectedness: The role of attachment-related avoidance. *Journal of Personality and Social Psychology, 98*, 573–586. doi:10.1037/a0017597.

Williams, P., & Aaker, J. (2002). Can mixed emotions peacefully coexist? *Journal of Consumer Research, 28*, 636–650.

Zautra, A. J., Reich, J. W., Davis, M. C., Potter, P. T., & Nicholson, N. A. (2000). The role of stressful events in the relationship between positive and negative affect: Evidence from field and experimental studies. *Journal of Personality, 68*(5), 927–951.

Zentner, M., Grandjean, D., & Scherer, K., R. (2008). Emotions evoked by the sound of music: Characterization, classification and measurement. *Emotion*, 8, 494-521.

Zimbardo, P. G., & Boyd, J. N. (1999). Putting time in perspective: A valid, reliable individual-differences metric. *Journal of Personality and Social Psychology, 77*(6), 1271–1288.

Zinchenko, A. V. (2011). Nostalgia: Dialogue between memory and knowing. *Journal of Russian & East European Psychology, 49*(3), 84–97.

12

The Addiction of Love: Sad Music and Heartbreak

Love Songs in Popular Music

While music has changed greatly over the centuries, one thing that has not changed in at least a thousand years is the dominant theme of our songs: love. It is a theme that has been prevalent throughout the arts across cultures and time periods. It is found in the earliest examples of Western literature (Hatfield & Rapson, 1993) and the imagery used to express the sensations of being in love has not changed in thousands of years (Ackerman, 1995). Folk music from all over the world carries similar themes of love, both its pleasant side, and the pain of love gone wrong. It is to be found in the *min-yo* folk songs of Japan (Matsubara, 1946), in the lyric songs of Russia (Propp, 1993) and the *shan'ge* folk songs of China (Schimmelpenninck, 1997), among others.

However, while love has been a prevalent theme for centuries, love songs themselves have both mirrored and shaped the shifting societal views towards love and relationships throughout the centuries. Our strong attraction to sad music in times of heartbreak can arguably be attributed both to the historical origins of the love song and to the physiological

S. Garrido, *Why Are We Attracted to Sad Music?*,
DOI 10.1007/978-3-319-39666-8_12

processes that occur when we fall in love. It is to the historical origins of the love song that we will turn our attention first.

William Jankowiak and Edward Fischer (1992) define romantic love as an "intense attraction that involves the idealization of the other, within an erotic context, with the expectation of enduring for some time into the future" (p. 150). Of course, fertility songs—performed to encourage procreation and abundance in humans, livestock and crops alike—are about as old as recorded human history. However, romantic love has also been featured in songs found on ancient papyri such as the Chester Beatty I Papyrus, and the vase fragments from ancient Egypt displayed in the Cairo Museum, which date from around 1300 BC (Ackerman, 1995). These songs have an intimate tone similar to that of modern-day love ballads which represents a clear departure from fertility songs (Gioia, 2015). Older literature from ancient Sumeria also contains a body of love songs dealing with the love, courtship and sacred marriage of the Mesopotamian love-goddess Ishtar, which dates from around 2100–1800 BCE (Sefati, 1998). These songs paint love in terms of the sacred and transcendent, an ideal that can also be traced throughout the history of the love song into the modern day (Gioia, 2015).

The most comprehensive history of love songs that has been compiled to date is Ted Gioia's *Love Songs: The Hidden History* (2015). In this book, Gioia traces the origins of many features of modern-day love songs right back to antiquity, through the times of the troubadours and the jazz age of the early twentieth century. He argues that love songs have frequently been the force behind social change. For example, in the early medieval period, the love song was the subject of ardent opposition by Christian religious leaders. The Council of Auxerre (651–665) prohibited *puellarum cantica* (songs of girls) that were commonly sung in villages in Spain because of their capacity of inciting love and lust. Similarly, other sources from the eighth to tenth centuries contain condemnations of love songs, particularly during church festivities.

However, according to Gioia, while this repression continued in the Christian world, the conquering of the Iberian Peninsula by Islamic forces meant that by the late medieval period, the mark of African music could be found in the music of Europe. This occurred in a foretaste of the way the forced migration of African slaves to America 1000 years later would further shape the course of music history. By the time of the troubadours, music would carry the evidence of both this Moorish influence and the idea of love as something mystical and supreme that was carried over from ancient Sumeria and from Christian influences.

These influences were apparent in the music of William IX, Duke of Aquitaine in southern France, along with his contemporaries and successors, who created an ideal of love that has come to be known as "courtly love". For several hundred years the romantic ideals of the troubadours were expressed through music and poetry in Europe and England, and they continue to shape our modern-day concepts of love and romance. Our current Western idea of marriage as an expression of the love and commitment between two individuals, rather than as a business transaction and alliance between two families as it was throughout much of human history, was strongly influenced by the same social forces that shaped the music of those periods (Coontz, 2006).

Music stayed in the realm of poets and lovers until the arrival of the printing press and the rise of an urban middle class in Europe, who would frequently number a piano among their possessions. With this development and then the advent of recording technologies in subsequent centuries, love songs were able to be mass-produced, and thus entered the world of commerce. Nevertheless, music has continued to both shape and lend expression to social revolutions. Thus the twentieth century saw love songs move from the intimate tone of the crooners, to the 'free love' movement in the music of The Beatles and Simon & Garfunkel, for example, through to the raw and deeply personal expression of the so-called 'indie' (independent) singer-songwriters of today.

Throughout these developments love in all its manifestations has remained a primary theme. A number of studies have analyzed the prevalence of love themes in popular music over the last few decades. Donald Horton (1957) found that 87.2 percent of the popular music in the 1950s in the USA was on the subject of love. In the 1960s this seemed to decrease slightly as political concerns became a topic for popular songs, but James Carey (1969) still found that in 1966 69.5 percent of the songs were about love. An informal survey of songs from the Billboard Hot 100 charts in 2015 seemed to indicate that love is back on the agenda, with four of the five songs examined being love songs (Temple, 2015).

While the prevalence of love songs does not appear to have changed radically over time, the ideals of love and the role of the individuals within them have changed greatly. Melvin Wilkinson (1976) looked at songs that were popular between 1954 and 1968 and found that the lyrics often echoed traditional sex-role expectations while others did not. He suggested that this demonstrated the desire for an equalizing in romantic love and provided an opportunity for men to express ideas generally considered unmasculine in Western society at the time. In this way they seemed to prefigure the social changes that were beginning to emerge during those decades. A similar study that looked at the 100 most popular songs between 1958 and 1998 (Dukes, Bisel, Borega, Lobato, & Owens, 2003) found that while the percentage of love songs did not change significantly over the period, there were developments in the lyrical content. The authors found that fewer love words were used over time, while references to sex, particularly by male singers, tended to increase. The authors attributed this change to the sexual revolution of the 1960s and 1970s.

One love song that has been around for centuries gives a quite clear illustration of the way songs reflect current social beliefs about love and relationships. My colleague Jane Davidson and I considered the song often known as 'Scarborough Fair' and some of its variants throughout the centuries (Garrido & Davidson, 2016). Of course, most readers would probably be familiar with the version 'Scarborough Fair/Canticle' recorded by Paul Simon and Art Garfunkel in 1966 and included on their album *Parsley, Sage, Rosemary and Thyme*. However, the song actually belongs to a family of ballads that date back to at least the seventeenth century. The earliest-documented version of this song-family is found in a black letter broadside from the collection of Samuel Pepys (1633–1703) held in the English Broadside Ballad Archive at the University of California (Magdalene College Pepys—Miscellaneous 358, EBBA ID: 32070). The song text consists of a dialogue between a female character and an 'elphin knight', in which the woman expresses a wish that the knight were in her bed. The two protagonists then go on to set each other a series of impossible tasks or riddles as a sort of love contest, including the sewing of a shirt with no cuts or seams.

The text of this version is filled with sexual imagery, which is often expressed by the female character. The ballad was evidently originally intended to be a sort of humorous and playful courtship song that was used largely in rural contexts (Douglas, 2004). However, it seems likely that the idea that the male protagonist was an 'elphin knight' or some kind of supernatural 'fairy lover' crept into the text in an effort to make the ballad more closely reflect the social mores of the time. While medieval courtly literature portrayed the virtuous woman as remote and undesiring, the passive recipient of pursuit by an ardent lover (Burns, 2001), during the seventeenth century female sexual desire and initiative was often associated with harlotry and witchcraft (Gowing, 2003). Thus, the originally humorous song was transformed into a moralistic tale that promoted the idea that female sexuality and agency were indicative of collusion with the devil or witchcraft.

By the Victorian era, in one version of the ballad—'Whittingham Fair'—the woman's role in the tale has been restricted even further. All reference to her sexuality and much of the sexual imagery is now gone. In fact, the male and female characters do not even communicate directly, employing an unnamed intermediary in much the same way that troubadour songs often involved the transmission of a lover's message to a far-off love through an envoy (Burns, 2001). Subtle changes in the tasks described in the ballad also reflect the fact of feminine economic dependency in the nineteenth century.

By the time Simon & Garfunkel recorded their version, the 'hippie' counterculture, which stressed the ideals of free love, freedom of speech and peace, was in full swing (Lund & Denisoff, 1971). Their version displays a simplicity of vocal style that reflects the revival in interest in folk music that accompanied this era, suggesting an idealization of the simple pastoral life. Against a backdrop of the Vietnam War, Simon & Garfunkel also added to the traditional ballad a counter-melody drawn from an anti-war song called 'The Side of a Hill', which Simon had written some years earlier. In addition, in the text used by Simon & Garfunkel the female protagonist in the original story never speaks at all. Rather, she is described performing the tasks alone. The effect of these changes is to shift the focus of the song from one of courtship to the image of a lonely, heartsick soldier pining for a distant love, while the women left at home must bear the load on the home front. In the context of the anti-war protests occurring at the time, the song thus depicts the pain and sense of futility that permeated public perceptions of the Vietnam war in many circles.

In its transformations, this ballad thus demonstrates the changing perspectives toward gender roles and love over time, metamorphosing from a humorous, bawdy courtship song, to a social commentary on female sexuality and a protest against war and social restriction. It is evident from this analysis that love songs are able to tell us a lot about relationships between men and women in the particular social and cultural climate in which the songs were created.

Evolutionary Links Between Music and Love

While the association between love and music in popular music throughout the centuries is clear, the link between love and music likely pre-dates by several millennia any physical evidence of the existence of love songs that archaeologists have been able to unearth. In fact, Darwin argued that sexual selection was closely linked to the evolution of music. He noted that among birds, the male of the species tends to have either ornate plumage, as in the case of the peacock, or to have elaborate vocal skills, as with the nightingale. This implies that for some bird species, song provides a similar function to the brightly coloured tail of the peacock—it helps them to attract mates.

Studies indicate that music is still the 'peacock tail' for many humans today. While women are mostly reluctant to accept the sexual overtures of an unknown male (Clark & Hatfield, 1989), one study of 300 young women in France found that women were more likely to comply when the male was carrying a guitar case (Guéguen, Meineri, & Fischer-Lokou, 2013). Thus, it seems that musical ability does increase the chances of reproductive success even in humans in the twenty-first century.

In some cultures the link between courtship and music is even more overt. For example, in southern Peru, the *charango*—a stringed instrument that looks much like a small guitar—is traditionally used as an integral part of courting rituals. Every young man will develop skills on the instrument and uses it in a series of elaborate rituals to signal his intentions to the object of his affections, and subsequently to signal the progress of the relationship to the community (Turino, 1983). In fact, the association between the charango and courtship is so strong that generally once married, a man will stop playing his charango altogether.

Biological evidence also points towards the link between music and mating. One neurological study, for example, showed that the same neural pathways were activated in female birds listening to the singing of male birds of their species as are activated when humans listen to music (Earp & Maney, 2012). In fact, it seems to be the case that the vocal sounds that an organism is able to produce can be suggestive of its physical state. Lower sounds, for example, tend to indicate a large resonator or vocal tract, and so can be indicative of the size of the creature and therefore its potential as a protector of offspring (Fletcher, 2004). Humans do seem to be able to accurately predict the physical appearance of an individual from hearing their voice. One study, for example, showed that the majority of participants in their sample were able to accurately match an unfamiliar voice to an unfamiliar face (Kamachi, Hill, Lander, & Vatikiotis-Bateson, 2003). Thus, it may be that the capacity of the voice to suggest physical size or strength is what lies behind the evident evolutionary connection between musical ability and sexual success.

However, other studies indicate that the *creativity* suggested by musical ability may be the evolutionary marker of sexual fitness that we find so attractive. Improvisation and novelty in performance, such as is displayed by the lyrebird, can indicate cognitive flexibility, another trait that could suggest potential usefulness as a mate. One study found that women at peak fertility within their menstrual cycle were more likely to be attracted to a penniless, but creative artist than to a rich man who displayed no creativity, while at low phases of fertility the opposite was the case (Haselton & Miller, 2006). The authors argued that this suggests that for a female who is biologically prepared to reproduce, creativity is a greater attractor than the amount of resources possessed by a potential mate.

The evidence reviewed in this chapter thus far has confirmed the idea that music is intrinsically linked to love, both biologically and culturally. It is used to attract a mate, to cement long-term bonds between individuals, and to express the joy of love. What about cases of unhappy love? As the next section will show, sad music and heartbreak are also closely tied to both our biological responses to rejection and to the historical origins of the love song.

Love and Sad Songs

The human experience of love has two sides: joy when the love is returned and pain in cases of rejection, loss or conflict. Our attraction to sad music to capture the pain of heartbreak and love-sickness is again indelibly tied up with its development throughout history. Even from antiquity, the pain of being separated from the beloved was a recurrent theme in love songs. Ted Gioia (2015) argues that the ancient Egyptian love songs, dating from 1300 BC, "reveal a fascination with romantic frustration, with thwarted desire and its impact on the emotions and imagination" (p. 19).

Gioia further argues that throughout much of their history, love songs have come largely from the marginalized and oppressed, such as prostitutes and slaves. It was their very origins that enabled these songs to become the impetus for both social and musical change. In speaking about the musical revolution that occurred in America in the twentieth century, with the growing popularity of music originating from black populations, Gioia says: "their very exclusions from the dominant culture freed them from the stiffness and decorum that made so many of the songs of white America seem vapid and sentimental by comparison ... above all, the slave wasn't hemmed in by the deep-seated Western shame ... at expressing heartfelt emotions in public" (p. 201). The unfortunate circumstances of their creators also meant that love songs became imbued with a feeling of wistfulness and longing, and created a longstanding connection in the popular imagination between love and enslavement.

In the courtly love of the troubadours, the theme of service or bondage to the beloved was also common, likely due to their influence by the music of Moorish slaves. Many troubadour lyrics concern themes of thwarted love and unreciprocated love for an unapproachable noble woman, and draw on Christian imagery of pilgrimage, sacrifice and knightly devotion. Songs of heartbreak are similarly found in cultures all over the world, such as the songs composed by the 6th Dalai Lama Tsangyan Gyatso in seventeenth century Tibet (Gyatso, 1993).

In more recent times, entire genres have sprung up around the expression of heartbreak and the anguish of regret. The Blues, for example—famously fatalistic—uses language that mimics that of real-life situations in expressing the longing for an unattainable lover (Kuhn, 1999). The tango, similarly, frequently recounts tales of tragic love encounters. In fact, even when not directly about heartbreak, love songs often have an ambiance of sadness, as if in anticipation of rejection or pain. These currents of sadness in many love songs thus appear to stem from two important historical influences on the development of the love song: the predominance of love songs from slaves and other oppressed individuals that became imbued with the sorrow of those who created them; and the religious influences that infused the love song with images of an unattainable love. There are, however, powerful biological reasons that also seem to pull us towards sad songs in times of heartbreak.

Romantic love is, of course, a part of the biological imperative to reproduce. It differs from a purely sexual drive, however, in that it motivates us to form a long-term attachment to a single individual in order to provide a stable and protected environment for any offspring that might result (Fisher, Aron, & Brown, 2005). Given the important biological function of romantic love, our brain is geared up to provide powerful incentives to select a mate and remain attached to them. Neurological studies indicate that when people are 'madly' in love, the areas of the brain that are responsible for critical thought become de-activated while the reward systems of the brain become activated (Bartels & Zeki, 2000). Thus, falling in love can feel much like a 'natural drug high', producing brain chemicals such as dopamine that are also produced during the consumption of narcotics like cocaine.

Just as in cases of addiction to narcotics, when the cause of that dopamine rush is removed, the motivation to regain it becomes more powerful. Thus, in situations of rejection or loss of the object of our love, our desire to be with that individual only increases. Studies have shown that those parts of the brain that are associated with the calculating of gains and losses becomes active when heartbroken, suggesting that there is an increase in our willingness to take large risks to reclaim the object of our desire (Fisher, Aron, & Brown, 2006). Helen Fisher and colleagues (2005) say that the brain patterns that are activated in rejected lovers demonstrate increases in "obsessive/compulsive behaviours, ruminating on the intentions and actions of the rejecter, evaluating options, and emotion regulation" (p. 9). Thus, it seems that, biologically, being in love is much like an addiction in that the craving to be with the person we love becomes even stronger in their absence. Music, in all its power to bring back vivid memories of a beloved individual and the feeling of being with them, may well be used in lieu of the individual themselves to induce a sense of connection with them.

However, music about heartbreak most likely provides similar psychological benefits to those discussed in relation to sad music in general in the previous chapters of this volume. The evidence suggests that we are particularly attracted to 'love-lamenting' music when we are discontented with our own romantic relationships (Knobloch, Weisbach & Zillmann, 2004). This appears to be particularly true for men. In one study, women who were highly lonely demonstrated a preference for love-celebrating music, while lonely men preferred love-lamenting music (Gibson, Aust, & Zillmann, 2000), implying that individual differences in coping style also play a role. It may be that for romantically disenchanted males hearing of the romantic successes of others increases distress (Zillmann & Gan, 1997), while some women may be able to enjoy a sense of romance vicariously through music, or to feel a renewed sense of hope in love through positive messages about love in the music. We also prefer to listen to music to love-lamenting music by performers of our own gender (Knobloch & Zillmann, 2003), perhaps deriving some sense of comfort from the knowledge that others of our sex have experienced similar frustrations. On the other hand, men and women who are in romantically satisfying relationships both tend to prefer love-celebrating music.

The authors of another study claim that the musical structure of many songs about heartbreak allows the listener to experience a cathartic effect. Chen-Gia Tsai and colleagues (2014) found that when listening to Chinese popular songs about heartbreak, participants demonstrated significant decreases in finger temperature during the first part of the songs, indicating an accumulation of negative emotions. Increased skin conductance in participants during the passage preceding the chorus and the entrance of the chorus suggests the arousing effect of this part of the song. The authors argued that the subsequent increases in finger temperature reported in the second half of the songs imply that the negative emotions evident at the beginning of the song were released during this period of arousal, resulting in a decrease in negative affect.

Whether or not the effects of listening to sad music are cathartic, it is evident that a strong connection exists between sad love songs and unhappy romantic experiences. My colleague Jane Davidson and I undertook a study designed to test whether people who listen to sad love songs would indulge in nostalgic remembrance of their own unhappy romantic experiences when listening to them (Davidson & Garrido, 2014). We also wanted to find out about the effect such memories would have on their mood. Data from this study came from a general questionnaire about music use in which we asked people to nominate a song that made them feel sad. Forty-seven participants nominated a love song that made them feel sad. We then randomly selected a further 47 participants as a comparison group from among those who did nominate a song that was not about love.

Participants completed various personality measures as well as listening to their selected song during the study, completing pre- and post-mood ratings, and rating 12 statements according to how well each statement fitted their perception of the effect of the music on their affective state. One statement of particular interest referred to whether the music made them remember personal experiences, stating: "it made me think of past events in my life".

Participants who had selected a love song as the song that made them feel sad scored significantly higher on the item indicating that the music made them remember past events. The same group also reported significantly higher scores in rumination and increases in depression scores after listening to their nominated song. Thus, as has been the case in the studies reported earlier in this volume, despite the attraction to love-lamenting music in cases of heartbreak, listening to sad music does not always seem to have a psychologically healthy effect. It also reconfirms our previous findings as discussed in earlier chapters in this volume, that sad music has an even more potent effect on our moods when it is connected to personal experiences or sad events in our mind. This appears to be particularly true of songs about heartbreak.

In a follow-up study[1] we surveyed 668 participants (188 males and 475 females), with a mean age of 33 years. Participants were asked to nominate both a song that they would listen to in a romantic situation and a song that they would listen to if they were feeling heartbroken. People with high scores in rumination and other less healthy coping styles such as denial, emotion-focused coping and behavioural disengagement were most likely to rate the song they nominated for when they were in love as negatively valenced. This could reflect either a tendency to view the songs negatively or to choose sadder songs in relation to love even when not heartbroken.

Our analysis of the reported reasons for song choices revealed that music was used in several ways to cope with heartbreak. The most frequently cited reason given was that the song expressed how the person felt about their situation. Others said that the music enabled them to "wallow in my heartbreak for a little longer" and to experience powerful memories of the beloved. Other frequently cited reasons were that it allowed them an outlet for their anger and disappointment and also that it validated their feelings about the situation. Some participants also selected music that made them feel closer to the person they loved. Only 6 percent of participants chose music that they said gave them hope and cheered them up. Thus, it appears that although some people are attracted to mood-improving music that can increase their hope, our strongest instinct in cases of heartbreak is to seek out music that reminds us of the beloved or times spent with them, and that allows us an outlet for our emotions.

That song choices are related to coping style was further confirmed by our analysis of the lyrics of the heartbreak songs nominated by our participants. We used LIWC[2] to look at patterns of word meanings in the selected heartbreak songs. Results revealed significant associations between the frequency of particular word groups in the lyrics of the chosen songs, and both personality traits and coping styles. Neuroticism from the Big Five Personality Inventory, for example, was correlated with lyrical content containing words about the past, she/he words, and words about death. This suggests that people with high scores in neuroticism

[1] Unpublished.

[2] See Chap. 2 for a more detailed description of this software for linguistic analysis.

tended to select songs with a high level of focus on past events and the beloved 'other' who was the subject of their heartbreak. The comparatively high level of words about death suggests a tendency to extreme responses to their situation. These results are not surprising given the strong associations between neuroticism and depression or other unhealthy mental health outcomes, and further confirms that the songs selected by participants to cope with heartbreak strongly reflect their own thoughts and coping styles.

Associations between lyrics and other less helpful coping styles were also found. Mental disengagement, for example, was correlated with the use of words related to anger, as was emotion-focused coping. People who cope by suppressing actions tended to select songs with lyrics that used a high number of words related to inhibition. Implicit mood measures also demonstrated that people who were feeling a sense of helplessness tended to select songs that used she/he words. The selection of songs like this likely expressed the participants' feelings of disempowerment in the situation. Helplessness is also associated with depression, since research indicates that when events are attributed to an external locus of control, the accompanying belief that one's happiness is in the hands of another tends to increase depression (Abramson, Metalsky, & Alloy, 1989).

On the other hand, significant correlations were found between adaptive coping styles and word patterns in the lyrics of songs selected to cope with heartbreak. For example, people with high scores in terms of extraversion tended to select music that expressed positive emotions and that contained a high number of personal pronouns, reflecting their people-oriented approach. Reflectiveness and active coping—which readers will remember are both regarded as coping styles most likely to result in positive outcomes (see Chap. 8)—were associated with words indicating a level of cognitive insight. Previous studies have found that the use of insight words suggests that a level of cognitive reframing or re-construal is occurring, processes that are themselves associated with positive health outcomes (Ayduk & Kross, 2010; Pennebaker et al., 1997). Active coping was also negatively correlated with the use of past-oriented words in our study.

These results confirm the strong relationship between personality and coping style, and one's choice of music. Participants tended to select music to cope with heartbreak that reflected and expressed their own feelings. The lyrical content of the songs demonstrated a wide range of thoughts and emotions, with participants who scored strongly on maladaptive coping styles or personality traits associated with mental health issues also tending to select songs that expressed a ruminative or past-oriented view of love experiences, as well as a sense of helplessness and inhibition. On the other hand, people with healthy personality traits such as extraversion or who scored strongly on scores of adaptive coping styles such as reflectiveness or active coping, tended to either select music that expressed positive emotions and that gave them a sense of renewed hope, or songs that could help them to engage in processes of reappraisal and reconstruction so as to allow them to gain insight into events and their own emotions in response to them.

Love and Longing in Music

Some scholars argue that much of the angst associated with love in modern-day contexts stems from the unrealistic and 'fairy-tale-like' concept of love that has been widely promoted by film and advertising in which the concept of an ideal mate—'the one'—has been advocated (Barker & Langdridge, 2010). As noted by other scholars, the concept of a lifelong partner fulfilling a multitude of personal needs is a relatively recent development in a historical record in which marriage and love have often been viewed as separate, and the institution of marriage had more to do with economics and connections than with satisfying individual emotional needs (Coontz, 2006). Studies have shown that even in the modern day people in non-Western cultures may be more likely to believe that romantic love is something temporary while marriage should be based on a more practical and enduring relationship (de Munck, Korotayev, de Munck, & Khaltourina, 2011).

The roots of the modern-day ideal of love that is commonly held in Western cultures again date back to the time of courtly love and the troubadours. Some scholars argue that these ideals have created a tendency to dissatisfaction with relationships in Western cultures in the modern day. Thus, as marriage has become more closely associated with love, there has been an undermining of the belief that marriage should be a stable lifelong commitment. Many of our love songs, therefore, still contain images of an unattainable, idealized love—themes that inevitably engender a note of wistfulness and sadness in such music. In the words of Gioia: "today fantasy stands out as a key element in our love songs … enabling the listener to experience vicariously the passion and intense feelings only rarely granted by our quotidian routine" (p. 19). Modern-day love songs often echo the "fascination with romantic frustration" that Gioia noted in the love songs of ancient Egypt (p. 19).

This was revealed in an interesting way in our study of 'Scarborough Fair' (Garrido & Davidson, 2016). As well as reviewing the historical contexts in which versions of the ballad were found, we asked 672 modern-day listeners about their response to the Simon & Garfunkel version. Participants listened to a recording of the song and were asked to describe any images or thoughts that were evoked by hearing the song. The majority of responses involved descriptions of some kind of pastoral or peasant-like imagery such as forests, villages, meadows of long grass or flowers, or 'long-haired, barefoot maidens'. Descriptions of personal memories evoked by the music were also numerous, particularly of the family members such as parents, grandparents or siblings who had introduced them to the music. Frequent descriptions were also made of the emotions evoked by the music with the music being variously described as calm, soothing, eerie, peaceful, sad and whimsical.

Several participants also mentioned the concept of love in their descriptions, describing romantic scenarios such as carriage rides, dancing, or picnics in fields, while other commented on its association with courtly love and chivalry or a time when love was 'simpler'. Some participants described the song as being a sad love song, about past love and loss. Others associated the music with medieval imagery such as knights, castles and troubadours. Only five participants appeared to know about the connection of this song with the anti-war movement, or anything to do with the historical origins of the music.

These results indicate that neither the original meanings of the songs (as far as we can understand them now) nor the emotional narrative created in Simon & Garfunkel's version were culturally available to the participants in our sample. Rather, the song had taken on a new meaning to listeners in the twenty-first century based on references far outside the narrative of the song. People who reported that they liked the song often did so because of its personal nostalgic connection to their youth or an idealized nostalgia for what they perceived to be a representation of chivalric love and a simple rustic lifestyle. Thus, even a ballad that has held many historical meanings over the centuries is understood in the twenty-first century in the light of the idealized concepts of love that are current today. Such attraction to the concept of 'chivalry' and romance as many people perceive them today, perhaps represents a discomfort in some with the difficulties of negotiating gender roles in modern relationships. Thus, on some level, the love songs of today often contain a note of mourning for an ideal of love that is rarely encountered in all the glory that it is in fantasy and fiction.

Does Music Help Us Cure the Addiction?

The predominance of love songs in all cultures for centuries of human existence testifies to the strong biological urges that romantic love involves for humans. More than just an expression of the sex drive, romantic love motivates the creation of long-term attachments, with the biological imperative so as to create a stable and protected environment in which to produce offspring. Although music has also served other evolutionary functions, song has likely played a role in mate selection since before prehuman times. It continues to influence our perception of sexual attractiveness today. Love songs have thus had an important influence both on the development of music over the centuries and also on social beliefs about love and gender roles. Those who are in love celebrate their joy in music. Those who desire love experience it vicariously in song, while those who have lost love express their laments in songs of heartbreak.

In much the same way as an addiction, when love is thwarted, our strongest instinct appears to be to listen to music that satisfies the craving for the beloved or for the sensations of love itself, turning to songs of love that both inspire and renew hope in love, and to songs that express the pain and hurt of heartbreak. Whether we choose to listen to love-celebrating music or love-lamenting music depends in turn on a number of variables, including gender, personality and coping style. A number of people are able to use songs that express heartbreak as part of the healthy psychological processes for working through their pain.

However, just as sad music generally can feed cycles of negative thinking in people with tendencies to depression, people with maladaptive coping styles also seem to turn to songs that express unhealthy viewpoints of love in times of heartbreak. Whether or not this has the effect of worsening their mood or helps them to recover and cope will require further testing in future studies. However, the studies reported here suggest that a highly past-oriented or emotion-focused approach to coping with heartbreak tends to be associated with negative mood outcomes in some people.

Nevertheless, as discussed above, the strong motivation we have to seek romantic love is biologically based, and the brain systems that are activated when in love provide powerful incentives to pursue love with energy and without regard for risk. Love songs, whether happy or sad, perhaps allow us a way to fill that need where real relationships are unsatisfying or unattainable. History and biology have come together to create an ideal of love that is often unreachable, a fact that often imbues our pursuit of love with some melancholy. Thus, love songs, even sad love songs, stories, or films, resonate strongly with so many listeners around the globe.

An even more painful part of the human experience is the separation that must be endured with the death of those we love. The next chapter will therefore discuss the role of sad music in grief and mourning.

References

Abramson, L. Y., Metalsky, G. I., & Alloy, L. B. (1989). Hopelessness depression: A theory-based subtype of depression. *Psychological Review, 96*(2), 358–372.

Ackerman, D. (1995). *A natural history of love*. New York: First Vintage Books.

Ayduk, O., & Kross, E. (2010). From a distance: Implications of spontaneous self-distancing for adaptive self-reflection. *Journal of Personality and Social Psychology, 98*, 809–829.

Barker, M., & Langdridge, D. (Eds.). (2010). *Understanding non-monogamies*. New York: Routledge.

Bartels, A., & Zeki, S. (2000). The neural basis of romantic love. *NeuroReport, 11*(17), 3829–3834.

Burns, J. E. (2001). Courtly love: Who needs it? Recent feminist work in the Medieval French tradition. *Signs, 27*(1), 23–57.

Carey, J. T. (1969). Changing courtship patterns in the popular song. *American Journal of Sociology, 74*(6), 720–731.

Clark, R. D., & Hatfield, E. (1989). Gender differences in receptivity to sexual offers. *Journal of Psychology and Human Sexuality, 2*(1), 39–55.

Coontz, S. (2006). *Marriage, a history: How love conquered marriage*. New York: Penguin.

Davidson, J., & Garrido, S. (2014). *My life as a playlist*. Perth: University of Western Australia Publishing.

de Munck, V. C., Korotayev, A., de Munck, J., & Khaltourina, D. (2011). Cross-cultural analysis of models of romantic love among U.S. residents, Russians and Lithuanians. *Cross-Cultural Research, 45*(2), 128–154.

Douglas, S. (2004). Ballads and the supernatural: Spells, channs, curses and enchantments. *Studies in Scottish Literature, 33*(1), 349–365.

Dukes, R. L., Bisel, T. M., Borega, K. N., Lobato, E. A., & Owens, M. D. (2003). Expressions of love, sex, and hurt in popular songs: A content analysis of all-time greatest hits. *The Social Science Journal, 40*(4), 643–650.

Earp, S. E., & Maney, D. L. (2012). Birdsong: Is it music to their ears? *Frontiers in Evolutionary Neuroscience, 4*, 14. doi:10.3389/fnevo.2012.00014.

Fisher, H., Aron, A., & Brown, L. L. (2005). Romantic love: An fMRI study of a neural mechanism for mate choice. *Journal of Comparative Neurology, 493*, 58–62.

Fisher, H., Aron, A., & Brown, L. L. (2006). Romantic love: A mammalian brain system for mate choice. *Philosophical Transactions of the Royal Society B, 361*, 1476.

Fletcher, N. H. (2004). A simple frequency-scaling rule for animal communication. *The Journal of the Acoustical Society of America, 115*(5), 2334–2338.

Garrido, S., & Davidson, J. (2016). Emotional regimes reflected in a popular ballad: Perspectives on gender, love and protest in 'Scarborough Fair'. *Musicology Australia, 38*(2), 65–71.

Gibson, R., Aust, C. F., & Zillmann, D. (2000). Loneliness of adolescents and their choice and enjoyment of love-celebrating versus love-lamenting popular music. *Empirical Studies of the Arts, 18*(1), 43–48.

Gioia, T. (2015). *Love songs: The hidden history*. New York: Oxford University Press.

Gowing, L. (2003). *Common bodies: Women, touch and power in seventeenth-century England*. New Haven: Yale University Press.
Guéguen, N., Meineri, S., & Fischer-Lokou, J. (2013). Men's music ability and attractiveness to women in a real-life courtship context. *Psychology of Music, 42*(4), 545–549.
Gyatso, T. (1993). *The Turquoise Bee: The Tantric lovesongs of the Sixth Dalai Lama* (R. Fields & B. Cutillo, Trans.). New York: HarperOne.
Haselton, M. G., & Miller, G. F. (2006). Women's fertility across the cycle increases the short-term attractiveness of creative intelligence. *Human Nature, 17*(1), 50–73.
Hatfield, E., & Rapson, R. L. (1993). *Love, sex, and intimacy: Their psychology, biology and history*. New York: HarperCollins.
Horton, D. (1957). The dialogue of courtship in popular songs. *American Journal of Sociology, 62*(6), 569–578.
Jankowiak, W. R., & Fischer, E. F. (1992). Cross-cultural perspective on romantic love. *Ethnology, 31*(2), 149–155.
Kamachi, M., Hill, H., Lander, K., & Vatikiotis-Bateson, E. (2003). "Putting the face to the voice": Matching identity across modality. *Current Biology, 13*(19), 1709–1714.
Knobloch, S., Weisbach, K., & Zillmann, D. (2004). Love lamentation in pop songs: Music for unhappy lovers? *Zeitschrift fur Medienpsychologie, 16*(3), 116–124.
Knobloch, S., & Zillmann, D. (2003). Appeal of love themes in popular music. *Psychological Reports, 93*, 653–658.
Kuhn, E. D. (1999). 'I just want to make love to you'—Seductive strategies in blues lyrics. *Journal of Pragmatics, 31*, 525–534.
Lund, J., & Denisoff, R. S. (1971). The folk music revival and the counter culture: Contributions and contradictions. *The Journal of American Folklore, 84*(334), 394–405.
Matsubara, I. (1946). *Min-yo: Folk songs of Japan*. New Delhi: Cosmo Publishing Company.
Pennebaker, J. W., Mayne, T. J., & Francis, M. E. (1997). Linguistic predictors of adaptive bereavement. *Journal of Personality and Social Psychology, 72*(4), 863–871.
Propp, V. (1993). *Russian folk lyrics* (R. Reeder, Trans. & Ed.). Bloomington: Georgetown University Press.
Schimmelpenninck, A. (1997). *Chinese folk songs and folk singers: Shan'ge traditions in Southern Jiangsu*. Ann Arbor, MI Chime Foundation.

Sefati, Y. (1998). *Love songs in Sumerian Literature*. Ramat-Gan: Bar-Ilan University Press.

Temple, I. (2015). The surprising, nomadic history of love songs. *Flypaper*. Retrieved from http://flypaper.soundfly.com/features/the-surprising-nomadic-history-of-love-songs/

Tsai, C.-G., Chen, R.-S., & Tsai, T.-S. (2014). The arousing and cathartic effects of popular heartbreak songs as revealed in the physiological responses of listeners. *Musicae Scientiae, 18*(4), 410–422.

Turino, T. (1983). The charango and the sirena: Music, magic and the power of love. *Latin American Music Review, 4*(1), 81–119.

Wilkinson, M. (1976). Romantic love: The great equalizer? Sexism in popular music. *The Family Coordinator, 25*(2), 161–166.

Zillmann, D., & Gan, S. (1997). Musical taste in adolescence. In D. J. Hargreaves & A. C. North (Eds.), *The social psychology of music* (pp. 161–187). Oxford: Oxford University Press.

13

The Role of Sad Music in Grief

At any given time a significant proportion of the world population is grieving the death of someone they care about, especially in war-torn countries or countries troubled by natural disasters. Music has close associations both with vocal expressions of grief and with processes for coping with grief, both historically and in the present day. However, music does not necessarily need to be sad in order to be useful for dealing with grief. In this chapter I will firstly discuss what grief is, before looking more closely at the role of music in mourning across different cultural contexts.

What is Grief?

The word 'grief' comes from a Latin word (via Old French) meaning 'burden'. The Oxford Online Dictionary defines it as 'deep or violent sorrow, caused by loss or trouble; a keen or bitter feeling of regret for something lost, remorse for something done, or sorrow for mishap to oneself or others' ("grief, n.," 2012). The term is most often used in relation to the loss surrounding the death of a loved one, although similar

S. Garrido, *Why Are We Attracted to Sad Music?*,
DOI 10.1007/978-3-319-39666-8_13

emotions are experienced in relation to other forms of loss as well, or even in anticipation of loss.

Grief, of course, bears a close relationship to sadness, although it is generally considered to be higher in intensity, and therefore arousal, than sadness (Jefferies, Smilek, Eich, & Enns, 2008). The exact distinction between sadness and grief is difficult to define, and is often believed to relate mostly to the triggers for the emotion (Neufeldt & Guralnik, 1988). Grief also tends to be experienced for longer periods.

As well as being an emotion of intense sadness, grief is often referred to as a long-term dynamic emotional process of gradual adjustment which is usually gone through by people experiencing loss. While psychologists in the past have spoken about 'closure' as the eventual aim of the grieving process implying an eventual end to grief, more recent understandings are of grief as an ongoing process in which the individual eventually reaches a state of reconciliation with their changed circumstances, and is able to comprehend the meaning of their loss (Silverman & Klass, 1996).

It has been proposed that the grieving process involves working through various emotional stages. Elizabeth Kübler-Ross (1969) outlined five stages of mourning, including denial and isolation, anger, bargaining, and depression, and ending in the eventual acceptance of the death. British psychologist John Bowlby similarly proposed that separation and loss involves four stages: a stage of numbness and protest, intense yearning, disorganization and despair as reality begins to sink in, and a final phase of reorganization (Bowlby, 1969).

Other scholars in the field of death and dying have focused on tasks rather than stages. James William Worden (1982), for example, proposed that there are four tasks that people need to accomplish in order to achieve psychological equilibrium: to accept the reality of the loss; to work through the pain of grief; to adjust to an environment in which the deceased is missing; and to find an enduring connection with the deceased while embarking on a new life. Another core part of healing process are the tasks of making sense of the loss, finding meaning in the occurrence of death and reconstructing one's own personal life-narrative in the light of the bereavement (Neimeyer, 2001). James Gillies and Robert Neimeyer (2006) propose that there are three aspects to finding meaning in the aftermath of loss: sense-making, benefit finding and identity change. The bereaved must assimilate the changes to their relationship with the deceased into their lives and redefine their identity with awareness of both the past relationship and the changes that have occurred (Humphrey & Zimpfer, 2008).

Grief can be accompanied by many symptoms that are similar to depression but that are not regarded as pathological. Rather, they are regarded as a normal part of the typically intense human response to death. While the intensity and duration of grief experienced differs greatly from individual to individual, in most cases, the mourning process eventually results in a return to emotional balance, although some level of grief may persist. However, it is suggested by research that around 7 percent of people suffering the death of a loved one will experience complicated grief, or grief that is unusually persistent or intense (Kersting, Brähler, Glaesmer, & Wagner, 2011).

Various factors contribute to the development of complicated grief, including the circumstances of the death, the relationship of the bereaved to the deceased, access to social support and mental health state. For example, where the death was of a child or spouse, complicated grief is more likely, in perhaps as many as 59 percent of cases (Meert et al., 2010). The rate of complicated grief among people with major depressive disorder may also reach as high as 25 percent (Sung et al., 2011). Thus, Sidney Zisook and Stephen Schuchter (2001) argue that there is a distinction between the normal grief that occurs with bereavement and the depression that some individuals experience along with it. It may be that when bereaved individuals with a history of depression focus on the negative emotions that accompany grief or slip into ruminative patterns of thinking, they may have difficulty adjusting to their loss in a healthy way (Nolen-Hoeksema et al., 1994).

Certain coping styles are also associated with differences in the outcomes of grieving. Problem-focused or task-focused grieving, such as active planning or engagement in behavior to overcome distress, is generally most closely associated with positive outcomes (Schnider, Elhai, & Gray, 2007). Emotion-focused coping such as venting, cognitive reframing, denial or distraction are less consistently associated with positive outcomes (Nolen-Hoeksema et al., 1994). Avoidance strategies can be useful in the early stages of grief in order to allow oneself to gradually face the reality of loss, but ongoing avoidance is associated with complicated grief if it continues long-term (Schnider et al., 2007). Some researchers therefore suggest that a healthy balance of all three broad coping style categories is most successful (Anderson et al., 2005).

While manifestations of grief differ greatly between individuals and cultures, rituals are used almost universally at various stages of the grieving process. The funeral may be the most prominent of these, but rituals continue to be of value throughout the grieving process and even once a level of acceptance has been reached. They play an ongoing role in continued remembrance of the deceased, and in acknowledging the importance of the deceased in one's personal history.

Scholars note that with the increasing secularization of Western cultures, grief rituals are not always as available for use in countries such as America and Canada, as they were prior to the twentieth century (Emke, 2002; Klass, Silverman, & Nickman, 1996). Similarly, in Australia after the First World War a deep cultural shift occurred which lasted until the 1980s in which thoughts and feelings about death were often avoided, rituals and expressions of grief were minimized and sorrow became a private matter (Jalland, 2006). This deterioration in the role of the traditional funeral has often led to insufficient grieving and inadequate grief resolution (Romanoff & Terenzio, 1998).

A reversal in cultural responses and attitudes to death and grief has occurred since then in many parts of the world, stimulated in part by waves of migration that have encouraged diversity in attitudes and approaches to grief. Psychologists have also contributed to the change by encouraging the view that open emotional expressions of grief can be healing (Kübler-Ross, 1969). Rituals are therefore becoming progressively a part of the grieving process once again.

Vocal and Musical Expressions of Grief

Music can be involved in both the immediate intense emotional experience of grief and the long-term experience of the grieving process. Throughout much of human history music has played an important part of rituals surrounding death (Becker, 2001). The anthropological literature reveals that in many cultures specialized music exists for use within the funeral ritual. Laments, for example, are found worldwide and in all historical periods and are an important part of a wake or vigil, a custom which itself has ancient origins (Wilce, 2009). Dirges and laments are also both found in ancient Greek traditions (Alexiou, 1974).

Such songs of lament from around the world often evoke the sound of a voice crying, wailing or keening, using series of descending figures which sound very much like vocal cries of distress. David Huron (2015) further describes the frequent use of ingressive phonation (vocalizing while inhaling), and a 'breaking' voice caused by constriction of the pharynx in vocal music that expresses grief. These telltale vocal signals of grief are repeatedly found in musical and performance conventions, such as the seventeenth-century use of descending minor tetrachords in the bass to symbolize lament (Rosand, 1979).

The vocalizations that are generally associated with grief, and from which the music of laments likely derive, seems to have a long historical relationship with separation and loss. Distress vocalizations have been extensively documented in the case of both domestic animals and primates who are separated from a parent, offspring or other members of their herd (Norcross & Newman, 1999; Seay, Hansen, & Harlow, 1962). While this does not necessarily indicate the presence of grief in the same sense that it is experienced by humans, it suggests the general adaptive functions that grief can serve in that it motivates a creature to remain close to its companions. However, some scholars suggest that in the case of death where closeness becomes impossible, grief is maladaptive: a cost of the human capacity to form social bonds. Others argue that the painfulness of grief ensures the creation of strong memories surrounding the circumstances of death (Nesse, 2005). In other words, since vocalizations of distress and grief are signals of the presence of death and therefore of possible danger, we are programmed to respond acutely to both the death of another and to the acoustic signals of grief.

David Huron (2008) further suggests that vocal cues signifying grief are social cues designed to evoke sympathy, as are the musical cues that signal the same. Similarly, Peter Kivy (1980) argues that music expressing grief typically evokes pity in the listener. Thus, a further function that may be fulfilled by expressions of grief is to evoke empathy in those around us, thereby signaling the need for social support. In any case, it seems that our biological programming is such that auditory signals of grief can evoke powerful responses in the listener.

How We Mourn with Music

This power of music to mimic vocalizations of grief and to evoke powerful emotional responses in the listener is one aspect that makes music such a potent element in rituals surrounding grief and mourning. While laments may be a part of mourning from the moment a death is discovered in some traditional societies, in most Western cultures the first opportunity for music to play a role in grieving is at the funeral. Christian music largely dominated funeral music in Western cultures until the 1970s. Much of this music was 'solemn' and 'grave', as was believed suitable for the occasion. Almost all funeral hymns in seventeenth- and eighteenth-century England, for example, were written in minor keys (Gammon, 1988). Similarly, a review of funeral marches reported in an Australian newspaper in 1910 contained around 60 songs for use in funerals, all of which, according to the author, showed evidence of having been 'composed under stress or sorrow' and were included presumably because of their mournful tone (TGR, 1910).

However, by the early decades of the twentieth century, dirges were becoming less common as mainstream churches began to consider the need to give funerals a less bleak atmosphere (Parsons, 2012). In the 1960s and 1970s a recognizable movement emerged to make mainstream church funerals more personalized and less austere. While choices were still necessarily limited by what was musically available, personal choice and the idea of celebrating the life of the deceased rather than focusing on loss began to have an influence on the music that was played. Thus modern day music choices in funerals do not always display the same mournful tone that they have in the past.

The concept of celebration within the context of mourning is also found in other cultural traditions. In fact, it was fairly common in many cultures until the twentieth century (Sakakeeny, 2011). One example of this is the jazz funeral that is found in Afro-American communities in regions of the United States. In this tradition, a wake is held prior to the funeral during which hymns are played. However, during the procession from the home to the church and cemetery, the band begins to play more upbeat, celebratory music, such as 'When the Saints Go Marching In'. The mourners often join in by dancing behind the musicians as the parade progresses, a moment known as 'cutting the body loose' (Secundy, 1989, p. 101). The spirit of celebration in this tradition is closely linked to the belief that the deceased has moved on to a better life in heaven.

Similarly, in parts of Latin America, the concept of rejoicing is also reflected in the use of *cantos de ángeles* (songs of angels) for the funerals of very young children. The death of a child was, traditionally, an occasion for festivity since it was believed that a child who died in a state of innocence was transformed into an angelic state (Schechter, 1994), thus escaping the sorrows and discomforts of a life of hardship on earth. In some parts of Latin America, such as Chile, the songs themselves were believed to form part of the process by which the child was able to be converted into spirit form (Orellana, 1990).

In modern-day funerals music may be selected to reflect a wide variety of tastes, preferences and meanings rather than just being chosen on the basis of tradition or 'suitability' to the setting. A survey of British funeral music conducted by Co-operative Funeralcare (2013) even reported some humorous choices such as: 'Always Look on the Bright Side of Life' by Eric Idle from Monty Python's *Life of Brian*, and 'It's Time to Face the Music' from *The Muppets*. An Australian funeral services provider reports some similarly ironic choices such as Queen's 'The Show Must Go On' or 'Another one Bites the Dust' (Kelton & Steward, 2008).

The desire to avoid extreme expressions of grief in funeral music, or to at least inject the occasion with some humour or positivity, was demonstrated in a series of studies that I conducted in collaboration with my colleague Jane Davidson (Garrido & Davidson, 2016a, 2016b). In our studies we found that the majority of our participants selected music of a positive valence rather than the mournful music that might have been expected. While some study participants were concerned with the concept of music that was "appropriate" to a dignified setting such as a funeral, others indicated a preference for joyful or even humorous music. As expressed by the participants, their choices were often motivated by a desire to minimize grief in the mourners, as well as to be personally remembered with joy and celebration. Thus the music associated with grief provides a complicated picture. Music used in grief rituals may not always openly express grief, nor will music that expresses grief necessarily evoke similar emotions in the listener.

What Psychological Functions can Music Serve in Grieving?

Charles Corr and colleagues (2008) argue that funerals themselves are a 'task-based' coping strategy because they allow the bereaved to take actions to begin to deal with the reality of the death and to ensure that the life of the deceased is both remembered and celebrated. Kastenbaum (2004) also argues that, despite the loss of many traditional rituals in contemporary society, we still have three things in common with bereaved people throughout time: (i) the desire to feel that our loved one is 'all right' even though dead; (ii) the need to continue a feeling of connection to the deceased; and (iii) a need to somehow keep something of that person alive in us so that we can continue to show our love and respect. Kastenbaum argues that the living can only move confidently ahead with their own lives if they feel they have succeeded in those three areas.

Music can form an important role in satisfying these needs. Angela Bourke, for example, suggests that the Irish traditional lament represents a structured expression of Kübler-Ross's stages of mourning (Bourke, 1988). Among other functions, it has been argued that music can help the bereaved to feel an ongoing sense of connection with the deceased and to celebrate the life of the deceased. It can also facilitate the expression of grief and the sharing of it with others, serve as a catalyst for confronting the reality of loss, reinforce religious convictions and create an atmosphere of the sacred around memories of the deceased, as well as helping to shape the emerging personal narrative of the bereaved in light of their loss (Garrido & Garrido, 2016). These functions will be discussed in more detail below.

Firstly, music serves both task-based roles and functions so as to help the bereaved to feel reassured as to the deceased's 'wellbeing'. In the context of the jazz funerals in Afro-American communities as well as in the *cantos de ángeles*, the providing of music or participation in its performance allow the bereaved to feel that they have taken practical steps to demonstrate their high regard for the deceased and to mark their loss in a meaningful way. These traditions also include beliefs that the musical performance itself ensures the reception of the deceased into heaven.

This is similarly found in lament cultures such as those found in Georgia and Finland, countries where it has customarily been believed that the lament itself is implicitly tied to the transition of the deceased into the spirit world. In Georgia, for example, the length and intensity of the lamenting expresses the social status of the deceased and how much their family valued them. It is believed that an appropriate send-off will ensure good treatment of the deceased in the hereafter (Kotthoff, 2006). Similarly, among the Karelian of Finland, the lament also was considered crucial in guiding the soul of the deceased into the spirit world (Tolbert, 1990). Thus the loved ones of the deceased in such traditions are able to feel that through the music they are participating in ensuring that the deceased will be taken care of in the afterlife.

The selection of music for modern-day funerals can also be a meaningful task for the bereaved in that it enables them to communicate a message about the deceased and their importance to those they have left behind. While funeral-goers may not have the same level of belief in the ritual power of music, the music played at contemporary funerals are often pieces of special significance to the deceased. The survey by Co-operative Funeralcare cited above reveals that bereaved families are increasingly choosing songs with which they or the deceased personally identify. For example, among the top ten most popular songs reported in 2012 were 'My Way' by Frank Sinatra and Shirley Bassey, 'Time to Say Goodbye' by Sarah Brightman and Andrea Bocelli, and 'Wind Beneath My Wings' by Bette Midler. My own research also indicates that the personal relevance of the music appears to have become the paramount criteria by which funeral music is chosen by people of most age groups today (Garrido & Davidson, 2016a, 2016b). Thus through music selections, grieving individuals are able to express much about the individual who has died, ensuring that they are remembered in the way they wanted to be remembered.

Both within the funeral setting and in post-funeral grieving, music also helps to facilitate the expression of grief, offering an opportunity for the release of sorrow and a sharing of the burden of grief with other mourners. As has been discussed in detail throughout this volume, two of the primary reasons that music has developed in human society are for the communication of emotion and to strengthen social bonds. The renowned sociologist Tia DeNora (2000) argues that in group settings music draws the listeners together in shared emotional experiences. Ritual lamenting, for example, provides a forum for shared grieving in which the lamenters provoke the listeners to tears enabling some shared catharsis (Kotthoff, 2006). It furthermore makes the bereaved feel less alone in their loss and strengthens social ties within the community. At the same time the setting puts limits upon the expression of emotion, providing a structure for its containment. Beyond the funeral, in therapy situations music can also help validate and express the emotions associated with grief (Dalton & Krout, 2005), often enabling the communication of feelings that are difficult to put into words (Magee & Davidson, 2004).

The second need enunciated by Kastenbaum—to feel an ongoing sense of connection with the deceased—can also be fulfilled, at least in part, by music. While individuals have differing needs in relation to grief and some people may benefit from a gradual detachment from the deceased (Stroebe, Schut, & Boerner, 2010), other bereaved people are assisted in coping by a sense that the relationship continues (Jalland, 2006). Music can help to provide a feeling of ongoing connection with the deceased in that it can trigger intensely vivid memories of the deceased and the emotions associated with them (Caswell, 2012).

These benefits often extend well beyond the funeral. In some Australian Aboriginal cultures, for example, dance performers commemorate the lives and loss of many previous performers every time they perform their dance ceremonies, even having a sensation that they are merging with their ancestral spirits in dance and thereby reinvigorating their relationships with deceased kin (Treloyn, 2016). Similarly, Clare O'Callaghan (2013) reported that in her study of music therapy in pre-loss care that participants in her study were unexpectedly comforted when hearing on a later occasion the music that had played at the funeral of a loved one, since it allowed them to feel the deceased's presence or to remember the message that they had intended to communicate by their music choices. In fact, Helen Dell (2016) points out the fact that people often seem to feel that the unexpected hearing of songs that were highly relevant to the deceased is some kind of communication from the afterworld, citing this as evidence of music's power to make us feel that the deceased is still with us. Thus music—both that associated with the funeral and that which reminds of the deceased in other ways—can act as an enduring symbol of the deceased individual in the minds of those they have left behind, enabling a sense of closeness to the individual to be created when hearing the same music in other contexts.

In addition, music can play a useful part of the long-term process of adjustment that grievers must undertake in the weeks and months subsequent to the funeral. A core part of the healing after the death of a loved one is the task of making sense of the loss, finding meaning in the occurrence of death and reconstructing the narrative of one's life in light of the bereavement (Neimeyer, 2001). James Gillies and Robert Neimeyer (2006) proposed that there are three particular aspects to this finding of meaning in the aftermath of loss: sense-making, benefit finding and identity change. The bereaved must assimilate their changed relationships with the deceased into their lives (Humphrey & Zimpfer, 2008). They need to redefine their own identity with awareness that their past relationship with the deceased is an integral part of who they have become. Music both forms part of the narrative of the loss itself, and can help to shape the emerging personal narrative of the bereaved. The music can tell the story of the deceased and of those who mourn, assisting the bereaved to formulate their shifting self-view in light of their loss. Music that comes to symbolize the deceased or the experience of loss becomes entwined within the narrative of the deceased's life and of those left behind.

A further function that music can serve is in strengthening religious conviction and hope. Religion is often a strong support for people who are mourning. Miriam Anderson and colleagues (2005), for example, showed that task-oriented and positive religious coping, when used together, resulted in a significant positive association with lower self-reported grief in grieving mothers. In people who are religious, music can remind mourners of their convictions in an afterlife and reinforce hope. Even in secular settings, many mourners are comforted by a belief that the deceased continues to exist somehow, or is someplace where they are happy and comfortable. Music can express such hopes, as well as imbue any occasion with a sense of the special. Music is inherently associated with spiritual experiences even in secular contexts (Penman & Becker, 2009). This helps the bereaved to feel that the passing of their loved one is being given the weight it deserves. In their study of funeral music, Sue Adamson and Margaret Holloway (2012) thus found that music played an important role in creating both a sense of public ceremony as well as in pursuing a "personal existential quest" (p. 33).

The Role of Coping Style in Music Selections for Grieving

The evidence reviewed above suggests that music has a valuable purpose to fulfill in helping mourners to grieve effectively, both at the funeral and in ongoing phases of grieving. Note, however, that while funeral music in many traditions has often been sorrowful in tone, it is not necessary for music to be sad to fulfill those functions. In fact, as noted above celebration is often an inherent part of the grieving process as well. In modern Western funerals as well as in traditional funerals in some cultures, mourners often choose to focus on celebrating the life of the deceased rather than on loss. Although feelings of sadness are both natural and healthy in the context of grief, since coping style is closely related to how people deal with issues like grief and death, the extent to which sad music is used or a more celebratory approach is taken, is likely associated with an individual's coping style.

This can be illustrated by briefly looking again at two of the participants we interviewed in the case studies discussed in Chap. 8 (Garrido & Schubert, 2011). Several years after the death of her father, one participant found that music that she associated with memories of her father evoked particularly acute levels of grief compared to music that was sad in a more general way. She tended to avoid such music unless she felt a need to reflect and to 'make sense' of events, thus suggesting an approach that balanced incorporating music in processes for working through her grief, with avoiding music that would trigger overly sorrowful thoughts at inopportune times. This mixture of coping styles is common, as individuals deploy different methods depending on their needs at the time. Some scholars in fact argue that while avoidance coping is generally considered maladaptive, in circumstances where the possibility of attaining one's goal is reduced such as where a death is involved, it can helpful (Carson & Polman, 2010), particularly as the grieving process progresses and the bereaved needs to be able to focus on the 'reorganization' of their life. Thus this participant displayed a helpful pattern in which she both allowed herself time to experience grief and remember her father, while avoiding repetitive focus on her grief.

Another participant in the same study also demonstrated a mixed approach to dealing with grief, pointing out the difference between natural and healthy grieving over the loss of someone important, and 'wallowing in depression'. She argued that the former is an important process in which the emotions being experienced need to be acknowledged, but that continual dwelling on sad thoughts is unhelpful. Thus, both these participants demonstrated an awareness of the usefulness of music within coping strategies to deal with their grief, and the helpfulness of putting sorrowful thoughts away at times so as to be able to continue with their own lives.

In a subsequent study, Emery Schubert and myself found that people with high scores in reflectiveness particularly reported using music to help facilitate their grieving (Garrido & Schubert, 2013). The relationship between music use, coping style and personality in dealing with grief was further confirmed in the study reported above in which Jane Davidson and I looked at funeral music selections (Garrido & Davidson, 2016b). In that study we found that people with high scores in the Big Five trait of Conscientiousness were most likely to choose music of a positive valence. Conscientiousness usually involves a high degree of consideration for the feelings of other people and a strong motivation to fulfill one's perceived duty (Gosling, Rentfrow, & Swann, 2003). It may be that people with this personality trait display an elevated desire to protect their mourners from an overly sorrowful occasion. On the other hand, highly neurotic people were more likely to choose negatively valenced music for their own funeral, a finding that tends to support the idea that sad music can be utilized as part of maladaptive coping strategies.

As with the other motivations for listening to sad music that have been discussed in previous chapters, the association between grief and an attraction to sad music can likely lead to both positive and negative outcomes depending on the coping strategy of the individual. While the process of grieving is a necessary and healthy one which music can help to facilitate (McFerran, Roberts, & O'Grady, 2010), in most people, the grieving process eventually reaches a point of resolution or acceptance in which the bereaved person is able to continue with their life, even though the grief may never fully disappear. However, in complicated grief, natural grief processes may become entangled with the more maladaptive thinking patterns associated with depression and the individual may have more difficulty resolving their emotions. These patterns can again be observed in the individual music choices. While music may serve to facilitate the expression and processing of grief in psychologically healthy individuals, in people with tendencies to depression or who are experiencing complicated grief, music listening may feed into a cycle of ruminative thinking that results in little psychological benefit.

The above discussion has highlighted that in the modern age the necessity still exists for rituals—albeit more secularized ones—and a sense of the sacred to surround the death of a loved one. Music has a large role to play in this re-ritualization of mourning both within the funeral and in post-funeral grieving. It can be an important vehicle for instilling occasions of mourning with the symbolic and the sacred whether music choices are traditional or modern. It furthermore provides a powerful tool for the rediscovery of personal expressions of grief and gives the bereaved a sense of being understood and comforted. In their choice of funeral music, mourners are able to celebrate and memorialize the life of the deceased in a very individualized way. In addition, music can help them to reconnect with positive memories and imbue past events with value and weight, providing an ongoing sense of attachment to the deceased individual and a continuing reminder of them. Music thus forms part of the changing personal narrative of the bereaved, assisting them to incorporate their past experiences into their understanding of who they are now in the light of their loss.

Although sorrow is a part of grief, grief also encompasses a celebration of the deceased, as seen in the jazz funeral and the *cantos de ángeles* as well as choices for funeral music in modern Western contexts. Thus, while sad music can facilitate grieving and play an important part in the processing of emotions and events, music does not have to be sad to play a useful part within the grieving process. In fact, individual coping style and personality will be involved in how people use music to deal with grief. Healthy coping styles will likely involve a combination of approaches including both facing, accepting, and allowing oneself to experience the intense sorrow that is a natural response to loss, as well as permitting oneself to eventually move forward with one's own life even while retaining a sense of connection with the past.

As demonstrated in the last three chapters, music holds an important place in helping us to deal with some of the most painful, although common experiences in human life: nostalgia for times and people in our past, heartbreak and separation from those we love, as well as the ultimate separation: death. What have we discovered about why we listen to sad music throughout this volume? The final chapter will attempt to pull together the strands of evidence we have considered, and summarize where we have arrived after the centuries of discussion that have surrounded the 'paradox of tragedy'.

References

Adamson, S., & Holloway, M. (2012). A sound track of your life: Music in contemporary UK funerals. *OMEGA, 65*(1), 33–54.

Alexiou, M. (1974). *Ritual lament in Greek tradition*. Cambridge: Cambridge University Press.

Anderson, M. J., Marwit, S. J., Vandenberg, B., & Chibnall, J. T. (2005). Psychological and religious coping strategies of mothers bereaved by the sudden death of a child. *Death Studies, 29*, 811–826.

Becker, J. (2001). Anthropological perspectives on music and emotion. In P. Juslin & J. Sloboda (Eds.), *Music and emotion* (pp. 135–160). Oxford: Oxford University Press.

Bourke, A. (1988). The Irish traditional lament and the grieving process. *Women's Studies International Forum, 11*(4), 287–291.

Bowlby, J. (1969). *Attachment and loss*. New York: Basic Books.

Carson, F., & Polman, R. C. (2010). The facilitative nature of avoidance coping within sports injury rehabilitation. *Scandinavian Journal of Medical Science and Sports, 20*(2), 235–240.

Caswell, G. (2012). Beyond words: Some uses of music in the funeral setting. *OMEGA: Journal of Death and Dying, 64*(4), 319–334.

Corr, C. A., Nabe, C., Nabe, C. M., & Corr, D. M. (2008). *Death and dying, life and living*. Belmont, CA: Cengage Learning.

Dalton, T. A., & Krout, R. E. (2005). Development of the grief process scale through music therapy songwriting with bereaved adolescents. *The Arts in Psychotherapy, 32*, 131–143.

Dell, H. (2016). Haunting music: Hearing the voices of the dead. In J. W. Davidson & S. Garrido (Eds.), *Music and mourning* (pp. 40–54). Oxon: Ashgate Publishing.

DeNora, T. (2000). *Music in everyday life*. Cambridge: Cambridge University Press.

Emke, I. (2002). Why the sad face? Secularization and the changing function of funerals in Newfoundland. *Mortality, 7*(3), 269–284.

Funeralcare, C.-o. (2013). *Funeral Music*. Retrieved from http://www.co-operative.coop/funeralcare/arranging-a-funeral/your-guide-to-arranging-a-funeral/Funeral-Music/

Gammon, V. (1988). Singing and popular funeral practices in the eighteenth and nineteenth centuries. *Folk Music Journal, 5*(4), 412–447.

Garrido, S., & Davidson, J. (2016a). The modern funeral and music for celebration: Part I. In J. W. Davidson & S. Garrido (Eds.), *Music and mourning* (pp. 9–17). Oxon: Ashgate Publishing.

Garrido, S., & Davidson, J. (2016b). The modern funeral and music for celebration: Part II. In J. W. Davidson & S. Garrido (Eds.), *Music and mourning* (pp. 18–30). Oxon: Ashgate Publishing.

Garrido, S., & Garrido, W. (2016). The psychological function of music in mourning rituals: Examples from three continents. In J. W. Davidson & S. Garrido (Eds.), *Music and mourning* (pp. 55–68). Oxon: Ashgate Publishing.

Garrido, S., & Schubert, E. (2011). Negative emotion in music: What is the attraction? A qualitative study. *Empirical Musicology Review, 6*(4), 214–230.

Garrido, S., & Schubert, E. (2013). Adaptive and maladaptive attraction to negative emotion in music. *Musicae Scientiae, 17*(2), 145–164. doi:10.1177/1029864913478305.

Gillies, J., & Neimeyer, R. (2006). Loss, grief, and the search for significance: Toward a model of meaning reconstruction in bereavement. *Journal of Constructivist Psychology, 19*(1), 31–65.

Gosling, S. D., Rentfrow, P. J., & Swann, W. B. (2003). A very brief measure of the Big-Five personality domains. *Journal of Research in Personality, 37*, 504–528.

grief, n. (2012). *Oxford English Dictionary Online*. Oxford University Press.

Humphrey, G. M., & Zimpfer, D. G. (2008). *Counselling for grief and bereavement* (2nd ed.). London: Sage.

Huron, D. (2008b). Why do listeners enjoy music that makes them weep? *Proceedings of the 10th International Conference on Music Perception and Cognition*, 236–242.

Huron, D. (2015). The other semiotic legacy of Charles Sanders Peirce: Ethology and music-related emotion. In C. Maeder & M. Reybrouck (Eds.), *Music, analysis, experience: New perspectives in musical semiotics*. Leuven, Belgium: Leuven University Press.

Jalland, P. (2006). *Changing ways of death in twentieth-century Australia: War, medicine and the funeral business*. Sydney: UNSW Press.

Jefferies, L. N., Smilek, D., Eich, E., & Enns, J. T. (2008). Emotional valence and arousal interact in attentional control. *Psychological Science, 19*(3), 290–295.

Kastenbaum, R. (2004). Why funerals? *Generations, 28*(2), 5–10.

Kelton, S., & Steward, F. (2008). Queen, Led Zeppelin and AC/DC now popular funeral songs. *The Daily Telegraph*. Retrieved from http://www.dailytelegraph.com.au/news/weird/queen-led-zeppelin-and-acdc-now-popular-funeral-songs/story-e6frev20-1111116793918

Kersting, A., Brähler, E., Glaesmer, H., & Wagner, B. (2011). Prevalence of complicated grief in a representative population-based sample. *Journal of Affective Disorders, 131*, 339–343.

Kivy, P. (1980). *The corded shell: Reflections on musical expression*. Princeton: Princeton University Press.

Klass, D., Silverman, P. R., & Nickman, S. L. (1996). *Continuing bonds: New understandings of grief*. Washington, DC: Taylor & Francis.

Kotthoff, H. (2006). Communicating affect in intercultural lamentations in Caucasian Georgia. In K. Buhrig & J. D. T. Thije (Eds.), *Beyond misunderstanding: Linguistic analyses of intercultural communication*. Amsterdam: John Benjamins Publishing.

Kübler-Ross, E. (1969). *On death and dying*. London: Routledge.

Magee, W. L., & Davidson, J. W. (2004). Music therapy in multiple sclerosis: Results of a systematic qualitative analysis. *Music Therapy Perspectives, 22*, 39–51.

McFerran, K., Roberts, M., & O'Grady, L. (2010). Music therapy with bereaved teenagers: A mixed methods perspective. *Death Studies, 34*, 541–555.

Meert, K. L., Donaldson, A. E., Newth, C. J. L., Harrison, R., Berger, J., Zimmerman, J., … Shear, M. K. (2010). Complicated grief and associated risk factors among parents following a child's death in the pediatric intensive care unit. *Archives of Pediatric and Adolescent Medicine, 164*(11), 1045–1051.

Neimeyer, R. (2001). Reauthoring life narratives: Grief therapy as meaning reconstruction. *The Israel Journal of Psychiatry and Related Sciences, 28*(3–4), 171–183.

Nesse, R. M. (2005). An evolutionary framework for understanding grief. In D. Carr, R. M. Nesse, & C. B. Wortman (Eds.), *Late life widowhood in the United States: Spousal bereavement in late life* (pp. 195–226). New York: Springer.

Neufeldt, V., & Guralnik, D., (Eds.). (1988). *Webster's new world dictionary* (3rd college ed.). New York: Simon and Schuster.

Nolen-Hoeksema, S., Parker, L. E., & Larson, J. (1994). Ruminative coping with depressed mood following loss. *Journal of Personality and Social Psychology, 67*(1), 92–104.

Norcross, J. L., & Newman, J. D. (1999). Effects of separation and novelty on distress vocalizations and cortisol in the common marmoset (Callithrix jacchus). *American Journal of Primatology, 47*, 209–222.

O'Callaghan, C. C. (2013). Music therapy preloss care through legacy creation. *Progress in Palliative Care, 21*(2), 78–82.

Orellana, M. (1990). Versos por Angelito: Poetry and its function at the wake of a peasant child in Chile. *Journal of Folklore Research, 27*(3), 191–203.

Parsons, B. (2012). Identifying key changes: The progress of cremation and its influence on music at funerals in England, 1874–2010. *Mortality, 17*(2), 130–144.

Penman, J., & Becker, J. (2009). Religious ecstatics, "deep listeners," and musical emotion. *Empirical Musicology Review, 4*(2), 49–70.

Romanoff, B. D., & Terenzio, M. (1998). Rituals and the grieving process. *Death Studies, 22*(8), 697–711.

Rosand, E. (1979). The descending tetrachord: An emblem of lament. *The Musical Quarterly, 65*(3), 346–359.

Sakakeeny, M. (2011). Jazz funerals and second line parades. In D. Johnson (Ed.), *KnowLA: Encyclopedia of Louisiana*. Louisiana Endowment for the Humanities: Louisiana.

Schechter, J. M. (1994). Divergent perspectives on the Velorio Del Angelito. *Journal of Ritual Studies, 8*(2), 43–84.

Schnider, K. R., Elhai, J. D., & Gray, M. J. (2007). Coping style use predicts posttraumatic stress and complicated grief symptom severity among college students reporting a traumatic loss. *Journal of Counseling Psychology, 54*(3), 344–350.

Seay, B., Hansen, E., & Harlow, H. F. (1962). Mother-infant separation in monkeys. *Journal of Child Psychology and Psychiatry Allied Disciplines, 3*, 123–132.

Secundy, M. G. (1989). Coping with words and song: The New Orleans jazz funeral. *Literature and Medicine, 8*, 100–105.

Silverman, P. R., & Klass, D. (1996). Introduction: What's the problem? In D. Klass, P. R. Silverman, & S. L. Nickman (Eds.), *Continuing bonds: New understandings of grief*. Philadelphia: Taylor & Francis.

Stroebe, M., Schut, H., & Boerner, K. (2010). Continuing bonds in adaptation to bereavement: Toward theoretical integration. *Clinical Psychology Review, 30*, 2.

Sung, S. C., Dryman, M. T., Marks, E., Shear, M. K., Ghesquiere, A., Fava, M., & Simon, N. M. (2011). Complicated grief among individuals with major depression: Prevalence, comorbidity, and associated features. *Journal of Affective Disorders, 134*(1–3), 453–458.

TGR. (1910). MUSIC. *The Queenslander*, p. 20. Retrieved from http://nla.gov.au/nla.news-article21881817

Tolbert, E. (1990). Women cry with words: Symbolization of affect in the Karelian lament. *Yearbook for Traditional Music, 22*, 80–105.

Treloyn, S. (2016). Restoring songs: On mourning and an 'everyday' performance genre in Northern Australia. In J. W. Davidson & S. Garrido (Eds.), *Music and mourning* (pp. 83–96). Oxon: Ashgate Publishing.

Wilce, J. M. (2009). *Crying shame: Metaculture, modernity, and the exaggerated death of lament*. Chichester: Wiley-Blackwell.

Worden, J. W. (1982). *Grief counselling and grief therapy: A handbook for the mental health practitioner*. New York: Springer Publishing Company.

Zisook, S., & Schuchter, S. R. (2001). Treatment of the depression of bereavement. *The American Behavioural Scientist, 44*(5), 782–797.

14

Towards A Model for Understanding Sad Music Listening

The discerning reader who has been following the arguments laid out in this volume will perceive that the number of reasons people have for listening to sad music and the effects it has on them are almost as numerous as the individual listeners themselves. Thus, the aim implied in the title of this chapter—to propose a model for understanding sad music listening—is in no way intended to suggest that the variety of individual responses to music can be summarized in a few trite sentences. In fact, it is this very limitation, inherent in many previous discussions of the topic, which the current volume seeks to overcome.

While philosophers have for centuries been discussing the subject of why we listen to sad music, little consensus has existed between them as to the answer. Rather, a multitude of explanations have been offered. Many of these are soundly logical, but are based largely on the observations of the individual scholars' own response to sad music. Thus, much of the apparently contradictory explanations offered in the literature to date may reflect the tendency to rely on personal experiences in forming hypotheses.

It is only in the last 5–10 years that any empirical research has been conducted into the question of why we listen to sad music. This research

S. Garrido, *Why Are We Attracted to Sad Music?*,
DOI 10.1007/978-3-319-39666-8_14

has finally enabled us to begin to see the many possible ways in which people can use sad music, the varying motivations they may have for listening to it, and some of the mechanisms that may underlie their response to it. From this research it has become apparent that there is no single answer to the question of why we are attracted to sad music. In this concluding chapter I will attempt to draw together some of the evidence that has been discussed in this volume about the many variables that seem to influence our attraction and response to sad music.

Qualities of the Music

Music that is perceived as sad by people in Western cultures is typically slow and in a minor key. It may tend to be low in pitch and have quite a narrow pitch range, as well as containing relatively smooth articulation and a small dynamic range. One of the reasons that these acoustic cues communicate sadness to the listener is because of their similarity to prosodic speech cues that similarly signify sadness. Due to the physiological changes that occur with the experience of sadness, vocal expressions of sadness do tend to be relatively slow, soft, low in pitch and with a somewhat slurred articulation. Thus, the listener generally perceives mimicry of these features in music, even in non-vocal music, as an expression of sadness by the listener.

In addition, there is some evidence that biological mechanisms can cause us to experience sadness in response to cues within the music. For example, music that is slow in tempo can cause our bodies to physically entrain to the slow rhythm, lowering arousal levels in the listener and inducing an emotion that may feel much like sadness. Furthermore, expressions of intense sadness, such as grief, may activate quite primitive brain stem responses designed to motivate us to escape danger. Since expressions of sadness and grief also serve the purpose of signaling the need for social support, music can also engender an empathic response in the listener. This likely takes place via the activation of mirror neurons, which cause an unconscious mimicry of, and instigation of the corresponding emotions in the listener.

In addition to musical features that may evoke emotional responses via biological mechanisms, culturally acquired knowledge also plays a role.

Minor keys, for example, are not universally perceived as sad, and, in fact, do not even exist in the music of some cultures. Rather, the minor key has come to be associated with sadness in Western cultures over a period of centuries. Thus, listeners who do not even have the musical knowledge necessary to be able to identify the key as minor could likely still perceive a piece of music in a minor key as sad. It has also been suggested that emotions are most often aroused in response to music in which there are violations of musical expectations based on our knowledge of common musical conventions (Huron, 2006; Meyer, 1956), thus suggesting that cues of sadness in music can differ from culture to culture.

However, as discussed in Chap. 2, the presence of the features commonly associated with sadness in Western music does not guarantee that a listener who is familiar with music of this culture will experience sadness in response to the music or even that they will perceive it as sad. Nor does it preclude the possibility of music that does not contain these musical features being experienced or perceived as sad. In fact, in the study I reported in that chapter, both tempo and mode were fairly evenly distributed across both the sad and happy listening conditions.

Of far more importance in my own study, and those of other researchers, were the lyrics. Songs that participants had categorized as happy typically contained more words in the present tense, more words expressing positive emotions, and more words expressing assent and agreement. Sad songs, on the other hand, contained more words expressing negative emotion such as sadness and anger. Other studies confirm that lyrics have a greater effect on both emotional response to music, and attitudes and outlook than pure music alone (Anderson et al., 2003; Brattico et al., 2011). Lyrics and other musical features typically associated with sadness may in fact work together to create a particularly compelling emotional experience for many listeners.

Personal Meaning

In addition to acoustic cues and the linguistic content of music, each individual brings to the music their own personal associations and experiences. Music acquires personal meaning where it has previously been paired with certain events, places or people. Where, for example, a certain song is repeatedly heard in a situation that causes stress or pain, such as in a dentist's surgery, the listener may immediately begin to experience feelings of anxiety upon hearing the song—even if the music is not intended to express such emotions. Similarly, a song that could be perceived as expressing sadness, could, if it has been heard repeatedly when in company with a person who is dear to us, cause an individual to experience feelings of pleasure and comfort. In addition to these unconscious associations, music can evoke specific episodic memories of times when it has been heard before.

Even when no particular memories are triggered, or when the music has not become specifically associated with anything else in the mind of the listener, music can trigger related thoughts and memories of a particular valence. For example, as the study reported in Chap. 9 demonstrates, sad music may cause an individual to think of sad times even where no specific associations with sad events have been formed with the music. Happier music tends to trigger thoughts of happy times, such as time spent with friends, on holidays or relaxing. Thus, music can take on personal meaning with very little need for specific reference to the past. Whether or not music triggers such thoughts and memories may have much to do with other individual variables that will be discussed further below.

Personality

The consideration of individual differences and the role of various personality traits has been a key focus of the research presented in this volume. Several empirical studies have suggested personality traits that may influence our response to, and hence our attraction to, sad music.[1]

One key personality trait that has been implicated in several studies (see Chap. 7) is absorption. Absorption—or the capacity to become deeply engaged in something—has been consistently found to be associated with a liking for sad music (Garrido & Schubert, 2011a, 2011b,

[1] See Chap. 7 for a more in-depth discussion.

2013; Kreutz et al., 2008), and is closely related to the way people use all kinds of music, both happy and sad, in their everyday life (Herbert, 2011). When listening to sad music, the capacity for absorption seems to enable some listeners to dissociate the emotion experienced from the displeasure that would often accompany an experience of sadness, allowing the listener to simply enjoy the emotional arousal and cognitive activation that occurs when listening to the music (Schubert, 1996, 2012a, 2012b). Since absorption is also a trait that is inherently adaptive and rewarding, helping individuals to cope with stress and to achieve states of intense concentration and 'flow', individuals with a propensity for absorption may find listening to sad music particularly rewarding since it provides an opportunity for deep emotional engagement that is highly pleasurable.

A related construct is that of openness to experience. Studies suggest that people with high scores in this personality trait are also more likely to enjoy sad music than others, and are likely to have more intense emotional responses to it (Vuoskoski et al., 2012). This may be because sad music often contains greater emotional variability and structural complexity than other music. Openness to experience involves an enjoyment of novelty, and it is likely that people with this personality trait require more complex stimuli in order to achieve their optimal level of stimulation.

Studies have also shown that sad music seems to be more attractive to people who are introverted. This may also be related to the motivation to regulate arousal and achieve an optimal level of stimulation. Introverts tend to be more easily overwhelmed by external stimulation and thus they may evince a preference for music that is relatively low in arousal potential, as is the case with much sad music. They may thus be attracted to sad music of a different type to people with high scores in openness to experience. It may be that the former prefer music that is slow and soft, while the latter may be attracted to sad music of greater intensity and variability, such as classical music. Alternatively, it may be that for people who find personal interactions with other people somewhat draining, i.e. introverts, sad music can provide a relatively low arousal way to experience a sense of social connection and solace.

One's capacity to feel sadness in response to music is likely also related to the degree of empathy an individual is prone to feeling. This is a trait that is also linked to absorption and to imaginativeness. Some degree of imaginativeness and fantasy proneness are necessary in order to be able to relate to sad music, since the individual needs to be able to both imagine the fictional character expressing the music or the storyline behind the music, and to imagine themselves within that story or experiencing the same emotions. Thus, a person's capacity to demonstrate empathy—to perceive and feel the emotions of others—is related to the attraction to sad music. Since empathy is also an adaptive and therefore rewarding behavior given its role in helping us to decode the emotional signals of others, the capacity to feel sadness in response to music likely makes listening to it a more enjoyable experience. Hence empathy has also been linked to an attraction to sad music. A more specialized form of musical empathy, in which people tend to be especially attracted to the emotional content of music and display a particular ability to relate to expressions of emotion in music, also appears to be related to our enjoyment of sad music.

One further personality trait that has been demonstrated to relate to our attraction to sad music is nostalgia-proneness (see Chap. 11). One's propensity for indulging in nostalgic remembering, as well as the degree to which one misses the past, influences the degree to which one likes to use sad music in order to induce nostalgic episodes. While nostalgia can involve mixed affective experiences, including both positive and negative affect, people are particularly prone to nostalgic reminiscing when feeling sad or lonely. Thus, sad music is often what an individual is drawn to when they wish to remember the past.

There is a considerable overlap between the personality traits that have been discussed in this volume. Not only do several of them tend to exist simultaneously in particular individuals (such as absorption and openness to experience), but they often work together synergistically to enhance one's emotional response to music. So, for example, a particularly empathic person who also has strong capacities to absorption may have an especially strong attraction to sad music since at least two adaptive cognitive processes are occurring and being rewarded by the brain. Similarly, the studies reported in this volume demonstrate that the relationship between nostalgia-proneness and a liking for sad music tends to be mediated by absorption, indicating that someone who has strong scores in absorption is more likely to experience frequent episodes of nostalgic remembering when listening to music. However, as previously indicated, one might be more likely to seek nostalgic experiences when feeling sad or lonely. Therefore, mood is also a variable that has an important influence on our attraction to sad music.

Mood and Mood Regulation Strategies

Mood influences our response to sad music in several ways. Firstly, people in a sad mood are more likely to *perceive* music as sad, since we have a tendency to view things in a negative light when we are ourselves in a negative mood. Just as they do with other stimuli, people in a sad mood are more likely to rate songs as of negative valence than people in a happy or neutral mood.

Secondly, people are more likely to *listen* to sad music when they are in a sad mood (Garrido & Schubert, 2011b; Garrido & Schubert, 2013; Van den Tol & Edwards, 2013). Sadness is, in general, an adaptive experience that motivates us to confront areas of our life where change may be needed. Thus, when experiencing heartbreak, grief, loneliness or a sense of disconnection from our past, individuals may be attracted to sad music as part of adaptive processes for dealing with these emotions. When experiencing negative emotions as a result of events in their lives, people are often attracted to sad music for several reasons: to experience a sense of connection with others who feel the same way; for the opportunity to vent their emotions; for distraction purposes; and to assist them in reflecting and thinking about their emotions and the events that have caused them.

These different motivations for listening to sad music reflect the different mood regulation strategies and coping styles that people have developed over the course of their lives. Emotions, which are our immediate response to an event or stimulus, have an influence on our long-term mood states. The effect an emotion will have on our moods is related to the thought patterns that are triggered by the event or stimulus, and our emotional response to it. These thoughts often stem from our habitual mood regulation strategies. While such strategies can change from situation to situation, they tend to reflect an individual's overall coping style, or habitual patterns of behavior in response to adverse events that tend to be fairly stable.

Mood regulation strategies and coping styles can be both adaptive and maladaptive. One example that has been featured prominently throughout this volume is the distinction between rumination and reflectiveness.[2] While both ways of attempting to modulate mood involve thinking about the event that has triggered a negative mood, reflectiveness involves positive thought patterns that eventually help the individual to move out of their negative mood state. Rumination, on the other hand, is the compulsive 'chewing over' of negative thoughts, feelings and occurrences. It tends to perpetuate sadness and depression, is often beyond the control of the individual, and is a difficult process to disconnect from once it has begun. These strategies for dealing with negative moods form part of broader overall coping styles. Rumination, for example, tends to be part of an emotion-based coping style, in which the individual focuses on the feelings and sensations they are experiencing. Emotion-based coping is generally considered less effective in resolving negative affective states than an active coping style, for example, which typically involves reflecting on, planning and executing practical steps towards changing the circumstances that are causing the negative mood.

An individual's learned mood regulation strategies and coping style can influence both whether they will choose to listen to sad music and also the effect that the music will have on them. These interact, in turn, with various other personality traits. For example, a person who is feeling sad due to some external event, may, if they are prone to absorption, be able to listen to a piece of sad music without feeling displeasure, and thereby experiencing some emotional catharsis in a relatively pleasant context. On the other hand, a person with low scores in absorption who favours an avoidant coping style may tend to avoid listening to sad music that may trigger unpleasantly sad responses. Similarly, a person who is feeling sad and who tends to use reflective mood regulation strategies may feel attracted to sad music because of the opportunity it gives them to confront their emotions and to engage in the cognitive work necessary in

[2] See Chaps. 6 and 8.

order to resolve them. Conversely, a ruminative person may be attracted to the sad music for the same reasons as the reflective individual, but find that rather than working through their negative emotions, the music only deepens cycles of negative thinking that exacerbate their negative mood.

Social Circumstances of Listening

A further variable that can interact with the musical and personal variables described above are the social circumstances in which the music is heard. As discussed in Chap. 10, music is a fundamentally social activity. Even where modern-day technology enables musical engagement to occur in solitude, a sense of social connection often continues to be involved in our experiences with music. The sharing of emotions through listening to music can often have the effect of strengthening social bonds. Social feedback also influences our musical preferences as well as our perception of the valence of music. In addition, processes of emotional contagion can mean that the affective power of music can be either intensified or diffused depending on the dominant affective response of the group to the music.

Thus, where sad music listening occurs in a group setting, the effect on individuals varies depending on the personalities of the individuals, and the thoughts, behaviours and group dynamics that occur in response to the music. For example, where the majority of people in a group have reflective mood regulation strategies and use sad music as an opportunity to gain needed social support or to collectively work through negative emotions, the individuals in the group will likely benefit from the listening experience. However, where 'group rumination' occurs, or a communal focus on negative thoughts and experiences in conjunction with listening to music that features dark and negative themes, particularly vulnerable individuals such as those with tendencies to depression may find that the process only deepens their dysphoria. Thus, while music can form a strong basis for the sharing of negative emotions, this can at times result in the intensification of depression and sadness.

The Model

Fig. 14.1 is an attempt to depict the musical, personal and situational variables described above that influence our perception of music as sad, our attraction to it, and the effects it will have on our mood and wellbeing.

As can be seen in Fig. 14.1, the features of the music itself do not alone determine whether an individual will perceive the music to be sad or experience sadness in response to it. Rather, the individual brings his or her own experiences, state of mind and temperament to the listening situation. The music takes on personal meaning through association with past events, and our perception of it is further coloured by our mood at the time of hearing, and social feedback from those around us.

Once perceived as sad, whether we are attracted to listening to the music depends on our personality, the life circumstances in which we find ourselves and thus our personal need to process negative emotions, and

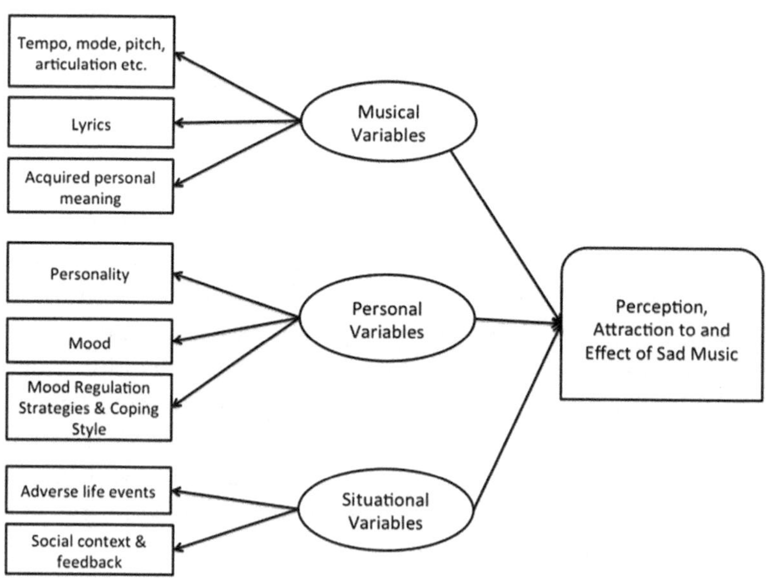

Fig. 14.1 A model of attraction to sad music

the strategies that we have learned for coping with difficult life events. We are further influenced by social feedback at this stage, as the response of people around us can influence our appraisal of the music as pleasant or unpleasant and hence our own emotional response to it. The impact that sad music then has on our mood is further influenced by interactions between our personality, our coping style and the context in which the music is heard. The interactions between these variables are shown in Fig. 14.2 as a pathway model.

As the model in Fig. 14.2 demonstrates, in order for sad music to have an influence on our mood or affective state, we must first perceive it as sad, based on the combined effect of the musical cues, and several personal and situational variables. Our perception of the music as sad then works along with other variables to determine whether we will be attracted to listen to it. Our attraction to sad music, in turn, interconnects with personal and situational variables yet again to determine whether or not the effect of the music on our mood will be a positive one.

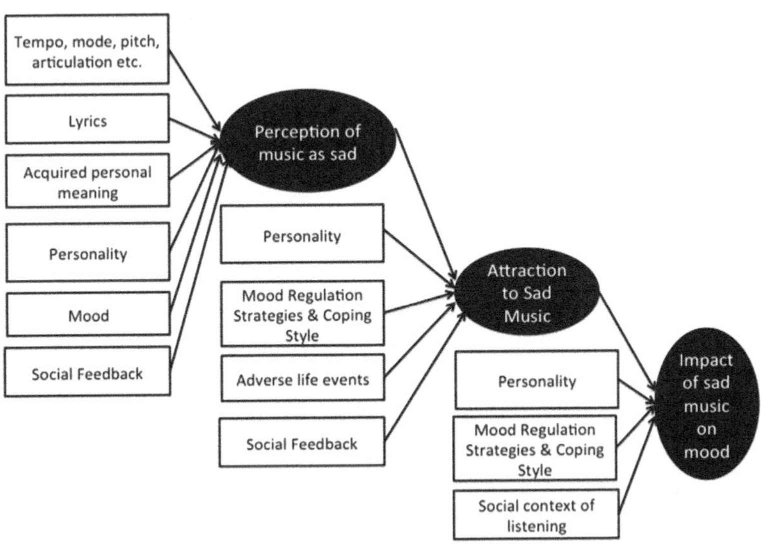

Fig. 14.2 A pathway model of sad music and its impact on mood

The Implications for Health and Wellbeing

As well as adding considerable insight to the philosophical question of why we are attracted to sad music and tragedy in other aesthetic contexts, the research discussed in this volume has important implications for our understanding of the role that music can play in health and wellbeing. While music therapists have long understood that music must be adapted to the individual needs of each patient, users of music in other contexts have often focused on the benefits of musical engagement without having any recognition of the interplay of the multiple variables above.

Music—particularly sad music and music evoking negative emotions—is neither universally beneficial, nor can it be completely blamed for the social instability and immorality with which it has been charged on many occasions in the past. Rather, the music itself, the individual, and the context in which it is heard all come together to create distinctly different affective experiences. Practitioners, music lovers and researchers interested in the use of music to improve mental health and quality of life face the dilemma of the need to cater to the tastes and preferences of the individual, while recognizing that personal choices do not always reflect healthy mood regulation strategies and that individuals display differing degrees of awareness of the effect of music on their mental health. Thus, while we might conclude that in general listening to sad music provides useful psychological benefits to the majority of listeners, some level of caution is needed, particularly in regards to people with mood disorders.

While the studies reported in Chap. 8 demonstrate that happy music is more likely to have a positive impact on the mood of people with tendencies to depression than sad music, Chap. 9 showed that simply 'prescribing' happy music for depressed people is of only limited value, particularly over the long term. Individuals tend to absorb music of any kind into their habitual coping style and thinking patterns. However, raising awareness of the impact of music on mood can be a useful way to raise the overall consciousness of behaviours that can contribute to depression. Furthermore, the findings presented in this book suggest that music that matches the arousal levels of the listener is likely to be most welcome to the listener, but that this music can be selected to as to trigger positive thoughts or memories.

Despite the mixed effects of listening to sad music, it is likely that it will continue to be prominent in the music charts of the future. Sad music reflects the human condition. In the words of Shakespeare's Richard III: "To weep is to make less the depth of grief" (*Henry VI*, Pt 3, Act 2, Scene 1). Furthermore, as this volume has attempted to make clear, sad music, like most music, has the power to persuade, embolden and deliver pleasure. Nevertheless, another lesson that has been documented herein time and time again, is that we might be advised to think carefully about the music we listen to. Listeners do well to ask themselves the question: 'Is my music helping me or perpetuating thoughts that make me feel worse?' So the question is not whether or not we choose to listen to 'sad' or 'happy' music, but whether or not the music we listen to is triggering thoughts that are helpful for our mental health and wellbeing.

References

Anderson, C. A., Carnagey, N. L., & Eubanks, J. (2003). Exposure to violent media: The effects of songs with violent lyrics on aggressive thoughts and feelings. *Journal of Personality and Social Psychology, 84*(5), 960–971.

Brattico, E., Alluri, V., Bogert, B., Jacobsen, T., Nartiainen, N., Nieminen, S., & Tervaniemi, M. (2011). A functional MRI study of happy and sad emotions in music with and without lyrics. *Frontiers in Psychology, 2*, 308.

Garrido, S., & Schubert, E. (2011a). Individual differences in the enjoyment of negative emotion in music: A literature review and experiment. *Music Perception, 28*(3), 279–295.

Garrido, S., & Schubert, E. (2011b). Negative emotion in music: What is the attraction? A qualitative study. *Empirical Musicology Review, 6*(4), 214–230.

Garrido, S., & Schubert, E. (2013). Adaptive and maladaptive attraction to negative emotion in music. *Musicae Scientiae, 17*(2), 145–164. doi:10.1177/1029864913478305.

Herbert, R. (2011). *Everyday music listening: Absorption, dissociation, and trancing*. Surrey, UK: Ashgate.

Huron, D. (2006). *Sweet anticipation: Music and the psychology of expectation*. Cambridge, MA: MIT Press.

Kreutz, G., Ott, U., Teichmann, D., Osawa, P., & Vaitl, D. (2008). Using music to induce emotion: Influences of musical preference and absorption. *Psychology of Music, 36*, 101–121.

Meyer, L. B. (1956). *Emotion and meaning in music.* Chicago: University of Chicago Press.

Schubert, E. (1996). Enjoyment of negative emotions in music: An associative network explanation. *Psychology of Music, 24*, 18–28.

Schubert, E. (2012a). Spreading activation and dissociation: A cognitive mechanism for creative processing in music. In D. J. Hargreaves, D. Miell, & R. Macdonald (Eds.), *Musical imaginations: Multidisciplinary perspectives on creativity, performance and perception.* Oxford: Oxford University Press.

Schubert, E. (2012b). Enjoying sad music: Paradoc of parallel processes? *Frontiers in Psychology, 10*, 312.

Van den Tol, A. J. M., & Edwards, J. (2013). Exploring a rationale for choosing to listen to sad music when feeling sad. *Psychology of Music, 41*(4), 440–465.

Vuoskoski, J. K., Thompson, W. F., McIllwain, D., & Eerola, T. (2012). Who enjoys listening to sad music and why? *Music Perception, 29*(3), 311–317.

Index

Note: Page numbers with "n" denote footnotes.

S. Garrido, *Why Are We Attracted to Sad Music?*,
DOI 10.1007/978-3-319-39666-8

FSC
www.fsc.org
MIX
Papier | Fördert gute Waldnutzung
FSC® C083411

Kolibri 360 GmbH
Ferdinand-Jühlke-Straße 7
99095 Erfurt, Deutschland
produktsicherheit@kolibri360.de